Differentiating Instruction *with* Technology

in Middle School Classrooms

Grace E. Smith
Stephanie Throne

International Society for Technology in Education
EUGENE, OREGON • WASHINGTON, DC

Differentiating Instruction *with* Technology
in Middle School Classrooms

Grace E. Smith and Stephanie Throne

© 2009 International Society for Technology in Education

Director of Book Publishing: Courtney Burkholder
Acquisitions Editor: Jeff V. Bolkan
Production Editors: Lanier Brandau, Lynda Gansel
Production Coordinator: Rachel Williams
Graphic Designer: Signe Landin
Copy Editors: Anna Raitt & Kathleen Hamman

Proofreader: Kathleen Hamman
Indexer: Seth Maislin, Potomac Indexing
Book Design: Signe Landin & Tracy Cozzens
Cover Design: Signe Landin
Book Production: Tracy Cozzens

Library of Congress Cataloging-in-Publication Data

Smith, Grace E.
   Differentiating instruction with technology in the middle school classroom / Grace E. Smith and Stephanie Throne. — 1st ed.
      p. cm.
   Includes bibliographical references and index.
   ISBN 978-1-56484-260-2 (pbk.)
   1. Individualized instruction. 2. Educational technology. 3. Teaching—Aids and devices.
4. Middle school teaching. I. Throne, Stephanie. II. Title.
LB1031.S623 2009
373.139'4—dc22   2009019542

First Edition
ISBN: 978-1-56484-260-2

Printed in the United States of America

International Society for Technology in Education (ISTE)
Washington, DC, Headquarters:
      1710 Rhode Island Ave. NW, Suite 900, Washington, DC 20036-3132
Eugene, Oregon, Office:
      180 West 8th Ave., Suite 300, Eugene, OR 97401-2916
Order Desk: 1.800.336.5191
Order Fax: 1.541.302.3778
Customer Service: orders@iste.org
Book Publishing: books@iste.org
Book Sales and Marketing: booksmarketing@iste.org
Web: www.iste.org

ABOUT **ISTE**

The International Society for Technology in Education (ISTE) is the trusted source for professional development, knowledge generation, advocacy, and leadership for innovation. ISTE is the premier membership association for educators and education leaders engaged in improving teaching and learning by advancing the effective use of technology in PK–12 and teacher education.

Home of the National Educational Technology Standards (NETS) and ISTE's annual conference and exposition (formerly known as NECC), ISTE represents more than 100,000 professionals worldwide. We support our members with information, networking opportunities, and guidance as they face the challenge of transforming education. To find out more about these and other ISTE initiatives, visit our website at **www.iste.org**.

As part of our mission, ISTE Book Publishing works with experienced educators to develop and produce practical resources for classroom teachers, teacher educators, and technology leaders. Every manuscript we select for publication is carefully peer-reviewed and professionally edited. We value your feedback on this book and other ISTE products. E-mail us at **books@iste.org**.

ABOUT THE AUTHORS

Grace E. Smith received a PhD in instructional (educational) technology from Wayne State University. Her experience includes 10 years as a teacher and reading specialist in public and private schools and 11 years as a technology curriculum coordinator and trainer for a school district of 10,000 students. She has also worked as the director of continuing professional education at a business college, as an educational consultant, as a curriculum coordinator and course developer for a Fortune 500 company, and as an adjunct professor at two universities, where she taught writing and technology courses.

Stephanie Throne received a PhD in Romance Languages and Literatures, Spanish, from the University of Michigan at Ann Arbor. She has extensive experience in developing online educational materials and was the first instructor at her institution to offer online foreign language classes. She currently works as an author consultant and presents at many conferences, workshops, and webinars. In addition, Throne teaches/tutors Spanish, math, reading, and writing for various instructional and private organizations. Throne is the co-author of a forthcoming Spanish text and is an editor/proofreader for several publications.

Acknowledgments

The work of educating children is more than a job; it is a calling. Thanks to the many teachers and colleagues who have inspired me, guided me toward the path I have followed, and have had a positive and special impact on my life. Thanks to my husband, children, and friends who continue to encourage me in my endeavors. Without their support, I would not have been able to write this book. —*Grace*

For my parents, who modeled excellent teaching at home and in the workplace and dedicated their lives to countless students. I would not be the person I am or where I am today without their amazing love and support. For my husband and my children, who continue to encourage me and love me unconditionally. I could not accomplish much without their laughter, smiles, and patience. —*Stephanie*

CONTENTS

INTRODUCTION

The purpose of *Differentiating Instruction with Technology in Middle School Classrooms* is to help you strengthen your teaching skills by adding technology tools to differentiated instructional strategies. As with most other endeavors, you'll probably find that the key to using technology with differentiated instruction is to move slowly.

You can try out as many or as few strategies in this book as you wish. Some strategies or activities require more preparation time than others, and some will be a more natural fit with your style of teaching. All chapters contain a variety of resources based on the topic at hand. These resources provide extra examples and ideas for trying out the activities in your own classroom. Throughout the chapters various strategies are explored in detail, and a glossary of strategies is also provided in Appendix A.

Here's a caveat from your authors. Although all websites in this book were tested prior to publication, websites change their addresses frequently. If you find that a link does not work, try searching on the title provided before each URL listing. In other words, if the link for the Center for Applied Research in Educational Technology (CARET) doesn't work, try searching on "Center for Applied Research in Educational Technology" or "CARET." You should be able to find the site without too much of a struggle.

In Chapter 1, we talk about technology's big picture, explaining what newer research has to say about modern skills, technology integration, and the impact of technology on student learning. Because of their busy schedules, classroom teachers are not always aware of important research studies or best practices. However, we strongly believe that educators must embrace current research data so that they can begin to modify their instructional strategies in order to reach more students, improve student learning, and become stronger teachers. Thus, we include several examples of recent studies in one convenient place.

In Chapter 2, we provide an overview of differentiated instruction traits and elements; discuss the complexity of the teenage brain and how understanding middle school students' emotional, physical, and intellectual development can lead to more effective teaching; and share insights on how to create an encouraging, exciting learning environment for this challenging age group. The authors rely on their experience as students, teachers, and parents, as both authors were once students, Grace is a former middle school teacher, and Stephanie is the parent of a current middle school student. We believe that knowing what the research shows about middle school minds, bodies, and emotions is essential to fostering positive learning environments. In other words, teachers must know how their students function to work with them in the best possible ways.

In addition, we realize that readers typically are well-grounded in either technology integration or in differentiated instruction but not usually in both. We think that these "twin" introductory chapters may help readers get up to speed in either or both fields.

We explain how to use the emerging Web 2.0 technologies and other tech tools in Chapter 3. The remaining chapters are devoted to demonstrating how to use technology to differentiate instructional strategies in middle school core and encore subjects and how to use technology to assess learning.

We've always liked books that feature overviews and "contents-at-a-glance" so we provide a snapshot of this book's chapters in Table I.1 (pp. 4–5).

Technology in Motion

We like to use a metaphor we call "Technology in Motion" (Fig. I.1) and because many of us are better at understanding pictures than words, the pinwheel illustrates four influential forces that produce energy and excitement about learning in our schools when they are in place and balanced

Imagine a pinwheel—the kind you used when you were a young child. Physicists tell us that the shape of the pinwheel captures wind in a way that makes the pinwheel spin. Moving air is converted to rotating energy in the pinwheel. Air that moves fast has more energy and causes the pinwheel to spin more quickly.

In our technology in motion pinwheel metaphor, each blade depicts a force or influence we see in education right now: 21st Century Skills and ISTE NETS, technology and learning research, differentiated instruction, and Web 2.0 tools and emerging technologies. When all four blades are equally weighted, the pinwheel spins properly, reflecting a cutting-edge position. If a blade is missing or incomplete, the pinwheel spins more slowly, if at all.

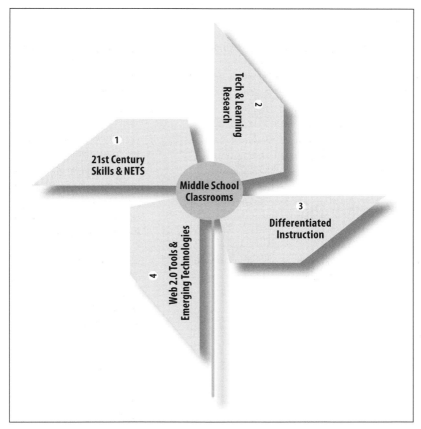

FIGURE I.1 ■ Technology in Motion pinwheel

As you can imagine, the schools that do not differentiate instruction and/or do not use technology with students have no pinwheel. In others, the pinwheel spins slowly because one or two blades are missing. In some schools, the pinwheel spins at top speed because all of the blades are in place and functioning well. This ideal position is technology in motion.

It is our hope that after reading this book, applying the differentiated teaching methods, and evoking creativity and determination, you'll have your class and school up to top speed.

TABLE I.1 ■ Strategies at-a-Glance

Chapter	Conventional Classroom Focus	DI Classroom with Technology
1. Technology's Big Picture: 21st Century Skills, NETS, and Current Research	Paper and pencil or low-tech tools to learn or extend learning	■ 21st Century Skills ■ NETS Skills ■ Research Studies
2. Differentiated Instruction and Middle School Learners	Paper and pencil or low-tech tools to learn or extend learning, teacher- and textbook-driven, sporadic attention to learning environment, affect, and distinctiveness of middle school learner	■ Links student passions with curriculum and fosters new interests ■ Cultivates a physically, emotionally, socially, and academically enjoyable learning environment ■ Allows technology to customize learning via collaborative projects and problem-solving tasks that enhance student affect
3. Using the New Web 2.0 and Other Technologies	Sometimes used if allowed and/or available	■ Safety concerns/sites ■ The Essential Nine Web 2.0 tools: Blogs Document Sharing Photo Sharing/Editing Podcasting RSS Social Bookmarking/Tagging Social Networking Video Sharing Wikis
4. Using Technology to Differentiate English/ Language Arts	Teacher and textbooks	■ Research activities for pre-reading and during-reading information ■ Author study, vocabulary study, characterization, culminating projects, connections to core content, multimedia ■ Technology for vocabulary, writing, spelling, speaking, and listening
5. Using Technology to Differentiate Math	Teacher and textbooks	■ Interactive/virtual games, simulations, manipulatives, software, competitions, and automated response systems ■ Digital tools and flexible groups for authentic product creation and sharing of information (PowerPoint, Webbes, blogging) ■ Streaming and Jigsaw

continued

TABLE I.1 ■ **Strategies at-a-Glance** *continued*

Chapter	Conventional Classroom Focus	DI Classroom with Technology
6. Using Technology to Differentiate Science	Teacher and textbooks	■ Pre-reading and pre-assessment activities ■ During-reading research activities and culminating project ideas, such as R.A.F.T.T., I-Search, comic strips, and social networking ■ Tech-driven flexible grouping ■ Tiered WebQuests
7. Using Technology to Differentiate Social Studies	Teacher and textbooks	■ Differentiating by interest with I-Search, Jigsaw, R.A.F.T.T. and WebQuests ■ Pre-reading and during-reading research activities ■ Culminating project ideas, such as newsletters, brochures, digital stories, timelines, Webbes ■ Choice Boards and web resources
8. Using Technology to Differentiate Encore Subjects: Art, Foreign Language, Music, Physical Education/Health	Often whole class, teacher-driven activities, with exception of pairing or grouping. Use of other DI strategies and technology dependent upon teacher knowledge and/or availability of funds for tech resources	■ Starting points for differentiation in encore classrooms ■ Cubing and ThinkDots tasks that link content and technology ■ "Conversing" about content via podcasts, audio drop boxes, collaborative projects, Skype, virtual field trips ■ Learning Contracts
9. Using Technology to Assess Learning	Teacher-driven	■ Alternatives for pre-, formative, and summative assessments ■ Websites and other resources

CHAPTER 1

Technology's Big Picture

21st Century Skills, NETS, and Current Research

Sometimes teachers ask why they should use technology in their middle school classes. After all, they have so much subject matter to teach, textbooks are laden with pages and pages of content, and the curriculum is vastly crowded. Getting to a technology project on top of all the other requirements is not easy. Tech is perceived as requiring another layer of preparation, especially if the teacher is not especially skilled in using it. Differentiating content is another matter, and, quite frankly, it's easier to teach only the whole group. Combining technology and differentiated instruction in a content subject requires some thinking and practice on your part to make it work. However, the payoff is that you will be a better teacher, and your students will be better learners and better prepared for the life skills they will need in a few years.

I (Grace) recently visited a few middle school classrooms and was astonished to observe few modern teaching techniques and a lack of technology. I felt as though I were in a time warp, traveling back to 30 years ago. Talk about déjà vu! Teachers were using overhead projectors with pre-made transparencies. Old, outdated maps were hanging on the walls. Chalkboards were filled with writing. And all the students had textbooks on their desks. Each teacher was the "talking head" for most of the class period. As I looked around at the faces of the students, it was easy to see how disengaged they were. I stayed, hoping each minute would get better. It didn't.

Later in the term, I visited another set of classrooms and experienced the same disappointment, but when the process hadn't changed by the halfway mark of each class, I left. On this particular day, though, I found the computer lab in each building and slipped in. In each of these labs, the climate was entirely different. The teachers talked for short lengths of time, usually to explain steps or how to do something with technology. Students asked questions, and teachers demonstrated solutions, using a computer projector. In some cases, students walked up to the teacher's computer and showed the class and the teacher how to perform a sequence of steps for a project. During the labs, students worked in pairs or groups on their projects. They collaboratively discussed approaches to learning a task. Not once did I see a bored expression, and when the bell rang, students seemed disappointed that they had to leave.

What was wrong with most of those regular classrooms? Though today's students are much different from those of 30 years ago, many teachers continue to teach in the same ways they were taught. Despite technological advances and tech availability, despite considerable research on the effectiveness of new presentation skills and differentiated instruction, the experiences in many classrooms mimic those of classrooms in earlier decades. These classrooms, so similar to Grandpa's and Grandma's, no longer engage today's students.

In this chapter, we lay out the framework for the rest of the book to demonstrate how four separate yet interconnected forces are converging to affect teaching and learning in middle school classrooms: (1) 21st Century Skills and NETS, (2) technology and learning research, (3) differentiated instruction, and (4) Web 2.0 tools and other emerging technologies. We also discuss research related to the 21st Century Skills and NETS•S and share information that shows how integrating technology into teaching and learning activities helps students achieve academically. Learning how to differentiate instruction with technology will transform your teaching and impact students' learning. As you know, the whole is greater than the sum of its parts, and as any student will tell you, using technology is more than cool—it's essential to learning and to life. Once you understand the synergy, you'll want to get on board!

The 21st Century Skills and the NETS•S

The 21st Century Skills

The 21st Century Skills set emerged out of research commissioned by the North Central Regional Educational Laboratory (NCREL), and conducted by the Metiri Group over a two-year period. In 2003, NCREL released a report titled "enGauge 21st Century Skills: Literacy in the Digital Age" (Lemke, Coughlin, Thadani, & Martin, 2003). The full report is available at www.metiri.com/features.html. A follow-up report, "Continua of Progress," is available on the same site. The 21st Century Skills embody the clusters of skills they deem most essential to today's learners, citizens, and workers. In its introductory "Message to the Reader," the report states the following:

> Without 21st-century skills, students are being prepared to succeed in yesterday's world—not tomorrow's. . . . To ensure that students will be ready to thrive in today's knowledge-based, global society, three significant things need to occur:
>
> 1. The public must acknowledge 21st-century skills as essential to the education of today's learner.
>
> 2. Schools must embrace new designs for learning based on emerging research about how people learn, effective uses of technology, and 21st-century skills in the context of rigorous academic content.
>
> 3. Policymakers must base school accountability on assessments that measure both academic achievement and 21st-century skills. (p. 2)

The 21st Century Skills were developed through a process that included research of the literature, workforce trends and analysis, and input from business and educational leaders and focus groups. The skills are clustered into four groups, shown in Table 1.1.

TABLE **1.1** ■ **enGauge 21st Century Skills**

Digital-Age Literacy	**Inventive Thinking**
Basic, scientific, economic, and technological literacies	Adaptability/managing complexity
Visual and information literacies	Self-direction
Multicultural literacy and global awareness	Curiosity, creativity, and risk-taking
	Higher-order thinking and sound reasoning
Effective Communication	**High Productivity**
Teaming, collaboration, and interpersonal skills	Ability to prioritize, plan, and manage for results
Personal, social, and civic responsibility	Effective use of real-world tools
Interactive communication	Ability to create relevant, high-quality products

© 2003 North Central Regional Educational Laboratory.

According to the Metiri/NCREL study, "Technology has catapulted us into a knowledge-based, global society" (2003, p. 7). Because of technology, what students learn and how and when they learn is changing. As a result of the study, NCREL advises that technology influences learning in three significant ways, summarized on the following page.

1. Technology is a driver for change. Success in this society will require significantly different skills than in the past.

2. Technology serves as a bridge to high academic achievement. More engaged, relevant, meaningful, and personalized learning lead to higher academic achievement. When technology is used appropriately, children learn more, even as measured by conventional tests.

3. Technology provides a platform for more informed decision-making and accountability, using timely, meaningful data to shape learning opportunities. This translates into more personalized learning based on continuous feedback available to students, teachers, and parents.

Partnership for 21st Century Skills

Partnership for 21st Century Skills is an organization that advocates infusing these skills into classrooms. Its mission is to "Serve as a catalyst to position 21st-century skills at the center of U.S. K–12 education by building collaborative partnerships among education, business, community, and government leaders." A listing of its organizational members, framework, and other information is available at www.21stcenturyskills.org.

NETS for Students

The International Society for Technology in Education (ISTE) developed a set of student standards in the 1990s and updated them in 2007 as a means to guide educators in the meaningful integration of technology into classroom activities. The National Educational Technology Standards for Students (NETS•S) both parallel and expand the competencies associated with the 21st Century Skills. The 21st Century Skills suggest areas of competency and responsibility that the NETS•S expand upon in relation to classroom learning. The two sets of skills are listed side by side in Table 1.2 to illustrate how the two sets of skills correlate. The NETS•S, available from ISTE at www.iste.org/nets/, are also included in this book as Appendix C.

TABLE **1.2** ▓ The 21st Century Skills and the NETS•S

The 21st Century Skills	NETS•S Skills
Digital-Age Literacy	**Research and Information Fluency**
Basic, scientific, economic, and technological literacies Visual and information literacies Multicultural literacy and global awareness	Students apply digital tools to gather, evaluate, and use information. Students: a. plan strategies to guide inquiry b. locate, organize, analyze, evaluate, synthesize, and ethically use information from a variety of sources and media c. evaluate and select information sources and digital tools based on the appropriateness to specific tasks d. process data and report results
	Digital Citizenship
	Students understand human, cultural, and societal issues related to technology and practice legal and ethical behavior. Students: a. advocate and practice the safe, legal, and responsible use of information and technology b. exhibit a positive attitude toward using technology that supports collaboration, learning, and productivity c. demonstrate personal responsibility for lifelong learning d. exhibit leadership for digital citizenship
Inventive Thinking	**Creativity and Innovation**
Adaptability and managing complexity Self-direction Curiosity, creativity, and risk taking Higher-order thinking and sound reasoning	Students demonstrate creative thinking, construct knowledge, and develop innovative products and processes using technology. Students: a. apply existing knowledge to generate new ideas, products, or processes b. create original works as a means of personal or group expression c. use models and simulations to explore complex systems and issues d. identify trends and forecast possibilities
Effective Communication	**Communication and Collaboration**
Teaming, collaboration, and interpersonal skills Personal, social, and civic responsibility Interactive communication	Students use digital media and environments to communicate and work collaboratively, including at a distance, to support individual learning and contribute to the learning of others. Students: a. interact, collaborate, and publish with peers, experts, or others employing a variety of digital environments and media b. communicate information and ideas effectively to multiple audiences using a variety of media and formats c. develop cultural understanding and global awareness by engaging with learners of other cultures d. contribute to project teams to produce original works or solve problems

continued

TABLE **1.2** ■ **The 21st Century Skills and the NETS•S**   *continued*

The 21st Century Skills	NETS•S Skills
High Productivity	**Critical Thinking, Problem Solving, and Decision Making**
Prioritizing, planning, and managing for results Effective use of real-world tools Ability to produce relevant, high-quality products	Students use critical-thinking skills to plan and conduct research, manage projects, solve problems, and make informed decisions using appropriate digital tools and resources. Students: **a.** identify and define authentic problems and significant questions for investigation **b.** plan and manage activities to develop a solution or complete a project **c.** collect and analyze data to identify solutions and make informed decisions **d.** use multiple processes and diverse perspectives to explore alternative solutions
	Technology Operations and Concepts
	Students demonstrate a sound understanding of technology concepts, systems, and operations. Students: **a.** understand and use technology systems **b.** select and use applications effectively and productively **c.** troubleshoot systems and applications **d.** transfer current knowledge to the learning of new technologies

Technology and Learning Research

As we were writing this book, we reviewed a number of research reports about technology and learning. In this section, the summarized results of several studies demonstrate how integrating technology into teaching and learning activities helps students achieve academically.

Research from the Center for Applied Research in Educational Technology (CARET)

According to the Center for Applied Research in Educational Technology (CARET), technology can help improve student performance in six ways. CARET is a project of ISTE in partnership with Education Support Systems and the Sacramento County Office of Education. For further details, visit the CARET site at http://caret.iste.org. We've added explanations after each of the research findings.

1. "Technology improves student performance when the application directly supports the curriculum objectives being assessed." In other words, technology is most effective when integrated with curriculum content.

2. "Technology improves performance when the application provides opportunities for student collaboration." Studies show that students' performances are enhanced when they use technology in pairs and collaborative groups.

3. "Technology improves performance when the application adjusts for student ability and prior experience and provides feedback to the student and teacher about student performance or progress with the application." This finding supports the differentiated instruction practices of coaching and mentoring, as well as sharing responsibility for how well students are learning when they use particular tech applications.

4. "Technology improves performance when the application is integrated into the typical instructional day." This finding supports classroom/content learning with technology as opposed to lab learning with technology.

5. "Technology improves performance when the application provides opportunities for students to design and implement projects that extend the curriculum content being assessed by a particular standardized test." Student-created products, multimedia, and video streaming are examples of how technology can broaden curriculum content beyond material assessed by standardized tests and can increase learning.

6. "Technology improves performance when used in environments where teachers, the school community, and school and district administrators support the use of technology." Along with administrative support for technology, (1) integration of technology with instruction, (2) professional development for teachers, and (3) computer use at home and in school with differentiated products and student entry points combine to improve performance.

Differentiated instruction focuses on teaching strategies that give diverse students multiple options for taking in and processing information, making sense of ideas, and expressing learning. Technology tools can support good instruction and offer personalized learning environments where students interact with software, conduct research, create products, and communicate with others outside their school. Both differentiated instruction and technology tools are important for digital-age learning.

Technology Use in Schools Reports

The use of technology in classrooms appears to range from none or minimal to frequent. Although various agencies and groups across the United States have collected data, neither the collection methods nor the types of data gathered are comparable. As a result, it is difficult, if not impossible, to know how much and how effectively technology is used in middle schools today.

Information from several important reports on the effectiveness of technology and how it is used in schools is presented in the following sections.

Technology Counts

Technology Counts is the main title of a report (in print and digital formats) produced by *Education Week* first in 1997 and annually since then except for 2000. *Education Week* surveys the entire United States to measure the status of K–12 educational technology. Using this data, researchers create individual state technology reports based on four criteria:

1. Access to Technology

2. Use of Technology

3. Capacity to Use Technology

4. Overall Technology

Education Week analyzes the data gathered. Every state receives a report card grade for each of the four categories and an overall grade. Readers can access the EdWeek site (www.edweek.org) to compare their states to others.

"Technology Counts 2007: A Digital Decade" is the tenth annual report completed by *Education Week*. Although many states have made great strides toward improving technology in the schools, it is disheartening to read these survey results. Of the 50 states and the District of Columbia, only three received an A for their overall technology grade: Georgia, Virginia, and South Dakota. Five states and Washington, D.C. (which ranked the lowest), received D grades: Hawaii, Oregon, Rhode Island, Delaware, and Nevada. The rest of the states range from Florida with a B+ grade down through eight states with C– grades. The average grade is C–/C+. To check out your state's score in the Technology Counts 2007 survey, see www.edweek.org/ew/toc/2007/03/29/. Individual states' grades from the 2008 and 2009 reports are also on the *Education Week* website. Entire reports for each year may be purchased from *Education Week.*

The USEiT Study

In the USEiT Study, a three-year study of several schools in Massachusetts completed in 2004, some typical findings were noted when middle school teachers were asked to rate which of 24 conditions provided obstacles for making more effective use of technology in their classrooms. Of the 24 conditions, 12 were especially meaningful. See Table 1.3.

Please note middle school teachers' perceptions of conditions 4, 5, 8, 9, and 10. These perceptions are commonly expressed in schools all over the country and reflect the larger message that many teachers believe they do not have enough time or do not know how to integrate technology into their day-to-day instruction or do not perceive it as important enough to include. More information about the USEiT study can be obtained at http://escholarship.bc.edu/intasc/25/.

TABLE **1.3** ■ USEiT Study Results

Condition	Not an obstacle	Minor obstacle	Major obstacle
1. Lack of computers in the classroom	12.5%	28.3%	59.2%
2. Difficult to access computers in labs and/or library	23.9%	39.2%	36.9%
3. Do not have enough computers for all of my students	19.9%	30.6%	49.5%
4. Professional development prepares me to use technology in the classroom, but I do not have enough time to "practice"	19.6%	37.7%	42.6%
5. Insufficient or inadequate support on how to use technology in the classroom	32.6%	44.4%	23.0%
6. Computers are too unpredictable—they crash or the software does not work right	30.8%	40.5%	28.7%
7. Increased speed and improved technology negates teachers' previous investments in technology	48.4%	39.0%	12.6%
8. There is too much course material to cover in a year to make room for technology use	21.5%	41.8%	36.7%
9. No idea how the district wants us to use computers in the classroom	49.3%	35.5%	15.3%
10. Not sure how to make technology relevant to my subject	54.8%	33.0%	12.1%
11. The computer skills of students in my class vary so widely that it's too difficult to manage computer use	55.5%	36.2%	8.3%
12. The academic skills of my students vary so widely that I cannot use computers usefully in my classroom	56.1%	34.0%	9.9%

The Unitedstreaming Study

"A Report on the Effect of the unitedstreaming Application on Educational Performance" (Boster, Meyer, Roberto, & Inge, 2002), says that those students who received instruction that incorporated unitedstreaming videos showed dramatic improvement in achievement. Unitedstreaming is a browser-based Internet content delivery system developed by Discovery Education. It consists of a collection of more than 5,000 videos and 50,000 chaptered clips of standards-based educational videos, teacher's guides, black line masters, student activities, clip art, quizzes, and teacher resources. The report analyzed experiments in science and social studies in Grades 3 and 8 from three school districts in Virginia. Classes were randomly assigned as part of the experimental group or part of the control group. Students in the experimental group received instruction incorporating the unitedstreaming application; students in the control group received instruction without exposure to the application.

Conclusions drawn from the study reveal three primary reasons that multimedia and technology are effective in the classroom:

1. Multimedia and technology engage students, leading to more attentive, knowledgeable, and higher-achieving students.

2. Multimedia and technology lead to better prepared and more effective teachers.

3. Multimedia and technology in the classroom change the nature of interaction in ways that help students learn. (2002, pp. 6–7)

A summary of the report is available at www.iste.org.

The Speak Up 2008 Study

The "Speak Up 2008 for Students, Teachers, Parents, and Administrators" report (Speak Up, 2009) from Project Tomorrow, a national nonprofit organization, summarized national data on technology use in education. Input was collected from 281,500 student surveys and 29,644 teacher surveys; 3,114 school leaders, and 21,309 parents also contributed their opinions.

The surveys focused on the technology products and Internet tools, including Web 2.0 and emerging technologies used by teachers and students, and how they are using them. Additional questions about 21st-century skills and schools' efforts to prepare students for the global marketplace were included. Surveys also focused on trends, obstacles, and issues, and student achievement through technology. The full Speak Up 2008 report, published in 2009, is available at www.tomorrow.org/speakup/pdfs/SU08_findings_final_mar24.pdf. Additional findings and special reports are published on Project Tomorrow's website (www.tomorrow.org).

Results from the survey show a gap between students' desire to use 21st-century technology tools, such as Web 2.0 applications and mobile electronic devices, for class-related tasks and the actual amount of time and freedom they have to access them. Here are selected facts from the survey data. Please note that some of the figures are close approximations (denoted by the word "about"), as some of the information was provided via bar graphs.

The following question provides a general overview of students' use of technology for school work and thus serves as a starting point for data analysis and reflection. When students in Grades 6–12 were asked, "Besides writing and Internet research, how do you use technology for school work?" they responded:

Use of Technology for School Work	Grades 6–8	Grades 9–12
Take an online test	About 31%	About 30%
Use an online textbook	About 26%	About 31%
Take an online class	About 12%	About 12%
Play educational games	About 44%	About 27%
Upload to a school portal	About 30%	About 38%
Use MySpace for collaboration	About 31%	About 47%
Create PowerPoints/videos	About 53%	About 63%
Communicate with others via e-mail, IM or text messages	About 47%	About 63%
Access class information	About 53%	About 64%

Mobile Learning

A significant increase between 2007 and 2008 occurred in middle school students' access to mobile electronic devices—cell phones, laptops, MP3 players, and smart phones. The 2008 Speak Up survey report showed:

- a 23% increase in cell phone access

- a 61% increase in laptop access

- an 85% increase in access to a smart phone for personal use (p. 4)

Students in Grades 6 through 12 access mobile devices with the following frequency (2009, p. 4):

Device	Middle School Students	High School Students
Cell phone	Just over 60%	70%
MP3	Just over 80%	Almost 90%
Laptop	50%	52%
Smart phone	25%	28%

However, students are often restricted from using mobile devices for school work. When students in Grades 6–12 were asked how they would like to use their mobile devices to help with school work, they said they would like to:

- Communicate with classmates (53%) or teachers (34%) via e-mail, IM, or text messaging

- Work with classmates on projects at home or at school (48%)

- Play educational games (32%)

- Conduct Internet research (53%)

- Record class lectures to listen to at a later time (32%)

- Receive alerts about upcoming homework and tests (51%)

- Access their schools' portals (24%) (2009, p. 4)

Are administrators and teachers opposed to integrating mobile devices into the classroom? It seems that there is much more resistance to these tech tools in the classroom; however, the Speak Up study showed some promising results. Seventy-five percent of all administrators and 50% of all teachers surveyed in 2008 believe that mobile devices boost students' interest in school and learning. One-third of the teachers and one-half of the administrators say the devices can be used to extend learning outside the classroom. One-third of the administrators and 20% of the teachers recognize the value of mobile learning devices in the development of critical thinking, communications, and collaboration skills. Teachers (25%) and administrators (33%) acknowledge that mobile devices can help to personalize instruction. Another positive finding was that half of the administrators and one-third of the teachers surveyed "recognize that using mobile devices for instruction would prepare students for the world of work" (2009, pp. 4–5).

Web 2.0

While Web 2.0 tools are extremely attractive to students and are heavily used outside of the classroom, opportunities for students to use them in their schools are limited and controlled. Middle and high school students reported in the 2008 Speak Up poll that they use these new tech tools and applications outside of school to communicate, collaborate, create, and contribute.

In terms of communication, 40% of high schoolers and 35% of middle schoolers update their profiles regularly on social networking sites, such as MySpace, Facebook, and Friendster. One-half use e-mail, text messaging, or IM to communicate with one another (2009, p. 5).

Students in Grades 6–12 collaborate via Web 2.0 tools by writing together (20%), creating a list of resources to share or remember (16%), notifying themselves of things that interest them (22%), and participating in online gaming (34%) and virtual reality environments (15%) (2009, p. 6).

How do teen students create and contribute via Web 2.0? Photo, music, or video sharing is the most frequent way (38%), while creating new videos, music, audio, or animation (32%) ranks a close second. Other popular responses were contributing to blogs (18%) and wikis (11%) and creating mashups by repackaging different pieces to create something entirely different (23%) (2009, p. 6).

Responses from teachers and principals to questions about their use of Web 2.0 tools and applications indicated lower numbers. However, they were closer in the areas of blogging (teachers: about 10%; principals: about 13%) and wikis (teachers: 5%; principals: about 7%). Principals and teachers responded equally (5%) in the areas of participation in online gaming and virtual reality. Principals (about 10%) collaborate and contribute by writing via Web 2.0 a bit more than teachers (5%) (2009, fig. 3, p. 5).

Online Learning

Comparisons of Speak Up data from 2007 with results from 2008 show that students' interest in online learning grew significantly, particularly at the middle school level. While high school students' interest jumped by 21%, responses of middle school students revealed a 46% leap! The primary reason for this upsurge in middle school interest was, as students said, "to get extra help in a subject (44%) in which they are struggling, thus viewing online learning as a tool for their own self-directed remediation" (2009, p. 6). High school students mentioned other reasons, such as to earn college credit (47%), to work at their own pace (43%), and to take a class that was not offered at their school (40%). About one-third of middle and high school students said that online learning increases their performance in school because they feel more comfortable asking questions and can review material as often as needed. Older students in Grades 9–12 say that online learning is more interesting because they have more control of their own learning. The 2008 survey shows that one-half of high school students long for more appealing classes. While one-third of parents and administrators think that students in Grades 6–12 should have to fulfill some type of online learning requirement in order to graduate from high school, only one-quarter of the students in those grades supported the idea (2009, pp. 6–7).

Student Perceptions about 21st-Century Learning and Preparation for the Global Marketplace

Students are innovative users of technology and adopt new technologies to support learning and lifestyles. Communication, collaboration, creation, and contribution are the four "C"s that drive their use of technology for learning and for personal use. The 2008 Speak Up survey suggests that producing content is often more important to them in their learning journeys than the outcome or end result. Students believe that technology enriches their learning experiences and prepares them for a competitive job market.

The poll highlighted some unsettling responses in students' perception of their schools, their (lack of) preparedness for future careers, and frustration with school policies on technology use.

Only one-third of high school students believe their schools are doing a good job of preparing them for future jobs; yet, over half (56%) of the principals think their schools are doing a good job. Parents responded even more harshly than the students. Sadly, only 25% of high school students think "their school cares for them as a person." More than half say that "if they were the principal, they would listen more to students' ideas as a strategy for improving education" (2009, p. 2). Forty-three percent of middle and high school students are frustrated with school filters and firewalls that are meant to protect them but instead limit their access and inhibit their learning. Thirty-five percent of students in Grades 6–12 believe that teachers are a major obstacle to technology use. In addition, 26% of middle and high school students specifically mentioned that school "rules" limit when and where technology is used at school. Many are disturbed by the rules that do not allow them to use their own devices and access their own communications tools (2009, p. 2).

Based on the responses from a cohort group of middle and high school students, teens wish that they could learn more about future careers in the following ways (2009, p. 8):

- By talking to field experts (46%)
- By getting on-the-job experience through part-time work (46%)
- Via podcasts and videos on "a day-in-the-life of ____," which they could download to mobile devices (26%)
- By using authentic tools to solve real-life problems with peers (26%)

Fifty percent of middle and high school students believe that science plays an important role in getting into college, and the same percentage of parents say they will encourage their children to pursue a STEM (science-technology-engineering-math) career. More than 40% of Grade 3–12 students think science is important because in the future they may have a job that uses science. Surprisingly, only 17% of students in Grades 6–8 and 21% in Grades 9–12 say they are very interested in pursuing a career in a STEM field (2009, p. 7).

How People Learn and Multimodal Learning Reports

Educators can take advantage of the research reported by two studies: "How People Learn: Brain, Mind, Experience, and School" (Bransford, Brown, & Cocking, 1999), available at www.nap.edu/html/howpeople1/, and a follow-up report, "Multimodal Learning Through Media: What the Research Says" (Metiri Group/Cisco Systems, 2008), available at www.cisco.com/web/strategy/docs/education/Multimodal-Learning-Through-Media.pdf.

In the conclusion of their 1999 report (p. 231), Bransford, Brown, and Cocking listed five ways that technology can help with effective learning environments.

1. Bringing real-world problems into classrooms with videos, demonstrations, simulations, and Internet connections to data and scientists.

2. Providing "scaffolding" support to augment what learners can do and reason about on their path to understanding.

3. Increasing opportunities for learners to obtain feedback from software tutors, teachers, and peers; to reflect on their own learning processes; and to receive guidance on how to improve their learning and reasoning.

4. Building local and global communities of educators, students, parents, and other interested learners.

5. Expanding opportunities for teachers' learning.

The researchers add,

An important function of some of the new technologies is their use as tools of representation. Representational thinking is central to in-depth understanding and problem representation is one of the skills that distinguish subject experts from novices. Many of the tools also have the potential to provide multiple contexts and opportunities for learning and transfer, for both student-learners and teacher-learners. Technologies can be used as learning and problem-solving tools to promote both independent learning and collaborative networks of learners and practitioners.

The use of new technologies in classrooms, or the use of any learning aid for that matter, is never solely a technical matter. The new electronic technologies, like any other educational resource, are used in a social environment and are, therefore, mediated by the dialogues that students have with each other and the teacher.

Educational software needs to be developed and implemented with a full understanding of the principles of learning and developmental psychology. Many new issues arise when one considers how to educate teachers to use new technologies effectively: What do they need to know about learning processes? What do they need to know about the technologies? What kinds of training are most effective for helping teachers use high-quality instructional programs? Understanding the issues that affect teachers who will be using new technologies is just as pressing as questions of the learning potential and developmental appropriateness of the technologies for children. (1999, p. 232)

The 2008 Metiri/Cisco report credits Richard Mayer, Roxanne Moreno, and other prominent researchers for the following data about visual and verbal learning: "Retention is improved through words and pictures rather than through words alone. . . . Students learn better from animation and narration than from animation and on-screen text" (2008, p. 12).

The Metiri/Cisco report also analyzes data from multiple studies, comparing multimodal learning with traditional, unimodal learning. The following is one of several interesting findings: "When the average student is engaged in higher-order thinking using multimedia in interactive situations, on average, their percentage ranking on higher-order or transfer skills increases by 32 percentile points over what that student would have accomplished with traditional learning. When the content shifts from interactive to noninteractive multimodal learning, the result is somewhat diminished, but is still at 20 percentile points over traditional means" (2008, p. 14).

Video Games in the Middle School Classroom

In their 2008 article, "Video Games in the Middle School Classroom," Elizabeth Simpson and Frances A. Clem report on research conducted by Beck and Wade (2004), Deubel (2006), Glasser (1998), Prensky (2001), and Bushweller (2006). Simpson and Clem recap interesting discoveries about our new generation of digital learners. We have distilled some of their findings that encourage the use of appropriate video simulation games as part of classroom instruction.

Digital learners:

- Process information at "twitch speed" with the ability to determine its usefulness in a matter of seconds;

- Relate to graphics first, not traditional text;

- Learn best through trial and error;

- Solve problems best within collaborative learning groups; and

- Perceive technology as an artifact of their culture, depend on it daily to meet their needs, and have a sophisticated community system built around technology.

Simpson and Clem believe that using video simulation games as classroom instructional tools is a great way to tap into students' affinity for graphics and technology. Their research concludes that video games encourage students' creativity, decision making, and role playing and help provide rich environments for learning. These authors say that many commercially available video games are not violent or titillating, and they list several good ones. Their article can be accessed at www.nmsa.org/Publications/Middle-SchoolJournal/Articles/March2008/Article1/tabid/1627/Default.aspx.

The 21st-Century Learner and Game-Based Learning

In their 2008 article, "The Twenty-First Century Learner and Game-Based Learning," Hiller A. Spires, John K. Lee, and James Lester report on research that illustrates the use of technologies by middle school students. The article is available at www.ncsu.edu/meridian/win2008/21st/.

The authors portray the connection between game-based learning and 21st-century skills, stating that game-based learning prepares individuals for managing complex information streams, the context for situated learning, and complex problem solving. They point out research that shows that game players have the ability to:

- Rapidly analyze new situations
- Interact with characters they don't really know
- Solve problems quickly and independently
- Think strategically in a chaotic world
- Collaborate effectively in teams

We are big fans of classroom games that connect with curriculum content. Games have broad appeal, and quite a bit of research supports gaming and learning. Here are a few names you may recognize:

Jean Piaget and Jerome Bruner both emphasized the importance of play for deep learning.

Robert Gagné's "Nine Events of Instruction" include "gaining attention" as step one. Games and multimedia capture the attention of students and make them curious. Other events in Gagné's list include practice, feedback, and assessment, all of which can be provided in gaming formats (Kruse, n.d., based on Gagné, 1985).

Mark Lepper and Thomas Malone's framework of intrinsic motivation is based on four criteria for engaging learners: challenge, curiosity, control, and fantasy. Challenge is created by clear, fixed goals that are relevant to the learner. Curiosity is both sensory and cognitive. Control is based on the feeling of choice, self-determination, and power. Fantasy encompasses emotions and the thinking process. These four criteria support gaming in education (Lepper & Malone, 1987).

Access, Adequacy, and Equity in Educational Technology

Results of a Survey of America's Teachers and Support Professionals on Technology in Public Schools and Classrooms

In this 2008 report by the National Education Association in collaboration with the American Federation of Teachers, researchers conclude that despite computer availability and use, no significant changes have been made in the way students are taught.

The report indicates that teachers still have not figured out how to use technology in innovative ways to improve learning and cites lack of teacher training as one of the problems. Another problem is that teachers tend to see technology use as another layer of preparation on top of what they teach. As a result of this finding, researchers recommend that professional development in technology be expanded to include integrating the use of technology as a learning tool in classrooms. Moreover, the researchers recommend, "All curriculum standards should include technology as an instructional tool and require students to use technology as an integral part of their class work and in a manner that enhances their creativity and learning of higher-order skills." The full report is available at www.digitaldivide.net/comm/docs/view.php?DocID=451/.

Technologies that Support Differentiated Instruction in Middle School Classrooms

Over the last 30 years, studies have shown that the most important factor affecting student learning is the teacher. Research from Robert J. Marzano, Debra J. Pickering, and Jane E. Pollock (2001), discussed in their book, *Classroom Instruction That Works: Research-Based Strategies for Increasing Student Achievement*, shows that nine categories of instructional strategies are most likely to help students learn in all grades and in any content area. In "Getting Acquainted with the Essential Nine," Laura Varlas (2002) explains each of the categories and suggests applications for them. Her article is available at www.middleweb. com/MWLresources/marzchat1.html.

The research by Marzano and his colleagues is important because it reveals nine essential instructional strategies that are most likely to improve student achievement. As states and districts become increasingly accountable for academic performance (due to the No Child Left Behind legislation), teachers need to learn how to employ instructional strategies that work to improve learning. These nine strategies can form a basis for differentiated instruction that uses technology tools.

In Table 1.4, Marzano's nine categories (in order of effectiveness) are listed in the first column. To explain how these strategies can be applied when teachers use differentiated instruction, we list corresponding elements in the second column. In the third column we list some commonly used technology tools, such as software and websites, that support differentiated instruction.

TABLE **1.4** ▣ Robert Marzano's Nine Categories of Instructional Strategies

Effective Instructional Strategies	Application to Differentiated Classrooms	Related Technology Tools
Recognizing similarities and differences	Graphic organizers, such as the Venn diagram and comparison matrix Representing similarities and differences in graphic or symbolic form Sorting, classifying, using metaphors and analogies	Inspiration software Web-based/downloadable graphic organizers Word-processing compare/contrast tables
Summarizing information and taking notes	Beginning, middle, end Clarifying information Teacher-prepared and student-prepared comments Webbing	Inspiration software NoteStar Read Write Think Notetaker Word-processing notes
Reinforcing effort and providing recognition	Effective praise and rewards Effort and achievement rubrics and charts Personalizing recognition Success stories of people who persisted during difficult times	Kids Are Authors (Scholastic) Microsoft Publisher or online certificates Personal Achievement Logs Word-processing feedback notes
Homework and practice	Planners/organizers Vary student and teacher feedback	Content-related software "Homework Help" sites to extend learning Word-processing planners, organizers, and notes BrainPOP and Discovery Education videos Multimedia and games

Nonlinguistic representations:
  Creating graphic representations
  Drawing pictures and pictographs
  Engaging in kinesthetic activity
  Generating mental pictures
  Making physical models
	Cause and effect organizers
	
	Concept organizers
	
	Drawing pictures, illustrations, and pictographs
	
	Graphic organizers
	
	Physical models and movement
	
	Time-sequence organizers
		Digital cameras
		
		Inspiration software
		
		Spreadsheet software
		
		Paint/draw tools
		
		Presentation software
		
		TimeLiner software
		
		Virtual manipulative software or websites
		
		BrainPOP and Discovery Education videos
		
		Multimedia and games

continued

TABLE **1.4** ■ **Robert Marzano's Nine Categories of Instructional Strategies** *continued*

Effective Instructional Strategies	Application to Differentiated Classrooms	Related Technology Tools
Cooperative/ collaborative learning groups by ability, interest, and other criteria	Flexible groups by interest, learning style, and/ or readiness Individual and Group Accountability Vary groups by size and objectives Think-Pair-Share strategy	Group investigations Individual and group assessments Jigsaw groups Multimedia software Scavenger hunts ThinkQuests/WebQuests Multimedia and games
Setting objectives and providing feedback	Learning contracts for achieving specific goals Ongoing assessment Praise Rubrics Self-assessment Student-led feedback Teacher feedback that is timely, specific, and constructive	Electronic journaling Project-based learning checklists RubiStar and other rubric generators Word-processing contracts
Generating and testing hypotheses	Decision making Historical investigation Invention Making predictions Problem-solving	Inspiration hypothesis Webs Internet research Online graphing generator Science Seeker software Simulations
Questions, cues, and advance organizers	Advance organizers Anticipation Guides Cubing and ThinkDots activities KWL Charts Pause after asking questions	Cubing and ThinkDots templates Inspiration advanced organizers Online or word processing KWL Charts Personal agendas

Source for effective instructional strategies (first column): Marzano, Pickering, & Pollock (2001).

What Does the Research Mean to Middle School Teachers?

We are reminded of some past conversations with school administrators who say they will embrace technology once they know it improves student learning. We say schools cannot wait for longitudinal data because, in the meantime, we are losing our students due to the preponderance of familiar but outdated instructional strategies that do not align with real-world work. The real world uses technology every day. Big corporations and small businesses use technology to plan, learn, communicate, assess, and produce. It is time for schools to embrace technology—wisely selecting the most effective tools, content, products, and processes it has to offer.

We realize that the research and skills sets we share in this chapter reveal challenges and opportunities for teachers. At the same time, we know that students are eager to learn with technology and want to "power up" when they go to school. We know this is true because we have used technology in our own teaching for many years and have observed students of all ages in numerous settings using technology. We have taught educators and K–16 students how to use software and web tools, how to produce products, and how to conduct research. In almost every instance, students' eagerness to learn and work with tech overshadows any fear of making mistakes.

In nearly every classroom, students enjoy helping each other figure out problems and, if allowed, are happy to show teachers how to use technology. Talk about problem solving! Students are natural tech problem solvers. Many teachers tend to disregard technology and learning research data. Some may fear changing their teaching techniques or hesitate to appear less than competent to students, some may not have time to study the data, and many others simply lack tech experience or work in districts so strapped for funds that the available technology is inadequate or unreliable. We understand all of these feelings and constraints—that's why we've written this book. As more teachers become comfortable using tech tools and experience how much prep time it can save them and how excited their students are to use tech in class, we believe they will encourage administrators to increase technology integration at all grade levels.

Summary

Studies show that technology is a highly motivating, interactive tool that can be used to personalize students' instruction according to their learning styles, interests, and readiness. Web resources and multimedia software greatly expand learning options and provide information access far beyond schools' textbooks and media centers. Technology can help teachers shape and deliver instruction to meet the needs of all students, assist in the improvement of students' thinking skills, provide research and presentation products, and improve communication.

Although many teachers still struggle with how to use technology and integrate it into classroom content, those who are more comfortable with technology may not have thought about how to use tech in a differentiated classroom. In other words, some teachers may be masters of differentiated instruction but not know how to use technology as a differentiation tool. Others may be techno whizzes but not know how differentiated instruction can improve their students' performances.

We believe that differentiated instruction supports what good teachers have always done and continue to do:

- Embrace the cultural–familial–academic differences among students

- Reach beyond text–chalkboard–lecture to stimulate student thinking

- Empower student-centered learning, in which planning, teaching, and assessment are focused on the needs, interests, and abilities of students

This book is about combining technology with differentiated instruction in ways that empower student learning and achievement. We explain the basics of differentiated instruction in Chapter 2 and in succeeding chapters offer strategies for combining it with technology to deliver middle school content in ways that motivate students.

Differentiated Instruction and Middle School Learners

Differentiated instruction continues to play a significant role in digital age classrooms. Due to its focus on modification of instruction for student diversity, student accountability for learning, and constructivist (student-centered) learning, differentiated instruction provides the flexibility teachers and students need. The curricular elements at the core of differentiated instruction (content—input, process—throughput, and product—output) mirror and marry nicely with technology. In addition, technology can assist us in our effort to engage students and personalize instruction according to students' interests, levels of readiness, and learning styles (the three primary student traits that guide differentiation). We'll share more about differentiated instruction in the next chapters as we challenge you to transform your classroom through the use of technology, not simply layer technology onto traditional instructional practices.

Overview of Differentiated Instruction, Student Traits, and Curricular Elements

Differentiated instruction (DI) is a way of looking at instruction that is centered on the belief that students learn in many different ways. It could be considered as a collection of best practices from gifted, special, and traditional education, but it's not really a new model. Back in the days of the one-room schoolhouse before the term was coined, teachers had to differentiate instruction for a range of ages and grades with no modern technology.

DI supplies teachers with a flexible framework that offers multiple learning approaches to meet learners' needs. It provides for an extensive array of instructional and management strategies to assist us in our effort to reach our very diverse learners. Within today's classrooms, we encounter an astonishing range of interests, levels of readiness, and learning styles, not to mention myriad cultural and familial differences that shape our students' social and learning personalities. DI recognizes and honors academic, cultural, and familial diversity. DI practitioners attend to that diversity and also meet curricular objectives via modification of instruction. Teachers, however, don't shoulder all of the responsibility for student learning and achievement; students are highly engaged and accountable.

As new trends and tactics are constantly emerging, you may wonder why differentiated instruction continues to be an influential educational approach in tomorrow's classrooms. This list of the fundamental components of differentiated instruction illustrates DI's value.

- DI encourages the modification of instruction to address student diversity and to meet curricular objectives.

- DI emphasizes student accountability for learning and high levels of participation via flexible grouping and simultaneous activities, such as Jigsaw and WebQuests.

- DI features group-driven tasks but also relies upon whole-class and individualized instruction to complement group work. It focuses on the quality of activities versus the quantity of work assigned.

- DI promotes a comfortable yet challenging learning environment. Teachers realize that their organization and presentation of content profoundly affects students' motivation to learn and their perceived ability to comprehend. Inspired students feel safe in their learning communities and are intrigued by the subject matter at hand.

- DI depends upon pre-, formative, and summative assessments that utilize both traditional and nontraditional evaluation methods, such as teacher observation, self-assessment, and project work.

■ Teachers who apply DI concepts show a willingness to learn more about their students and to modify instruction to support students' needs. As a result, using surveys and other tools to learn about students is important.

■ DI is guided by the constructivist or student-centered approach to teaching and learning. Constructivism, one of the big ideas in education that arose during the early 1990s, is the belief that students create or construct their own knowledge and understanding by building on previous learning. Constructivist learning is active rather than passive. Constructivist teachers relinquish their traditional role of "sage on the stage" (the omnipotent keeper of knowledge) to become the "guide on the side" (the facilitator of experiences and opportunities for students to learn).

■ In student-centered classrooms, planning, teaching, and assessment are focused on the needs and abilities of students. Why? Because constructivists believe learning is most meaningful when topics are connected to students' needs and interests, and when the students themselves are actively engaged in creating, understanding, and connecting with knowledge. Students are motivated to learn when they feel they have a real share in their own learning. In a student-centered classroom, students are given options and are included in decision-making processes. The focus in these classrooms is on choices, rather than on one size fits all. Students are regarded as individuals with ideas and needs that merit consideration and thoughtfulness.

■ DI practitioners make instructional decisions based on students' readiness, interests, learning profile, and affect; the learning environment; and the curricular elements of content, process, and product.

Now that we've shown DI's promise for longevity, let's examine the student traits and curricular elements that guide differentiation, as well as some common strategies that you might use for each. Please note that the ideas in Tables 2.1 and 2.2 are not an exhaustive list of strategies! (We will leave our exploration of student affect and the learning environment until later on in the chapter.) Differentiation of one or more of these essential curricular elements or student traits, translates into multiple learning approaches that will benefit students.

TABLE **2.1** ■ Definition of Student Traits and Possible Strategies for Differentiation

Readiness What students know; current preparedness	**Interest** Students' curiosities or passions	**Learning Profile** Preferred way to learn (shaped by intelligence, learning style, cultural-influenced and gender-based preferences)
Tiering	R.A.F.T. (Role, Audience, Format, Topic) and R.A.F.T.T. (Role, Audience, Format, Topic, and Technology)	Activities based on multiple intelligences theory
Curriculum Compacting	WebQuest	Tic-Tac-Toe or Choice Board
Varied Graphic Organizers	I-Search	Activities based on cognitive styles (auditory, kinesthetic, tactile, visual)
Learning Contracts	Jigsaw	Stations or Centers
	Stations or Centers	Various options based on interest or readiness

TABLE **2.2** ■ Definition of Curricular Elements and Possible Strategies for Differentiation

Content What is taught and learned (input)	**Process** The activities students do to make sense of ideas, concepts, and information (throughput)	**Product** The assessments or demonstrations of learning, such as the artifacts students produce (output)
Curriculum Compacting	Flexible Grouping	R.A.F.T. or R.A.F.T.T.
Learning Contracts	Cubing	Tic-Tac-Toe or Choice Board
WebQuests	ThinkDots	Numerous options based on interest
I-Search	Jigsaw	Numerous options based on readiness
Centers or Stations	Centers or Stations	Numerous options based on learning profile

In case you might not be familiar with some of the strategies referenced above, see Appendix A, Glossary of Strategies at the end of the book that briefly describes each one. In the remaining chapters of this book, we'll implement some of them in our suggested classroom activities, so you'll come upon some of these old friends again.

Whether you're an experienced DI practitioner or a novice, you are special because you work with what many believe to be the most difficult age group of students. If you are experienced, we're certain that you've witnessed firsthand the benefits of incorporating differentiated instruction into your classroom. Let's turn for a moment to the unique nature of middle school learners, who face a series of social, emotional, and intellectual changes. Can you anticipate why DI might provide the best approach for students at this level?

The Inner Workings and Complexities of the Teenage Brain

Emotional, Physical, and Intellectual Development and How They Impact Middle School Learners

Students in eighth grade often vary in appearance and maturity. One member of the football team might be 6 feet, 6 inches tall and weigh 180 pounds, a member of the wrestling team might be 5 feet tall and weigh 85 pounds. Another peer who plays on the football and wrestling teams might be 5 feet 9 inches tall and weigh 280 pounds. Talk about disparity! This example illustrates the huge variety that exists solely in the physical stature of our middle school students. On a daily basis, you also witness a wide range of diversity in their social, emotional, and intellectual levels of development. We are only beginning to understand the reasons for the unique behavior that our middle school students demonstrate, as well as the different paces at which they mature socially, emotionally, and intellectually. We usually have from 45–50 minutes, five days a week, to reach the young teens in our classrooms. Not only is there a great deal of academic ground to cover, but there's also a whole lot of psychology going on. In order to connect with our students intellectually, we need to understand and appreciate them emotionally and socially. Therefore, we'd like to explore some of the research on the teenage brain and the social, physical, and emotional development of adolescents.

In 2000, PBS aired a documentary about the teenage brain called "Frontline: Inside the Teenage Brain." You may view it online and see the great resources associated with the program at www.pbs.org/wgbh/pages/frontline/shows/teenbrain/. Other organizations, such as the National Middle School Association (NMSA) and the National Education Association (NEA), have published information about the teenage brain and how it affects learning styles, personalities, and behavior in the middle school classroom. Frontline's documentary describes a study in which teens and adults were asked to identify the emotions expressed on several pictures of faces, and neuropsychologists monitored how their brains responded to the photos via MRI images of the participants' brains. Even the medical practitioners were stunned that the teens had trouble identifying some of the emotions correctly (fear in particular) and that they used a different part of the brain to do so. The adults relied on the frontal cortex, which is known as the CEO of the brain, as it is the organizer, planner, and mood controller. The teens, however, utilized the amygdala, which is responsible for directing instinctual or gut reactions. It's found in the lower part of the brain and is considered to be "inferior" to the prefrontal section. The neuropsychologists concluded that the frontal cortex was not yet functioning at full capacity in the teen brain, resulting in teens' greater impulsivity, risky behavior, and a failure to think through possible consequences before acting. Furthermore, they discovered that the males' reactions were much stronger than the females' (PBS, 2002c). Based on the personalities in your classroom, do these results surprise you?

Further research has shown that the brain grows during the teenage years. Although 95% of the brain's structure is complete by age five or six, the brain experiences additional growth just before puberty. The growth occurs just behind the forehead in the prefrontal cortex, the portion of the brain mentioned previously. Once the growth phase is over, the brain turns to "pruning" of synapses. In other words, gray matter is lost, but myelin is wrapped around the most-used connections to strengthen them. The most daunting aspect of this whole process is that what our teens do at this time of growth can affect them forever. For example, if they use connections for sports and drama, those will be strengthened, but those for music and art may be pruned back. The connections they prefer and use most frequently (even if they're not so positive, such as those for TV viewing and playing couch potato) are hardwired to stick around, but those they ignore or fail to develop will fall by the wayside and literally die. This phenomenon is called the "Use It or Lose It Principle," coined by Jay Giedd, a neuroscientist at the National Institute of Mental Health who was a part of the Frontline show. Teens tend to tune us out at times about major issues, such as drugs and alcohol, but the research described above only underscores the fact that dangerous substances can do nothing but harm the growing brain and have lasting effects (PBS, 2002b).

The "Use It or Lose It Principle" also applies to the cerebellum (at the base of the brain—at the back of the head just above the neck), which changes more than any other part of the brain during adolescence. The cerebellum supposedly aids physical coordination, but scientists have found out that it also helps the brain process mental tasks that require higher order thinking—even those involving a teen's social skills. This section of the brain appears to be much more sensitive to environmental stimuli because it's not controlled by genetics (PBS, 2002b).

The corpus callosum is yet another section of the brain that undergoes growth during puberty. The corpus callosum transmits information between the hemispheres of the brain via a series of fibers. The fiber system that shapes language learning and associative thinking grows more quickly than those of proximate regions both before and during puberty. However, that rapid phase of development declines rather abruptly. For all of you language teachers (including me, Stephanie) who have been encouraging students, parents, and administrators to start language learning at a young age, we were right! It's much more difficult to begin learning a new language after age 12 (PBS, 2002a).

Interestingly, we viewed a video posted on Edutopia, "The Heart-Brain Connection: The Neuroscience of Social, Emotional and Academic Learning" (www.edutopia.org/ richard-davidson-sel-brain-video/). In this video, neuroscientist Richard Davidson (2007) echoes the notion of brain plasticity (changeability) that was publicized in the Frontline program on the teenage brain. Like Giedd, he maintains that there are "more sensitive periods" when the brain might be less plastic than others, and he believes that its plasticity never disappears completely. Studies that Davidson has conducted on the brain speak volumes about the influence of affect, the fourth DI student trait, which is how students feel about themselves, their work, and the classroom. Just to clarify, we hear a variety of terminology related to affect, such as affective domain or emotional intelligence and social and emotional learning (SEL). It is not our intent to devote many pages of text to comparing and contrasting these theories or relationships, but here are a few working definitions with some brief background:

Emotional Intelligence

Defined by psychologist and author Daniel Goleman (1995)

> Per Goleman: emotional intelligence is "the capacity for recognizing our own feelings and those of others, for motivating ourselves, and for managing emotions well in ourselves and in our relationships." (1995, in Edutopia, 2001a)

Affective Domain

Defined by David R. Krathwohl, Benjamin S. Bloom, and Bertram B. Masia (1964)
Best known as Krathwohl's Taxonomy of Affective Domain, a part of Bloom's Taxonomy of the three domains of educational goals and activities.

> Karin Kirk quotes Krathwohl et al. on affective domain: the "learning objectives that emphasize a feeling, tone, an emotion, or a degree of acceptance or rejection." (1964, in Kirk, 2007)

Social and Emotional Learning (SEL)

More of an outgrowth of Goleman's book (*Emotional Intelligence*), Gardner's book (*Multiple Intelligences*), in addition to educational research on prevention and resilience.

> Zins and Elias (2006) define SEL as the "capacity to recognize and manage emotions, solve problems effectively, and establish positive relationships with others."

We have read studies about how SEL programs have decreased violence in schools, improved test scores, increased cooperation and unity, and strengthened emotional control. (See, for example, "Emotional Intelligence Research: Indicators Point to the Importance of SEL" (2001b) at www.edutopia.org/emotional-intelligence-research/ and "Emotional Intelligence: The Missing Piece" at www.edutopia.org/emotional-intelligence-missing-piece/.)

Davidson shares in his presentation (2007) that if we invest time in SEL, not only do we impact the affective domain, but we impact brain function and structure. Training students to respond in emotionally and socially appropriate ways actually affects concrete brain circuits, particularly those in the prefrontal cortex (something that medication is unable to do as effectively). In addition, SEL reduces the production of the stress hormone, cortisol, which is beneficial for the body and the brain. When there is a high level of cortisol in the brain due to anxiety, working memory is disrupted. If students can learn effective, calming responses to negative emotions, they improve cognition. Moreover, what many have considered as inherent traits or characteristics in the past, such as kindness, patience, and calmness, can indeed be developed in students as skills via this form of character education.

How do these developments in the teen brain's structure manifest themselves in students who enter through the doors of our classrooms for a mere one to three years, depending on the grade levels and subjects we teach?

In terms of anatomical development, we've learned that 11- to 16-year-olds go through rapid physical changes, similar to what they experienced during infancy. At no other stage of human development will such extensive physiological changes occur in such a short period of time. Peter Lorain explains that young teens endure the hardening of the skeletal structure (tailbone included), which often results in sciatic nerve pain if they are forced to sit for a long period of time. Muscles are stretched to the limit because bone growth exceeds muscle growth, so students literally feel "growing pains." The stomach actually increases in length and activity, so our students are hungry all the time, and the body needs that food to help with the other areas that demand energy for growth. The hormones that have already begun to rage through some bodies manifest themselves in acne, physical awkwardness, and distraction. As you might expect, there is no way to predict exactly when a teen will develop. Girls mature earlier than boys, but both genders experience different rates of change, and those changes are taking place sooner than in times past (Lorain, n.d. a).

When we think about challenges that present themselves in our classrooms, one that you might mention has to do with noise control. Our middle schoolers are constant chatterers and like to get in the last word, especially if a friend has made a wisecrack that demands a reply. We often forget that talking affords them the chance to work through the developmental and social experiences they're tackling. It's no secret that adolescents feel a strong need to belong to a peer group. In fact, their friends' opinions frequently matter more to them than those of their parents or teachers. Nonetheless, they seek and definitely need at least one adult in whom they feel they can safely confide. They feel comfortable testing out different roles or identities within a group, but they will conform in order to avoid rejection. This intent to conform is particularly evident in forms of dress and behavior, which can appear rather questionable or drastic at times. Our initial reaction is to scold them or judge them, but what they really need is the exact opposite. If we do not allow them the time and the space to come to grips with their own identities, they'll continue or escalate the behavior, unusual clothing, hair style, or anything else for shock value (Lorain, n.d. b).

Though teens seem to be more apathetic than passionate, more cruel than kind, such is not the case. During the middle school years, adolescents begin to contemplate moral issues, such as right versus wrong, social injustice, and inequality between the quality of life of various cultures or peoples. Take advantage of these budding concerns by constructing hands-on tasks, such as a community service or school improvement project, interviews of community leaders, letters to trigger change or protest unfairness, or some type of communicative exchange with middle schoolers in another state or country. When we extend our lessons beyond the classroom walls in a way that's relevant to our students, we deepen our connection to them, and help our students to cement key information into long-term memory.

The Learning Environment

A Critical Component for Success

Learning environment, the management or climate of the classroom, is DI's fourth curricular element, and it's a bit more difficult to manipulate than the other three. It is an extremely vital yet somewhat more intangible DI curricular element. Obviously, the learning environment is an actual, physical place. When we think about the learning environment as a curricular element, however, we are referring to the classroom climate, which we often measure in subjective terms. The learning environment, as you know, exerts a huge influence on our learners, so it's essential to cultivate a healthy one and monitor it vigilantly. However, it's inherently subjective and, as scholars Adelman and Taylor (2005) point out, founded on perception: "classroom climate is a perceived quality of the setting." As we have multiple students in the classroom, we might have 25 or 30 disparate assessments of the classroom climate. What we do know is that our middle school students thrive in a task-oriented classroom with active learning, flexible groups, peer tutoring, focus on improvement, room for mistakes, and, of course, technology. Because the fear of failure is particularly intense at this age level, the traditional, performance-oriented classroom wherein grades, test scores, and correctness reign supreme is not always the best fit (Maddy, 2008). Unfortunately, it's pretty commonplace. We persist with our mantra that student choice, whenever possible, is empowering, as it fuels motivation and achievement. In addition, activities that supply ample opportunity for the exploration of personal interests are of the essence. Old curiosities quickly fade, and new interests replace them, so continue to assess throughout the year. Whatever the current trend may be, your middle school students will express intense passion about it, intensity unmatched by any other age group.

Although learning environment is largely based on perception, we can change the physical surroundings and our own teaching styles to effect a positive change for our students. The three additional curricular elements, content, process, and product, enable many more concrete strategies for differentiation; nonetheless, the learning environment is something that we must attend to in order to differentiate effectively.

Time allotment in middle school class periods does not truly accommodate or enhance community building, nor do the social, intellectual, and emotional challenges that your adolescent students undergo. For those two reasons in particular, it is even more vital to dedicate time and energy to fostering a safe learning environment. My (Stephanie's) classroom personality tends to be somewhat strict, particularly at the beginning of the year, and then I ease up as I see fit. I find it's much more difficult to toughen up with students if you've started off too leniently. My students know my expectations and classroom policies—even my college-age learners. However, rigor does not mean exclusion. Involving students in decision making is empowering. If students genuinely feel a part of the process, they just may be more respectful of your rules and of their classmates. In other words, if you value their input, they might give more weight to yours. Second, students recognize that you are presenting them with an opportunity that does not come around too frequently in other classrooms, so something is at stake. If they are fearful or troubled by particular aspects of the learning environment, they have a chance to address those issues via the avenue you've made available to them. If you begin by including students, you set a tone for the classroom environment that is key to future success, particularly for collaborative projects. It does not ensure that your classroom will be totally free of conflict, but a set of common values and practices decided upon by all (the democratic process at work) is powerful. Furthermore, it may help to minimize the unattractive features of middle school learning in your classroom, such as bullying, unkindness, and disrespect, which consume precious learning time and have negative impacts on all those in the classroom including the teacher.

The social, academic, physical, and emotional challenges specific to middle school learners are just the tip of the iceberg for middle school teachers. We haven't begun to mention additional obstacles that present themselves in classrooms of all levels, such as unruly behavior, self-centeredness, dysfunctional family situations that affect individual students and those around them, copious assessments, movement to other classes, and various interruptions from P.A. announcements and phone calls to bomb threats and other safety-related concerns. Building an effective learning community is definitely an emotionally laden task that can be tricky.

Yet another significant element of the middle school learning environment that we tend to overlook is the physical space and layout of the classroom. Although elementary teachers consider organization and placement of materials and desks and special classroom areas for interest centers, free reading, or group meetings, the traditional middle school classroom can be an uninviting place. Many of the middle school classrooms we've visited have desks with immovable chairs (the desk and the chair are joined together with the desktop's surface on the right-hand side) that are aligned in rows. If left-handed students are fortunate, they might find one desk that has a writing surface on the left-hand side. In order to accommodate group work, students must move their entire desk (as opposed to just a chair). The desks are usually made of hard wood and metal, and the chairs are not adjustable or comfortable for growing teens. Our students are forced to hunch over, slump, and stretch out their legs almost to the point that they're lying back in their chairs, just to try to get more comfortable. While we can't modify the basic physical layout of the classroom, we can make minor improvements to create an appealing environment. Pleasing physical surroundings translate into an increased comfort level for our students, and an upbeat learning atmosphere is well worth the effort. Music and images that appeal to and reflect students' interests and concerns (celebrities, current movies, sports, etc.)

make your classroom an inviting place. Students who feel at home in their classrooms typically work with more confidence and success.

Finally, if we spend quality time educating our students about emotional intelligence and affect, we equip them with better defenses to handle the stress associated with the transitions to middle school and adolescence. Proponents of SEL claim that such training also improves focus and recall in the classroom, along with a multitude of other benefits mentioned earlier in this chapter. Moreover, attention to affect via SEL helps students to develop coping mechanisms to deal with family and other personal issues that trap them emotionally and cognitively (Richardson, 2002). The "appropriate" social and emotional responses that we teach them are those that they will need for success in their future professions, too.

A must-see for students, teachers, and parents is PBS' **It's My Life** site (http://pbskids.org/itsmylife/). It offers videos, games, journal activities, interviews with teen celebrities, and offline activities in the following areas: friends, family, school, body, emotions, and money. When you click on the "School" icon, there is a drop-down menu that says "More topics" further down the screen, just above the "Games" section. Choose "Middle School."

Celebrate your students! There's a fun read at **Fifty Great Things About Middle Schoolers!** (www.education-world.com/a_curr/curr097.shtml).

Check out the numerous resources at the **Collaborative for Academic, Social and Emotional Learning** (www.casel.org/home.php). It has a wealth of information about SEL, particularly a long list of programs used by schools across the nation.

Summary

As you invest yourself in the "tweens" in your classrooms—those with developing, ungainly adult bodies and still malleable children's hearts—we encourage you to assimilate DI strategies and technology. Differentiated instruction powered by technology assists us in our endeavor to meet the physical, intellectual, and emotional challenges and needs specific to middle school learners that we have examined throughout this chapter. As a differentiator, technology helps us to personalize learning for our extremely varied students through collaborative learning and problem solving, which are excellent activities for the growing brain and for our students' future professions in the world of work. Technology facilitates modification of instruction in several areas to meet the needs of diverse students by making changes to subject matter (content), channels of throughput (process), means of output (product), and the learning environment. As a great motivator, technology has a powerful influence on our students' affect levels.

In Chapter 3, we're going to explore some of the tech tools and strategies available to us through the read/write web also known as Web 2.0. We'll identify its nine technologies that have the most impact on teaching and learning and investigate how you might use them in your classroom.

Using the New Web 2.0 and Other Technologies

You've probably heard of Web 2.0 and may even use some aspects of it. So what's the buzz about Web 2.0? And what exactly is it? Why is it causing a social and cultural shift that affects student learning? How will Web 2.0 technologies impact your teaching? And what do you need to do to get on board?

Quite simply, Web 2.0 applications change the nature of Web 1.0 from distributed to participatory. In Web 1.0 users obtain information by searching for it and accessing, printing, or downloading the information from a website. Information is distributed down to each user, and the user is the receiver of the information.

In Web 2.0, users control the tools of access, production, and publication and use them to collaborate. Users can add to and change others' work online (if permitted), share openly, and produce information as well as receive it. Web 2.0 is transforming education because every educator and every student can be an author, a knowledge producer, and a collaborator. In fact, Web 2.0 is often referred to as the read/write web because that's exactly what it is.

Web 2.0 is grounded in constructivism in which students create, produce, and have responsibility for their own learning. The role of the teacher shifts to facilitator/manager, rather than the only keeper of knowledge. This is a major cultural change for teachers, who may find themselves in the position of knowing less about technology than many of their students and feel uncomfortable about using technology when they didn't grow up with it or use it in college. Yet as The Partnership for 21st Century Skills (2002) states,

> Today's education system faces irrelevance unless we bridge the gap between how students live and how they learn. When students use 21st century technologies, they are able to meet their intrinsic needs to form communities, ask questions, and earn audience and attention. Today's students will spend their adult lives in a multitasking, technology-driven, diverse world, and they must arrive equipped to do so.

Safety Concerns

Although Web 2.0 changes teaching and learning by opening up new frontiers, it also brings the need for greater monitoring of student access, activities, and projects. Educators must emphasize acceptable use of the Internet and Internet safety as well as teach it. One of the most exciting aspects of the Web 2.0 technologies is that many of the tools are free as well as collaborative. Free and collaborative makes for compelling economics in financially strapped districts. At the same time, throwing caution to the wind and opening the doors wide open to Web 2.0 is sheer stupidity. Schools are legally bound by the Children's Internet Protection Act (CIPA) to protect students (www.fcc.gov/cgb/consumerfacts/cipa.html).

Despite the fact that school districts uphold the law, passed in 2000, by using content filters and other means to protect students, no system is perfect. Inappropriate content still slips through. And students who are smarter than the filters can find ways around blocked sites to access inappropriate content.

So how do you deal with the equation of free + collaborative + safety concerns? We find the best way is also another equation: acceptable use policies + curriculum content that educates staff and students about keeping safe online + filtering + parental involvement = safe Web 2.0 schools.

Organizations, such as CyberSmart, GetNetWise, NetSmartz, Web Wise Kids, and Wired-Kids have superb resources for helping you and your students learn about Internet safety.

A great starting point for in-class tasks is the free CyberSmart curriculum (www.cybersmartcurriculum.org). Here you will find lesson plans and activities, printable posters, family letters in PDF format that outline what students will be studying about cyber safety in class and what families can do together to reinforce learning, and many excellent resources organized by topic. Each lesson includes an overview, lesson objectives, related ISTE standards, websites to preview for use with your students, online resources, activity sheets, plans and teaching instructions, and extension activities.

In addition, CyberSmart offers professional development and short videos made by high school students for K–8 students. GetNetWise (www.getnetwise.org) is another terrific source of information with numerous tutorials that show parents how they can change computer settings/preferences using Flash to heighten security and privacy.

NetSmartz (www.netsmartz.org) provides activities for collaborative or independent learning. It has a wealth of resources in English and Spanish for students in Grades K–12. Some of its outstanding resources include:

- SchoolTube: an Internet video publisher.

- NetSmartz 411: a knowledge base for parents with an "ask the experts" option.

- A bi-monthly newsletter called BNetS@vvy that gives adults tips as to how to encourage online safety.

- Activity cards that correlate with online activities. These are handy printables with the following features: list of materials, overview, educational objectives, overarching Internet safety message, discussion questions, dialogues, suggested answers, and instructions for one to two activities. Middle school students watch a vignette and then complete various tasks, such as answering questions in groups, playing a game, writing a paragraph, letter or dialogue, developing an Internet safety plan, and so on.

- Online games and vignettes.

- Downloads, such as posters, PDFs of safety pledges, screensavers, media player skins, and situation cards with hypothetical, what-should-you-do? problems/issues.

- Internet vocabulary, certificates, and licenses.

Web Wise Kids (http://webwisekids.org) features an Internet safety program for parents and other intriguing solutions for classroom use. The Missing School Kit includes materials for youth leaders and community groups in the format of the Missing game (luring, predators, chat rooms) for students ages 11–14. A high school series is also available: "Mirror Image" (cyberstalking/modeling scam game) and "Air Dogs" (piracy, bullying, illegal downloading game). The website also includes a number of resources.

WiredKids (www.wiredkids.org) offers an ever-growing database of safe sites that pass through rigorous inspection before they may be approved. Three team members, who have completed several training courses, evaluate the site and search for negatives, such as foul language, nudity, online shopping, gambling, violence, intolerance, and so on. If the site passes inspection, it is rated according to age appropriateness. A knowledge base of questions and answers for parents is available, as is the opportunity to submit questions. In addition, WiredKids provides communities for students through which they may take classes and participate in clubs and activities, play games, become reporters, and review sites. In order to become members, students must obtain approval by submitting a signed code of conduct form, a signed parental consent form, and a letter from their school that shows they are in good standing.

The Difference between Web 1.0 and Web 2.0

According to Tim O'Reilly, whose firm brainstormed a comparison, Table 3.1 shows the big differences between Web 1.0 and Web 2.0 (O'Reilly, 2005).

TABLE **3.1** ■ Differences between Web 1.0 and Web 2.0

Web 1.0	Web 2.0
User as consumer	User as producer
Read only	Read and write
Individuals	Social groups and communities
Homepages	Blogs and wikis
Portals	RSS and aggregators
Bookmarks/favorites	Tags (keywords)
Owning	Sharing

To help you more fully understand the effects of the change from Web 1.0 to Web 2.0, we encourage you to watch any or all of the following videos and read one article. They offer insights into the changing world of technology, teaching, and learning.

Social Media in Plain English: www.commoncraft.com/show

The Machine Is Us/ing Us: www.youtube.com/watch?v=NLlGopyXT_g

A Vision of Students Today: www.youtube.com/watch%3Fv=dGCJ46vyR9o

Did You Know? 2.0: www.youtube.com/watch?v=pMcfrLYDm2U

"A Day in the Life of Web 2.0" by David Warlick:
www.scribd.com/full/2299957?access_key=key-1y2sjdd3bujjcd4xqgxd
www.iste.org/Content/NavigationMenu/EducatorResources/YourLearningJourney/
Web20/A_Day_In_the_Life_of_Web_2_0.pdf.

This article gives a description of how Web 2.0 tools can be applied in a middle school setting.

The Essential Nine

Learner Web 2.0 Tools You Should Know and Use

To help you understand Web 2.0, there are nine key terms you especially need to know. They are the nine technologies that have the most impact on teaching and learning. You might think of Table 3.2 as a choice board. As you learn about and understand one of the topics, cross it off and move on to another one until you complete the grid. Unlike tic-tac-toe boards commonly used in differentiated classrooms, this is a "cover all" board. In this chapter, you'll be learning about all nine applications so that you can decide which ones will work best for you and your students.

TABLE **3.2** ■ Choice Board for Web 2.0

1. Blogs	2. Document Sharing	3. Photo Sharing/Editing
4. Podcasting	5. RSS	6. Social Bookmarking/ Tagging
7. Social Networking	8. Video Sharing	9. Wikis

We briefly discuss in the next few pages each technology, ideas for using the tool in your classroom, and sites you can use to investigate each technology.

Blogs

A blog (weblog) is a website that allows an author or authors to publish information from any location without having to know programming code or file transfer protocol (FTP). Blogs encourage communication and discussion through the use of comments, and many blog services allow users to upload images and videos so that blog spaces can also be used as webpages. Blogs are organized around short writings called posts. The front page of a blog generally shows a list of posts in reverse chronological order along with the author's name and the date of the posting.

Educators often use blogs to keep parents and students up to date on what is happening in the classroom. They display student work (without students' names), share news and/ or announcements, and post links to explore.

Look at a few classroom blogs to see how teachers use them:

Mr. Jay Monson's Classroom Blog:
http://classblogmeister.com/blog.php?blogger_id=59644

Ms. Howard's Class Writing Blog:
http://dl1.yukoncollege.yk.ca/takpilotblog/

Mr. Fisher's Colonization Blogs:
http://mr-fisher.edublogs.org/2007/06/05/colonization-blogs/

Middle Web Middle School Diaries: www.middleWeb.com/mw/aaDiaries.html

Here are some additional suggestions for how blogs might be useful for the middle school classroom:

- Student writing

- Current events

- Posting of events, calendar, assignments

- Reflections and discussions on readings or activities

- Prompts for finding facts and for investigations

- Links to resources

- Sharing ideas

- Class portal

- Access to class materials (aka online filing cabinet)

- E-portfolios

- Online book club

- Class newsletter

Unless blogs are hosted on your private school server or their settings are marked private, blogs are public spaces that anyone can enter. Our recommendation is that if you want to start a blog with middle school students, you should host the blog on your own school or district server so that the general public cannot access the blog. Some blog software, such as WordPress, can be downloaded to your server and configured to use with your student population. Moodle and Blackboard both have blog tools, so if you already use either of these content management systems in your district, you can use their built-in blog features. Alternately, you can use a blog service from ePals, Gaggle, or Class Blogmeister, all considered secure and safe for students.

Getting Started with Blogs

Round up support. We believe that it's vital to earn the support of your administrator, the tech director, and the parents of your students. Although it's unreasonable to seek confirmation about every project, blogging can be a touchy subject, as it is often perceived as dangerous to students. Your tech director and associates will be excited to work with you if you approach them and ask for support/advice. (We know this firsthand, as Stephanie is married to a tech director, and Grace was the instructional technology coordinator for a school district of 9,000 students.) Your principal or department chair will appreciate the heads-up, and parents will be more willing to participate if you allow them to be involved from the get-go.

Provide ample training and make your objectives clear. Your students' parents in particular will welcome any instruction and hints about how blogs work, how they are monitored, how to keep their children safe, what your objectives are, and so forth, especially because many of them have never used blogs and may not understand them. Your students need to know what is expected of them and why you have chosen to use this medium. Any tutorials and helpful links would benefit both your students and their parents so that you all can begin on the same page.

Research and share results. Ask your students to investigate and complete activities that deal with blogging and safety. You might require that they produce an artifact, such as a Webbe, PowerPoint presentation, or some other type of collaborative project on the safest blog sites for students. If possible, have an informational session in which they share their results with staff, other students, and parents.

Talk about blogging in person. Establish ground rules and talk about consequences for possible infractions. Involve your students in this discussion in class, face-to-face, and use a computer system and projector to build a document or checklist for distribution or posting. Think about the rules you want to use with students when they blog. Bud the Teacher offers some insight on high school blogging that you can review for similar ideas for middle school students (www.budtheteacher.com/wiki/index.php?title=Sample_Blog_ Acceptable_Use_Policy).

Insist on a signed contract that students and parents must sign. Reiterate rules, guidelines, and consequences of infractions that you discussed with your students in class. Include the extremely important, non-negotiable safety-related issues, such as publication of personal information, language use, and respect.

Model first and start simply. You might want to begin simply with announcements and homework assignments and then allow students and parents to view one of your own blogs as a model. That way, they can see examples of appropriate entries.

Invite feedback and assess use. Encourage parents to voice concerns and praise about your blogging efforts and their children's involvement. Remember that everyone works at a different speed, and it may take longer for some children and their parents to embrace your strategy than it will others. Self-assessment is important, too. Ask yourself whether your goals were met. Did the blog work as you had intended? What needs to be changed or improved to make it work better?

Blog Resources

Video: Blogs in Plain English: www.commoncraft.com/show

Blackboard: www.blackboard.com

Blogger: www.blogger.com

Blogs on Educational Blogging:
http://supportblogging.com/Links+to+School+Bloggers

Class Blogmeister: http://classblogmeister.com

EduBlogger: http://edublogger.org

ePals: www.epals.com

Gaggle: www.gaggle.net

Google Blog Search Tool: http://blogsearch.google.com/?hl=en&tab=wb

Moodle: http://moodle.org

Technorati Blog Search Tool: www.technorati.com/search?advanced

WordPress: www.wordpress.org

Document Sharing

Online document sharing sites feature software applications that can be used jointly by two or more people. Instead of having to create a document in traditional software and then e-mailing it or placing it in a shared folder on the same network for further editing, users can either upload or create a document (Google Docs) or create it online (Zoho tools also allow importing) and invite others to add to or edit its content. Another type of document sharing is shown at the SlideShare site, where users can upload PowerPoint presentations for other users to view or download for their own use. These three sites can be accessed from anywhere in the world.

Because Web 2.0 is all about collaboration, you and your students can take advantage of these easy-to-use online tools that empower people to work together, no matter where they live. Document sharing is especially useful for collaborative writing projects, data projects, group presentations, and similar classroom applications.

Google Docs features an online word processor similar to Microsoft Word, a spreadsheet, and a presentation editor. SlideShare is a site where you can post your work and download presentations shared by others. Zoho offers a suite of online products that can be shared, including a word processor, spreadsheet, planner, blog, wiki, and other tools.

Document Sharing Resources

Google Docs: http://docs.google.com

SlideShare: www.slideshare.net

Zoho: www.zoho.com

Photo Sharing and Editing

Photo sharing and editing sites are places to upload your images and view or download those contributed by others. Along with these standard features, some sites provide very cool tools to enhance the images or use them into another format. Here are some ideas for using online photo resources.

Say your students are working on a digital story about the Civil War, and there is limited class or lab time for students to search for images, or you want to restrict the images to a certain theme. So, you find images from various sources and place them in an online account. Students can go to the online account and select from the images you provide.

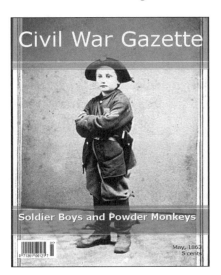

FIGURE **3.1** ■ Magazine cover created using Big Huge Labs.

Or you want to embellish some digital photos to enhance your curriculum handouts or presentations. Or, you want to have a discussion with your students about some thought-provoking photos. All of these ideas can be easily implemented using some of the new photo sharing and editing tools.

Big Huge Labs (http://bighugelabs.com) is a site where teachers can generate unique and appealing products using digital images. Using online tools, you can create imaginative products, such as magazine covers, movie posters, and trading cards. Figure 3.1 shows a magazine cover created by using Big Huge Labs' template and adding text and a public domain Civil War photo. Image generators are fun to use and useful for conveying messages. *Note:* this site contains a blog and forum, and there is no privacy policy. Children under 13 are not permitted to use the service.

Flickr (www.flickr.com) is an online photo sharing site that uses keyword "tags" to create categories and connections between photos and site users. Flickr is a fast-growing site with millions of images that can be used for including visual literacy in your classroom but is probably blocked in most districts due to the possibility of inappropriate images. However, teachers can search for photos by keyword and upload photos for class projects. You can create a private group and invite your students to view the images you have selected and posted, or you can post the images you have found to your blog or wiki. As an example, Meriwether Lewis Elementary School in Portland, Oregon, makes a set of photos available for its students (www.flickr.com/photos/lewiselementary/).

VoiceThread (http://voicethread.com) is an online, interactive media album in a slide show format that uses any type of media—images, documents, and videos—and permits users to add comments in four different ways: using voice with a microphone or telephone, text, audio file, or video with a webcam and share them. The result is a collaborative digital discussion within each VoiceThread. The final product can be exported to an archival movie for offline use on a DVD or video-enabled MP3 player. You can register to receive a free teacher account.

North Carolina teacher Bill Ferriter shows how he uses VoiceThread with his sixth graders for collaborative thought in his blog (http://teacherleaders.typepad.com/the_tempered_radical/2007/11/using-voicethre.html). He offers two handouts, one on "Previewing VoiceThread" and another on "VoiceThread Commenting." Bill's wiki about using Voice-Thread (http://digitallyspeaking.pbwiki.com/Voicethread/) offers useful examples. We like how Bill encourages student participation by engaging them in digital discussions.

VoiceThread also has a school version called Ed.VoiceThread that has been designed to address safety and security issues flexibly within the K–12 environment. Students may participate in the community only after being added by their teacher, and student e-mail addresses are not required. All VoiceThreads are private by default, and you can block VoiceThread.com to prevent students from seeing content not in the Ed.VoiceThread network. One nice feature is that you can block so that students interact and collaborate only within your school domain or only with students in the Ed.VoiceThread community. You can visit the Ed.VoiceThread community to see how other teachers are using this product (http://ed.voicethread.com/#q/).

Photo Sharing and Editing Resources

Video: Online Photo Sharing in Plain English: www.commoncraft.com/show

Big Huge Labs: http://bighugelabs.com

Flickr: www.flickr.com

VoiceThread: http://voicethread.com

Podcasting

Podcasting is an exciting and popular technology. There are three kinds of podcasts: audio, visual, and video. School-produced audio podcasts are mostly amateur shows, similar to radio broadcasts, that can share class content and student projects. Visual podcasts include graphics and images, and video podcasts include videos. Video podcasts are sometimes called vodcasts or v-casts.

You don't have to create podcasts to enjoy them. You can subscribe to podcasts or a series of podcasts and listen to them on your computer or on your MP3 player. You can subscribe using an aggregator like Bloglines. (See the RSS section in this chapter for more information.) There are a number of podcasts available on the web that you can listen to and use in your classroom.

Take a look at Mr. Mayo's Podcast Page (http://mrmayo.typepad.com/podcasts/), Coley-Cast (www.mrcoley.com/coleycast) or Mabry Online (http://mabryonline.org/podcasts/) to see how some teachers use podcasts in their classroom. Mr. Linden's Library (http://district.dearbornschools.org/schools/long/podcast/Long Elementary/Mr Lindens Library/Mr Lindens Library.html) is another example. Check out some of the podcasts organized by category at The Education Podcast Network (http://epnweb.org) or Radio WillowWeb (http://millard.esu3.org/willow/radio/). Think about serial stories students can create, family oral histories, summaries of events, reviews for tests, career interviews, book reviews, and language practice. Ideas for using podcasts abound.

If you want to produce podcasts, you and your students will probably enjoy creating them. Here are the stages and key steps to creating a podcast:

- **Preproduction or planning stage:** In this stage, you determine the audience and the goal and objectives of the podcast. This step also includes writing the script, finding appropriate music and/or sounds, and practicing the script.

- **Recording stage:** A podcast can be recorded using a computer, microphone, and audio editing software such as Audacity, a free editing program for Windows and Mac computers. Apple's GarageBand software is another option for producing podcasts on Mac computers.

- **Postproduction stage:** This stage includes editing the voice recording and adding the music and sound effects. The final audio file is saved in MP3 format.

- **Publishing stage:** This stage includes uploading the audio file to a server and creating the RSS feed file so others can subscribe to the podcast. You may also need RSS feed software; however, you can also use the free Feedburner and Blogger method (http://learninginhand.com/podcasting/blogger-feedburner.html).

Tony Vincent's site, Learning in Hand (http://learninginhand.com/podcasting/), offers more details about how to podcast.

Podcasting Resources

Video: Podcasting in Plain English: www.commoncraft.com/show

Examples of Educational Podcasts:
http://podcasting-in-education.wikispaces.com/Examples+of+Educational+Podcasts

The Education Podcast Network: www.epnWeb.org

Get Free Podcasts (Apple): http://movies.apple.com/movies/us/apple/
ipoditunes/2007/tutorials/apple_itunes_getpodcasts_r640–10cie.mov

Podcasting in the Classroom: http://userwww.sfsu.edu/~nshelley

Ideas for Podcasting in the Classroom: http://fcit.usf.edu/podcasts

Creating Podcasts from Learning in Hand by Tony Vincent (tutorial):
http://learninginhand.com/podcasting/create.html

Radio WillowWeb and Segment Planning Book:
http://millard.esu3.org/willow/radio
http://learninginhand.com/podcasting/RadioWillowWeb.pdf

Jake Ludington's MediaBlab:
www.jakeludington.com/podcasting/20050222_recording_a_podcast.html

Audacity software and Audacity tutorial: http://audacity.sourceforge.net

GarageBand software and GarageBand tutorial:
www.apple.com/ilife/garageband
www.apple.com/support/garageband/podcasts

RSS

RSS brings information to you automatically rather than having to search for it or receive it in your e-mail account. In other words, the news comes to you, rather than you having to go to the news. RSS can save you a huge amount of time! What's great about RSS is that you can have your own unique collection of content that is personalized to your interests. You can receive local, national, and world news; sports and technology updates; and info on just about any other topic.

So what exactly is RSS? RSS stands for Really Simple Syndication or Rich Site Summary. It's a technology tool used for bringing information to you and placing it all in one account so that all you have to do is visit your account and find all of your information in one place. RSS aggregators periodically check for new items in the feeds you are subscribed to, usually once every hour.

How do educators use RSS? You first set up an RSS account called an aggregator or news reader. Then you subscribe to your favorite blogs or news services, and other sites that regularly publish content. Each subscription sends a feed to your aggregator account, and you visit your aggregator account to read your feeds. Until you set up an account for the first time and subscribe to a few feeds, our explanation may not seem very clear. We recommend that you watch the video "RSS in Plain English" (www.commoncraft.com/rss_plain_english/) as it does an excellent job of explaining RSS and how it works.

There are a number of web-based and downloadable RSS services. Google Reader and Bloglines are two of the most popular web-based readers. Bloglines is a useful aggregator because it stores your RSS account online so that you can access it from any computer, and it's simple to set up and use. You can make your RSS account public so others can see which blogs and sites you read, or you can make your listing private. The list of blogs in your newsreader is referred to as a blogroll. Here's a peek at the Bloglines site of one of your authors. Note the feeds subscribed to and organized in the left column.

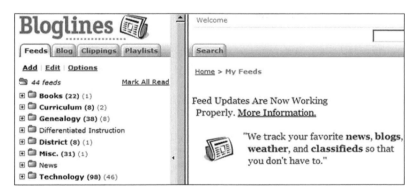

FIGURE **3.2**   ■   A Bloglines site

Take a look at blog guru Will Richardson's Bloglines public account (www.bloglines.com/public/wrichard/). Click on the title of any of the feeds to which he has subscribed to see what they are about. You can subscribe to some of them yourself.

Once your account is created, you can create and use folders to organize your feeds; and Bloglines has information on its site about how to do this. You may also want to look at these two video tutorials, (http://andyrush.net/screencast/bloglines/) and (www.htc.honeywell.com/eLibrary/Bloglines/), and a tutorial in PDF format (www.dupagepress.com/uploads/media/Kelly_Watson__s_Bloglines_Tutorial.pdf).

With the millions and millions of websites now online or even the few hundred you've bookmarked and follow, it is physically impossible to visit each site daily to see if new content has been posted. For this reason, educators use aggregators to subscribe to and read content that is brought to them via RSS. Some common uses are listed below:

- Keep track of headlines in news, education, professional organizations and other fields.

- Research a topic.

- Receive updates of your favorite blogs.

- Receive data from customized searches at Google.

- Receive info on hobbies and sports

- Track student blogs and wikis.

RSS Resources

Video: RSS in Plain English: www.commoncraft.com

Bloglines: www.bloglines.com

Google Reader: www.google.com/reader

Social Bookmarking with Tagging Features

Social bookmarking is an organized and personalized system for saving websites online rather than in an Internet browser. Instead of saving your favorite sites as bookmarks only to your computer, you can save them to a website that is accessible from any computer. You can also keyword or tag your bookmarks to associate them with a topic or more than one topic. Using a social bookmarking system, you have the option of sharing your bookmarks or saving them as private. One practical feature of social bookmarking is that you can view what other teachers have made public and found useful. The same sites may be useful to you.

After you have assigned a tag and saved it, you can find the object later by searching on the tag or key term. You can assign more than one tag to an item and other people can also assign other tags to the same object.

After you have saved a number of bookmarks on a site like Delicious (http://delicious. com) and tagged them, you can view them as a cloud. This feature lets you sort your sites by the tags themselves. You can next click on the tag you choose and the sites associated with the tag are listed. The process of tagging supports sharing and producing information for others to use. Tagging represents a noteworthy change in the way data can be saved, sorted, searched, and shared.

One of the issues everybody runs into is this: you've saved a site on your home computer and want to use it at school but you can't find it or vice versa. Or you want to share your bookmarks but don't have time to locate and e-mail them. A social bookmarking site means that your bookmarks will be available to you wherever you are. Another benefit is that you can easily share bookmarks publicly with your colleagues.

As we wrote previously, student Internet safety is always a concern. For that reason, we do not advocate using public social bookmarking sites with students who can too easily search for inappropriate links. Social bookmarking sites, such as Delicious, cannot be installed on district or school networks as they are considered security risks. However, all hope is not lost.

Scuttle (http://sourceforge.net/projects/scuttle/), an open source social bookmarking application, offers features similar to Delicious but without the safety and security short-comings. Scuttle allows users to specify one of three types of security settings for each bookmark—public, private, or shared with watchlist. Public bookmarks are available to anyone. Private bookmarks are available only to you. Shared with watchlist bookmarks are available to registered users but not to unauthorized users. You may want to test Scuttle in your district to see if it meets your needs.

BuddyMarks (http://buddymarks.com) is an online, closed, social bookmarking system that may also be suitable for middle schools. Using it, you designate your "buddies" (i.e., students) who can have access to your sites. You may want to try this site for a research project and allow students to add their sites to yours while you monitor their activity.

Social Bookmarking Resources

7 Things You Should Know About Social Bookmarking:
http://net.educause.edu/ir/library/pdf/ELI7001.pdf

13 Tips for Effective Tagging:
www.techsoup.org/learningcenter/Webbuilding/page5508.cfm

BuddyMarks: http://buddymarks.com

Delicious and tags: http://delicious and http://delicious/help/tags

Scuttle: http://sourceforge.net/projects/scuttle

Video: Social Bookmarking in Plain English: www.commoncraft.com

Social Networking

In Web 2.0 terms, social networking means an online community of people who share similar interests and activities. Social network services are web-based and offer a variety of ways for users to communicate, including e-mail and instant messaging services. Social networking has changed the way we communicate and is being used by millions of people every day on a regular basis. If you don't believe that millions are using social networking sites, check out some statistics at Wikipedia (http://en.wikipedia.org/wiki/List_of_social_networking_websites/).

Educators don't generally use social networking sites with students. Think about the number of times that Facebook has been in the news. Although teens gravitate to Facebook, most districts block it and similar social networking places because of issues with privacy and controversial content. Nonetheless, educators should know about social networking sites, why they are blocked, and whether any social networking sites should be opened to teens at all. Two sites aimed at teens and tweens have been launched on the Internet, Whyville, and FreshBrain. Both are virtual worlds geared for teen and pre-teen girls and boys.

According to the Whyville website (www.whyville.net),

> Whyville was launched in 1999 by Numedeon, Inc. to apply over 20 years of research in education and cooperative learning to develop new web-based tools for education. Researchers have identified the middle school years as a time when children, especially girls, lose their interest in math and science. Studies suggest that exposure to engaging educational and in particular scientific activities during this critical period can substantially influence future academic and career choices. We launched Whyville as a virtual city, which engages young people in constructive educational activities while promoting socially responsible behavior. It is an outgrowth of the company's extensive research and practical experience related to learner-centered, hands-on, inquiry-based education.

> Inside Whyville, citizens learn about art history, science, journalism, civics, economics, and really so, so much more. Whyville works directly with the Getty, NASA, the School Nutrition Association, and Woods Hole Oceanographic Institution (to name just a few) to bring incredible educational content to kids in an incredibly engaging manner.

> Today, there are countless learning games and activities on Whyville . . . which is probably one of the reasons *Education Daily* states that Whyville is one of edu-gaming's biggest successes.

> Increasingly, Whyville is finding its way into the classroom, from elementary schools to post-graduate courses for preservice teachers. We encourage you to introduce Whyville to your students and even incorporate it into your curriculum. Registering as a teacher in Whyville allows you to bring your students on and manage their accounts. If you and your class join Whyville, we'd love to hear about your experience.

FreshBrain

The creators of FreshBrain describe their mission as the following: FreshBrain is focused on enhancing the education and development of our youth in the areas of business and technology by providing hands-on real world experience.

On the website (www.freshbrain.org), they provide the following description of Fresh-Brain's purpose and structure:

> At the core of FreshBrain is an open and free website that provides teens with the opportunity to explore, engage, and create through activities and projects. FreshBrain takes advantage of the latest technologies, such as web conferencing and social networking, to provide a very progressive environment where teens can complete activities and work together on projects. This experience is enhanced with Advisors, available to support and mentor teens who are working on projects, with the intention of increasing the likelihood of success. In addition, FreshBrain provides teens with tools and training in the latest technologies to complete these projects.
>
> Providing the latest tools in technology, and a social interactive networking environment, has enabled teens to explore, create, and share with others. A result of pulling these two key online arenas together into one solution has enabled FreshBrain to attract teens comfortable with technology and communicating online. Creations from FreshBrain users range from music videos to logo designs.

Social Networking Resources

FreshBrain: www.freshbrain.org

Whyville: www.whyville.net

National Cyber Security Alliance (lessons for cyber safety): http://staysafeonline.org

Video Sharing

Teachers use video hosting sites to find interesting multimedia for classroom content to engage learners. Subscription sites, such as Discovery Education Streaming (http://streaming.discoveryeducation.com) and BrainPOP (www.brainpop.com), offer wonderful videos and other materials. Other sites, such as ICue (www.icue.com) and the Memorial Hall Museum (www.memorialhall.mass.edu/activities/tools/), offer free streaming videos, but these sites are not categorized as sharing because users cannot upload their own videos.

Video sharing sites are actually server-based services that store professional, educational, and/or videos made by amateurs like the rest of us. To access or post videos, users first create an account. Once the account has been created, users may search for videos by tags or keywords and play them on their computer screens or download them for other uses, such as including them in blogs and PowerPoint presentations. Users may also upload videos to share with others if an account has been created.

Due to the community nature of Web 2.0 and video sharing services, users may also rate videos, add comments or responses, and connect with other users. Problems with video sharing include the variable quality of the videos themselves and access to inappropriate videos. Schools tend to block video sharing sites because they cannot adequately filter video content. Until such filtering technology is available, we suggest you do not advocate opening up YouTube to students. Opening YouTube to faculty is another matter because teachers should be able to review what is available on YouTube and save any resources that are appropriate to show to their students.

Two other sites, SchoolTube (www.schooltube.com) and TeacherTube (www.teachertube. com), seem to be much better filtered by the hosting services themselves. These sites may be totally acceptable for students to view, but as with any site you recommend to students, you should review the content first to see how appropriate it is for your grade level and content area. We feel it is much safer for teachers to use SchoolTube and TeacherTube and save the resources to use with students later.

Educators can create accounts with TeacherTube. Once an account is created, teachers can upload, tag, and share videos, support files, notes, and lessons plans. They can also create video groups and playlists, integrate TeacherTube videos on websites, and make videos public or private. SchoolTube is a similar service, as is YouTube.

Video Sharing Resources

SchoolTube: www.schooltube.com

TeacherTube: www.teachertube.com

YouTube: www.youtube.com

Wiki

A wiki is both a shared website and an authoring tool that permits users to add, remove, and edit content. The term *wiki* derives from the Hawaiian word *wiki-wiki* meaning quick. A wiki is an easy and useful tool for collaborative authoring. A wiki space is text-based, and it can include graphics, audio, video, files, and animation. Wikis have enormous potential as educational tools for educators and students because they encourage collaborative learning, and foster thinking and sharing of resources. Wikis are used in the business world to manage information and documents, for brainstorming, and for discussion. They can be used the same way in the classroom. In fact, a wiki offers the opportunity for students to share findings as they work on a collaborative research project. Look at Wikibooks and Wikijunior to see how others are collaboratively writing books (http://en.wikibooks.org).

In the school environment as in the business world, wiki software can be installed on a district or school server, requiring logins and passwords. Doing so protects students. There are many software options for building wikis, but we like Wikispaces where K–12 teachers can register for a complimentary, ad-free, and private wiki tool.

Here are some school-focused wikis that illustrate how they are being used in classrooms:

Mr. Berkowitz's Seventh Grade Class:
http://loislowryauthorstudy.wikispaces.com

Team 8 Blue Saves the World!: http://team8bluesavestheworld.wikispaces.com

Adams News Wiki: http://adamsnews.wikispaces.com

Ms. C's Middle School Information Technology wiki!: http://msit.wikispaces.com

Wikis are extremely versatile and can be used in a variety of ways by educators. Here are a few activities wikis excel at facilitating in the classroom:

- Brainstorming ideas
- Class notes and handouts
- Collaborative textbooks
- Collaborative writing
- Collaborative notetaking
- Creation and organization of content and study guides
- Dissemination of classroom information
- Exploratory projects
- Lesson summaries
- Literature circles
- Post PowerPoint presentations, podcasts, and images
- Resource collections
- Serialized writing

- Sign-up sheets
- Staff development documentation
- Vocabulary study

Wiki Resources

Educational Wikis:
http://educationalwikis.wikispaces.com/Examples+of+educational+wikis

Things You Should Know About Wikis:
www.scribd.com/full/2329317?access_key=key-15ceyq5uv7p8onanqny4

Video: Wikis in Plain English: www.commoncraft.com

Wikibooks: http://en.wikibooks.org

Wikijunior: http://en.wikibooks.org/wiki/Wikijunior

Wikispaces: www.wikispaces.com

Wikispaces for Teachers: www.wikispaces.com/site/for/teachers

Other Tech Tools

Along with Web 2.0 tools, many wonderful technology tools are available. Consider content software, content websites, game creation tools, product makers or generators, teacher tools, streaming video, and Webbes. As we suggest use of these tools throughout the book, there are mini-descriptions of each of these technologies and some examples.

Content Software

By content software, we refer to software that relates directly to curriculum content, such as social studies, math, or ELA software that delivers content or supports content. In the old days of technology, software was installed via a floppy disk or CD. Some changes in the concept of software have evolved over the past few years.

In the past, software has been installed on a district or school server and distributed to local, individual computers or installed directly on local computers. With the advent of thin client technology, some software can be installed and processed at the server level rather than the local computer level, so that a hard drive is not needed in the local computer. Commonly used software, such as Microsoft Office, can be installed in this manner.

In the past, software has been considered proprietary with individual licenses or network licenses purchased for each machine using the software. Some open source software programs in which the source code is available to the general public for use and/or modification from its original design is now available free of charge (examples: Open Office, Moodle). Some software is also free but not open source. Downloads may be needed (examples: Google Earth and Google SketchUp, Tux Paint, and Tux Typing).

Until recently nearly all content software has been installed on local computers or servers. Now some content is entirely web-based (examples: WriteOnline, Destination Math/Reading).

Content Software Resources

Destination Math/Reading: http://hmlt.hmco.com

Google Earth: http://earth.google.com

Google SketchUp: http://sketchup.google.com

Microsoft Office: http://office.microsoft.com

Moodle: http://moodle.org

Open Office: www.openoffice.org

Timeliner XE: www.tomsnyder.com/timelinerxe

Tux Paint: www.tuxpaint.org

Tux Typing: http://tuxtype.sourceforge.net

WriteOnline: www.cricksoft.com/uk/writeonline

Content Websites

By content websites, we mean sites that relate directly to curriculum or support curriculum content, such as social studies, math, or science. Examples of rich sites are listed here.

Content Website Resources

Ad*Access: http://library.duke.edu/digitalcollections/adaccess

American Memory: http://memory.loc.gov/ammem

Library of Congress: www.loc.gov

Middle Ages: www.learner.org/interactives/middleages

National Geographic for Kids: http://kids.nationalgeographic.com

Read Write Think: www.readwritethink.org

Smithsonian American Art Museum Interactives:
http://americanart.si.edu/education/interactives

XPeditions: www.nationalgeographic.com/xpeditions

Game Creation Tools

Game creation tools are the sorts of products that teachers and/or students can use to create educational games. Two examples are Microsoft's PowerPoint and Publisher. PowerPoint can be used to create slide show games or board games. Publisher can be used to create board games. Quia has fabulous tools that can create game-like activities. We also like the commercial products from FTC Publishing.

Game Creation Resources

Games and Puzzles: www.teachertools.org/games_dynam.asp

Quia: www.quia.com

FTC Publishing: www.ftcpublishing.com

Product Generators

By product generators, we mean software that helps teachers and students produce products or artifacts. Microsoft Office and Open Office are suites of applications that enable users to produce products, such as presentations, worksheets, spreadsheets, newsletters, and so forth.

Teacher Tools

By teacher tools, we mean Quia, RubiStar (rubrics maker), 4Teachers, Puzzlemaker, and similar tools that teachers can use to create activities for their students.

Teacher Tools Resources

4Teachers: www.4teachers.org

Puzzlemaker: http://puzzlemaker.discoveryeducation.com

Quia: www.quia.com

RubiStar: http://rubistar.4teachers.org

Streaming Video

By streaming video, we mean the sequence of video images that are sent in compressed form over the Internet and displayed on the viewer's screen as they arrive. Streaming video means that the web user does not have to wait to fully download a large file before starting to watch the video. Instead, the media is sent in a continuous stream and is played as soon as it arrives. The advantage of using streaming video is that multimedia supports various learning styles and helps students learn.

Streaming Video Resources

BrainPOP: www.brainpop.com

Discovery Education Streaming: http://streaming.discoveryeducation.com

iCue: www.icue.com

Open Vault: http://openvault.wgbh.org

Webbes, e-Books, Interactive Books, e-Portfolios, and Digital Stories

Using software you may already have or some free downloads, you and your students can create any number of products that encourage writing tied to content. Webbe refers to both web-based and word-processed books that can be printed or viewed online. A Webbe is also an e-book but not the only kind of e-book. E-books with sound can be created with presentation software (such as PowerPoint). E-portfolios are collections of students' work. They can be created and linked in presentation software. Digital stories are another fun way to use technology and tie the stories to content. You can use the free downloads Movie Maker, iMovie '08, or PhotoStory 3 to create digital stories.

Webbes, e-Books, Interactive Books, e-Portfolios, and Digital Stories Resources

Webbe software: www.realebooks.com

Webbe templates: www.everythingdi.net

Creating e-books with PowerPoint:
http://drscavanaugh.org/ebooks/creating_ebooks_with_powerpoint.htm

How to Create Talking Books in PowerPoint:
http://atto.buffalo.edu/registered/Tutorials/talkingBooks/powerpoint.php

Interactive books, such as "Choose Your Adventure," can be made using PowerPoint: www.microsoft.com/education/interactivestory.mspx

Creating Electronic Portfolios with PowerPoint: www.clarion.edu/41907.pdf

Electronic Portfolios for Students:
www.uen.org/Lessonplan/preview.cgi?tid=64513&LPid=7134

iMovie '09: www.apple.com/ilife/imovie

Movie Maker:
www.microsoft.com/windowsxp/downloads/updates/moviemaker2.mspx

Photo Story 3:
www.microsoft.com/windowsxp/using/digitalphotography/photostory/default.mspx

Summary

As you can see, the many new Web 2.0 tools and some older favorites combine to make digital learning and digital producing amazing and fun experiences! Successful technology integration is achieved when curricular goals and learning are enhanced. Tech tools permit real-world connections to experts and research, foster active engagement, and personalize learning.

CHAPTER 4

Using Technology to Differentiate English/Language Arts

Today's English or language arts (ELA) classroom does not have to imitate grandma's or grandpa's classroom. Adding technology to ELA helps to differentiate, modernize, and bring excitement to traditional content.

At the same time, technology engages students and personalizes their learning. Technologies help students conduct research and create products, similar to the way in which digital-age workers respond to new situations by bringing together information to create timely documents that drive businesses to thrive. When instruction is active and students are engaged, learning soars!

This chapter is divided into two parts. The first part focuses on some of the ways teachers can use technology to differentiate literature instruction and learning. The second part shares a number of additional strategies for differentiating vocabulary, writing, spelling, speaking, and listening in the ELA classroom. In both sections we list resources for content-based software, websites, Web 2.0 applications, video streaming and podcasting resources, and product producing software.

Before jumping in, we'd like to remind you that it's a good idea to begin the year by knowing students' reading abilities. Reading is such a fundamental part of ELA that you will want to know right off which students struggle, which are at grade level, and which excel. Teachers can use district assessment information or mini-assessments using released state reading tests or other instruments. A simple, informal way to assess students is by using the Lexile Map via individual oral reading mini-sessions.

The Lexile Framework for Reading (www.lexile.com) is an approach that measures reader ability and text difficulty on the same scale. To use the Lexile Framework as a mini-assessment, print the Lexile Map (www.lexile.com/tools/lexile-map/), which is available in both English and Spanish. Starting at a level below which you suspect the student will perform fluently, have each student read to you every paragraph, moving upward until the student no longer reads easily. Then record (on the printed copy, on a note card, or in another file or location you choose) the student's independent reading level—the last paragraph at which the student read fluently. Lexile scores are recorded in this manner: 740L. The level 740L is the average reading ability for a student ending the fourth grade. The Lexile score will reflect the student's current measure and assist when searching for books to match to reading levels in your class. Books lexiled at a higher level than the student's independent reading level can be used with the expectation that some scaffolding may be needed. We show the Lexile score next to each of the literary works profiled in this chapter. The Lexile website offers additional tools including a searchable database of leveled books.

Once you know the range of skills in your classroom, you can design instruction to meet the needs of the diverse learners in your class, and you will be able to group students by readiness and other means.

Differentiating Literature

We selected a representative literary work for beginning the conversation in this section: *The True Confessions of Charlotte Doyle* (1990) by Avi, a historical novel read in middle schools across North America, often in Grade 7. Following the section on this book, we also suggest a few resources for some other literary works commonly read in Grades 6–8.

Bear in mind that the strategies we show with *The True Confessions of Charlotte Doyle* can apply to many literary works taught in middle schools. If you use this novel at a different grade level in your district, you may have to make adjustments to the strategies we offer in this chapter. By adjustments, we mean making accommodations for the diverse learners you teach, reflected by their readiness, learning profiles, and interests.

We offer two approaches for differentiating a literary work. One approach is based on the premise that the entire class is reading only one novel at the same time. Using *The True Confessions of Charlotte Doyle* as an example, we propose a set of literature-based research and activities links, and product-producing software that you can easily use to differentiate learning with technology in your classroom. We also include menus of choices based on student interests so that student activities and products differ, even though the whole class reads the same book.

An alternate method of differentiating instruction would be to ask students to choose from a set of related books based on genre and/or time period. The teacher then divides the students into flexible groups or literature circles for activities and discussion. The tricky part of dividing students into literature groups is adjusting for their various readiness levels.

Although students may be interested in a particular theme, their reading abilities may not correspond well with their initial book choices. Or, their sophistication level may not jibe with their reading ability. It will take time and skill to steer students to books appropriate for their levels of readiness and interests.The teacher also needs multiple lesson/activity plans, one per book, to guide groups along.

We find that either method—whole-class-one-book or small-group-multiple-books—works equally well when students have choices. Literature circles seem to require extra preplanning by the teacher so that they work smoothly, but students usually enjoy reading a self-selected book and discussing it with equally interested peers. Not every teacher, though, knows how to work effectively with groups or feels comfortable managing literature circles in middle school. Group work can be chaotic unless it is managed effectively and ground rules prevail. Discussing a novel as a whole class can be exciting when the text itself is the foundation for lessons, discussion, and activities.

In the sections that follow, we present the following: a whole-class approach using technology resources to differentiate *The True Confessions of Charlotte Doyle*; a series of snippets for using technology to differentiate additional works often read during the middle school years; a choice board for differentiating any novel by interest and learning profile using technology; and two strategies for using literature circles with several novels.

Differentiating *The True Confessions of Charlotte Doyle*

The True Confessions of Charlotte Doyle (740L) is a fast-paced tale about a 13-year-old girl who takes an extraordinary sea voyage in 1832. While crossing the Atlantic Ocean to be reunited with her family in Rhode Island, Charlotte Doyle is the only female and non-crew member aboard *The Seahawk*. During the voyage, she faces several challenges before she is reunited with her family. A surprise ending tops off this engaging historical novel.

In teaching any novel, instructors generally follow a sequence of steps. Pre-reading activities include having students predict what the novel is about based on the cover, blurb, title, or book jacket. When the teacher introduces the novel enthusiastically, most students will want to read it.

During-reading activities typically include having students work on characterization worksheets, plot flowcharts, family trees, vocabulary, reading response journals, sequencing of key events, predictions and foreshadowing, and map locations.

The teacher uses during-reading activities to build understanding and provide fodder for discussion. Not every chapter needs to be processed in depth, nor do comprehension activities need to be used with each chapter. In fact, one of the major purposes of a novel study is to allow students to become immersed in a good read.

After-reading activities involve having students write summaries of the plot, create storyboards, write comparisons/contrasts of characters, write alternate endings, investigate information about the author, and develop other culminating or final assignment activities. The teacher assesses students via tests or final projects. Students may also assess themselves.

In Table 4.1, we compare and contrast the typical, traditional instruction of *The True Confessions of Charlotte Doyle* with technology-enhanced, differentiated instruction of the same novel. To develop this table, we first looked at several reading guides available to ELA teachers for teaching *The True Confessions of Charlotte Doyle* and similar novels. We compiled typical steps for teaching the novel in column one. In column two, we added strategies we would personally use in teaching *The True Confessions of Charlotte Doyle* to our fictional class of seventh graders.

Note that adding technology to differentiate instruction does not mean that you should use technology in every step of reading the novel. There are many ways to differentiate instruction, and we provide enough choices to tech-enhance novel teaching so that you can pick and choose those that work best for you. Start slowly and honor your comfort zone.

Nearly any kind of technology will help to differentiate from straight text reading. On top of that, technology appeals to middle school students and may even motivate them to do more careful reading so that their technology piece is just right.

TABLE 4.1 ■ Differentiating *The True Confessions of Charlotte Doyle*

Typical/Traditional Instruction	Tech-Enhanced/Differentiated Instruction
Pre-Reading Motivation	**Pre-Reading Motivation**
Word web or map on the term "confessions" (chalkboard or overhead transparency)	Use Inspiration software (www.inspiration.com) or Bubbl (www.bubbl.us) to generate a word web on the term "confessions" as a whole group, in pairs, or by individuals. Discuss word maps/webs as a whole group.
During-Reading Activities *Background Reading on 1832 Nautical Terms*	**During-Reading Activities** *Background Reading on 1832 Nautical Terms*
Graphics (text, encyclopedia, or paper handout of brig, book appendix) Map of the world in 1832	Pair students to research crossing the Atlantic and shipboard life with directed sites, such as: www.jeaniejohnston.ie/history.html www.theshipslist.com/ships/descriptions/brig.htm www.brigniagara.org http://allan.tompkins.com.au/austpix/brig2.gif www.royal-navy.org www.ayrshirehistory.org.uk/jsmith/brig.jpg www.boatsafe.com/nauticalknowhow/gloss.htm Students take notes and discuss them with each other or in the whole group.

continued

TABLE **4.1** ■ Differentiating *The True Confessions of Charlotte Doyle*   *continued*

Typical/Traditional Instruction	Tech-Enhanced/Differentiated Instruction
During-Reading Activities *Gender Roles in 1832*	**During-Reading Activities** *Gender Roles in 1832*
Chalkboard, discussion, background reading in text or encyclopedia	Compare gender roles in 1832 vs. today. Using a word processor, create a three-column table with "Topics" as the header for column 1, "1832" as the header for column 2, and "today" as the header for column 3. Next, add the number of rows needed for the topics to be compared in columns 2 and 3. The topics may include work, family, school, and leisure (and others) and look something like this sample: {SAMPLE_TABLE} Show the file using a digital projector, typing in words and phrases as students discuss them. Better yet, ask students to do the typing while you facilitate. You can also post the file to Google Docs and ask students to work on the project collaboratively prior to class. As a summary activity, ask pairs of students to write descriptions of men's and women's fashions in 1832 and draw them using Microsoft Paint or a similar product. Resources for 1832 fashions: www.printsgeorge.com/Fashion%2019.htm www.victoriana.com/lady/palmer.html www.connerprairie.org/HistoryOnline/clothing.html www.pastpatterns.com http://locutus.ucr.edu/~cathy/weev.html
During-Reading Activities *Author*	**During-Reading Activities** *Author*
Background information from text	Share video/web interviews with Avi using computer /digital projector: www.avi-writer.com/about_avi www.readingrockets.org/books/interviews/avi#interviews/ Students can take notes as they listen to and watch Avi. Discuss findings with whole group.
During-Reading Activities *Plot Diagram*	**During-Reading Activities** *Plot Diagram*
Worksheet with fill-in blanks for exposition, rising action, climax, falling action, resolution	Ask paired students to discuss the plot, then use the Read Write Think plot diagram tool (www.readwritethink.org/materials/plot-diagram/). Print the finished product.

Sample table (embedded within the Gender Roles cell):

Topics	1832	Today
Work		
Family		
School		
Leisure		

continued

TABLE 4.1 ■ Differentiating *The True Confessions of Charlotte Doyle*   *continued*

Typical/Traditional Instruction	Tech-Enhanced/Differentiated Instruction
During-Reading Activities *Vocabulary Study*	**During-Reading Activities** *Vocabulary Study*
Glossary, word study	Students can use an online dictionary and create their own glossary in a word processing program or, if your school allows, a wiki of terms from *The True Confessions of Charlotte Doyle*. Online vocabulary quiz can be used as a checkpoint (http://205.126.22.50/reading/books/charlottedoyle.html).
During-Reading Activities *Characterization*	**During-Reading Activities** *Characterization*
T-charts or other forms of character charts	After discussion of the main characters and listing of some their key traits, ask students to use the Character Trading Cards at Read Write Think (http://readwritethink.org/materials/trading_cards/). Students should print the cards and in small groups, trade them and discuss.
During-Reading Activities *Activities*	**During-Reading Activities** *Activities*
Comparison/contrast worksheets Cause and effect worksheets	After discussing the traits of the main characters, ask students to consult their notes as they use the two-circle Venn diagram (www.readwritethink.org/materials/venn/) or the three-circle Venn diagram (http://interactives.mped.org/view_interactive.aspx?id=28&title=). After discussion of key points/problems in the novel, ask students to use the cause and effect organizer (http://readwritethink.net/lesson_images/lesson925/blank-go.pdf or http://my.hrw.com/nsmedia/intgos/html/igo.htm). Print the products.
After-Reading Activities *Culminating Project/Assessment*	**After-Reading Activities** *Culminating Project/Assessment*
Book cover Book report Assessment/test	**Newsletter format:** Create a 1–2 page newsletter with images and articles after Charlotte arrives in Rhode Island. Use publishing or word processing software or try the printing press at Read Write Think (http://interactives.mped.org/view_interactive.aspx?id=110&title=). **Brochure:** Using word processing/desktop publishing software or free online software at www.mybrochuremaker.com, ask students to create a brochure to entice Europeans to travel to America on the Seahawk in 1832. **Story:** Using Photo Story 3 or PowerPoint or similar software, ask a team of students to retell Charlotte's story. **Timeline (Our Timelines):** Ask students to create a timeline (www.ourtimelines.com/create_tl_2c.html) of the world events during Charlotte's life from her birth to 1832 and another one of their own life. Then ask them to compare/contrast three or more common elements in each timeline, using a comparison table or Venn diagram.

Technology "Snippets" for Differentiating Other Literary Works

A Wrinkle in Time (770L)

A Wrinkle in Time, written by Madeleine L'Engle (1963), is the story of Meg Murry, her younger brother Charles Wallace, and her friend Calvin O'Keefe. The three young people are transported through space via a tesseract—a sort of "wrinkle" in space and time—to rescue Mr. Murry, a gifted scientist, from the evil forces that hold him prisoner on another planet.

Technology Enhancements

Author Study

Share websites about *A Wrinkle in Time* at which students can learn about the author:
www.madeleinelengle.com
www.kidsreads.com/series/series-time-author.asp.

Vocabulary Study

Students can use an online dictionary and create their own glossary in a word-processing program: www.wordcentral.com.

Review practice for chapters 1–4 vocabulary:
www.quia.com/cm/27351.html
http://books.quia.com/cm/27351.html.

Review chapters 5–8: http://books.quia.com/pop/46636.html.

Review chapters 9–12: http://books.quia.com/jg/390377.html.

Characterization

Create running records of character notes on Meg, Charles Wallace, and Calvin in a word processing program, Google Docs, or a wiki: www.wikispaces.com.

Create a character attribute web in Inspiration software or Bubbl: www.bubbl.us

Culminating Project

Board Game: Using MS Publisher or PowerPoint or similar software, create a board game. See http://drb.lifestreamcenter.net/Lessons/Wrinkle/Wrinkle1.gif for an example.

My Brother Sam Is Dead (770L)

My Brother Sam Is Dead, written by James Lincoln Collier and Christopher Collier (1984), is a novel about a family living in Connecticut during the American Revolution. The story is told through the eyes of the younger son, Tim Meeker, as his older brother joins the rebel forces while the rest of the family tries to stay neutral in a Loyalist town.

Technology Enhancements

Author Study

Author profile: www.mcelmeel.com/writing/collier.html

Interview with Christopher Collier:
http://nutmeg.easternct.edu/connecticutstudies/ChristopherCollierInterview.htm

Social Studies Connections

At GoogleLit, students use Google Earth to explore the several locations described in the novel. The file includes discussion questions and resources:
http://web.mac.com/jburg/GoogleLit/6-8/Entries/2007/4/14_My_Brother_Sam_Is_Deadby_James_Lincoln_Collier_%26_Christopher_Collier.html.

About Redding, Connecticut: www.historyofredding.com/HRmbsd.htm

Liberty news chronicles about the Revolution:
www.pbs.org/ktca/liberty/chronicle.html

The Global Village: www.pbs.org/ktca/liberty/perspectives_global.html

Software

In the Thinking Reader program by Tom Snyder Productions (www.tomsnyder.com) students can read the novel, working at their own pace. They can use text-to-speech to hear words, enlarge the font size, and access Strategy Help. The program provides seven research-based reading comprehension strategies: summarize, question, clarify, predict, visualize, feel, and reflect.

Culminating Project

WebQuest: http://projects.edtech.sandi.net/ofarrell/mybrosam

"The Tell-Tale Heart" (1350L) and "The Raven" (1350L)

"The Tell-Tale Heart" (1843) is a short story and "The Raven" (1845) is a poem written by Edgar Allan Poe. Students in Grade 8 usually read some of Edgar Allan Poe's short stories and poetry. Here are some technology enhancements to help differentiate instruction.

Technology Enhancements

Author Study

Poe Museum: www.poemuseum.org

Knowing Poe: http://knowingpoe.thinkport.org/default_flash.asp

Multimedia

The Tell-Tale Heart animated movie at YouTube: www.youtube.com/watch?v=W4s9V8aQu4c (7:48).

The Raven read aloud by an actor: www.repeatafterus.com/title.php?i=1740.

Interactive *Raven:* www.teachersfirst.com/share/raven

The Raven Interactive Literary Devices: www.teachersfirst.com/share/raven/start.html

Culminating Project

Read Write Think Printing Press: Tell the story of Poe's life and describe one of his products in a brochure, booklet, newspaper, or flier: http://interactives.mped.org/view_interactive.aspx?id=110&title=/. Your audience should want to buy or subscribe to Poe's product based on your sales pitch.

Edgar Allan Poe WebQuest: www.geocities.com/educationplace/poe/wqpoe.htm.

Anne Frank: The Diary of a Young Girl (1080L)

Discovered in the attic in which she spent the last years of her life, Anne Frank's diary (1947) is a powerful reminder of war and a moving testament to the human spirit. Her diary was published in 1947 by her father, Otto Frank, the only member of her immediate family who survived World War II. The book was published in Dutch and translated into English in 1952.

Technology Enhancements

Author Study

Biographical information from the Anne Frank Center: www.annefrank.com/who-is-anne-frank/

Multimedia

Anne Frank: The Diary of a Young Girl (05:47): http://streaming.discoveryeducation.com. As described by Discovery Education, "A journal is a collection of thoughts and experiences. This part presents a video about Anne Frank to show that her journal can teach us about the time period in which she lived." This movie requires a subscription.

Anne Frank the Writer: An Unfinished Story: www.ushmm.org/museum/exhibit/online/af/htmlsite/. The U.S. Holocaust Memorial Museum made this exhibition in 2003 honoring Anne Frank's life and writing.

Map tracing Anne Frank's movement through Europe: www.ushmm.org/wlc/article.php?lang=en&ModuleId=10005210/

Timeliner XE or 5.0: Use software to construct a timeline of the key dates in the diary.

Culminating Project

Using the Anne Frank Guide (www.annefrankguide.net/en-US/bronnenbank. asp?step=1e/), students can research and develop projects and talks and send in projects they have made. Although registration is necessary, students do not have to use their e-mail addresses and can invent a name and login. Specially designed by the Anne Frank House team for students, it contains photos, a timeline, and data. The teacher guide is available at www.annefrank.org/upload/downloads/ AFGTeacherManual.pdf, and there is a teacher blog for ideas: www.annefrank.org/ diaryprojects/.

A Christmas Carol **(1080L)**

Charles Dickens' classic holiday tale, published in 1843, provides a marvelous way to introduce students to one of the great authors in the English language.

Technology Enhancements

Author Study

Timeline of Dickens' life: http://charlesdickenspage.com/timeline.html.

Animated story of Dickens' life: www.bbc.co.uk/drama/bleakhouse/animation.shtml.

Multimedia

Dickens and Christmas: www.fidnet.com/~dap1955/dickens/christmas.html.

A Christmas Carol—audios in three parts: http://storynory.com/category/dickens/.

Surviving Charles Dickens' London (game): www.bbc.co.uk/arts/multimedia/dickens/.

Culminating Project

A Dickens of a Party WebQuest from Read Write Think: www.readwritethink.org/lesson_images/lesson238/dickens_WebQuest.html.

Choice Board for Differentiating Any Novel

By offering choices based on multiple intelligences and interests, we show a table of students' process activities for creating the components of a digital news journal, broadcast, movie, digital story, or similar product.

Consider the technology resources you have available in your district. Then, look in Table 4.2 to see the sorts of tasks students may perform to work on a group project about the literary work they are studying.

TABLE **4.2** ■ Choice Board

1. Interpersonal	2. Intrapersonal	3. Math/Logic
Present the product to the class (presentation software) "Sell" the product to the school, parents, others (presentation or publishing software, podcasts)	Maintain journals or logs on the project (word processing software) Research data for the project (online search tools)	Create assessments and rubrics to assess the project (word processing, Rubistar, Rubric Maker) Manage time and tasks via checklists and timelines (word processing or spreadsheet software)
4. Bodily-Kinesthetic	**5. Visual**	**6. Musical**
Rehearse and act as news anchors or reporters during the project (tech video equipment) Pose for publicity shots (digital camera)	Create still shots and art for materials (digital camera, drawing tools) Shoot/create the video or digital product (video cam)	Create the soundtrack (Audacity, Photo Story 3) Create a commercial for school announcements (PowerPoint, iMovie, Movie Maker, podcast, etc.)
7. Linguistic	**8. Existential**	**9. Naturalist**
Write the script for the product (word processing software) Write the PR materials (presentation, word processing, publishing software)	Create/direct/produce the theme/product (word processing for the theme and direction notes, digital storyboard) Work with others to stay on theme; regroup or combine groups as needed (refer to documents and edit as needed)	Design and create the props and stage them in their proper environment (design/drawing tools) Manage the lighting, makeup, and special effects (design/drawing tools)

Off- and Online Literature Circles

In a literature circle, small groups of students join together to discuss a literary work in depth. The discussion is guided by students' responses to their reading. Discussion may include events, character traits, reflection, critical thinking, response journals, vocabulary work, summaries, and so on. TeenReads (www.teenreads.com) is a place for students to check book reviews by peers.

There's a wonderful overview for getting started with literature circles at Read Write Think (http://readwritethink.org/lessons/lesson_view.asp?id=19/) and a look at roles students play at www.npatterson.net/litcircleroles.html. Additional excellent information is available at www.saskschools.ca/curr_content/bestpractice/litcircles/.

In general, here is how to start the process. Select a set of books appropriate for grade level and readiness of students. Use the Lexile searchable database to help; assign 4–6 students to each literature circle based on interest and readiness. To allow student selection, each student can be given a choice among two or three of the books in the set. Provide a description of each book ahead of time or read a passage from it to the whole class.

Assign roles for the members of each circle or let students choose them. These roles, such as scribe, group leader, and reporter, rotate throughout the chapters so that everyone has the opportunity to play all roles. Assign reading to be completed by the circles inside or outside of class; capable students may also help set up the assignments. You may also want to use student contracts.

Select circle meeting dates or let students help to plan the dates. Help students understand and prepare for their roles in their lit circle. During meetings, "cruise" the lit circles and facilitate when needed. Evaluate the process with the students, using self-assessments and discussions.

Table 4.3 is an example of a literature circle set of historical fiction books with a readability range of 650–950L for a middle school class of 30 students. This set of books shares a nautical theme.

TABLE 4.3 ■ **Nautical Books Literature Circle**

Title	Pirates	The Buccaneers	The True Confessions of Charlotte Doyle	The Stowaway	Stowaway	A Night to Remember
Author	Jennifer Holm	Iain Lawrence	Avi	Kristiana Gregory	Karen Hesse	Walter Lord
Era	1854	1700	1832	1818	1768	1912
Lexile	690L	720L	740L	820L	830L	950L
Grade Level Reading Equivalent	3–4	3–4	4–5	5–6	5–6	7–8
Students per group	5	6	6	4	5	4

At Literature Circle Roles Reframed: Reading as a Film Crew (www.readwritethink. org/lessons/lesson_view.asp?id=877), students are asked to think like filmmakers while reading a text. Read Write Think has information about online literature circles for teen girls (www.readwritethink.org/lessons/lesson_view.asp?id=970) and for teen boys (www. readwritethink.org/lessons/lesson_view.asp?id=997).

At the San Antonio, Texas ISD website, online literature circles are described and some helpful resources are posted (http://itls.saisd.net/index.php?option=com_content&task= view&id=78&Itemid=101/). While attending the NECC 2008 conference in San Antonio, we talked with students and a teacher who had participated in an online literature circle during the 2007–08 school year. Both students and teacher were very enthusiastic about the process and wanted to continue using online literature circles in the next school year.

Online literature circles can be easily created with wiki or course management software, such as PBWiki, WikiSpaces, Blackboard, or similar platforms. For safety and security reasons, it's best to house a wiki on a private server in your district or to use a secure platform that is not open to the public. (Wiki tools are discussed in Chapter 3.) If you would like to work with another classroom not in your school or district, try ePals (www.epals.com).

Differentiating Vocabulary, Writing, Spelling, Speaking, and Listening

Let's face it. Working through language arts textbooks can be boring. In fact, without literature to spice up discussion, day after day of ELA skills work can drag down the class and the teacher.

In this section, we offer general suggestions and some interactive sites to help brighten up ELA and make it more appealing to students who may not enjoy working on skills but love technology. First, we provide some broad ideas for differentiating ELA. Second, we zoom in on Webbes and digital stories and how you can use them in your ELA classroom. Third, we provide a number of resources that will enhance this material and make learning it more fun and interactive for students.

Ideas for Differentiating Vocabulary, Writing, Spelling, Speaking, and Listening

We invite you to consider the following broad ideas.

Use digital presentation software, web tools, and music and digital art tools to reflect research and learning. Teach copyright and citation information. Information about copyrights is located at www.copyrightkids.org, and there are multimedia clips about copyrights available from the Library of Congress (www.loc.gov/teachers/copyrightmystery/).

Software and online tools spark creativity and allow students to produce products that demonstrate learning. Students can work individually or in groups to use and create products that will help them listen, speak, spell, write, and improve vocabulary. Starter ideas include PowerPoint book reports, PowerPoint "choose your own adventure" stories, word-processing or publishing software to create newspapers and magazines, electronic books, bookmarks, and more.

Use word-processing and writing tools to create, edit, and mark up changes. Word-processing tools often include a track changes tool that when turned on can be used as a markup or editing tool. Some teachers like to receive their students' work digitally so that they can use the markup tools to provide feedback to students electronically. Of course, students can also do peer editing this way.

Another helpful Word tool is the auto-summarize feature. This tool uses selections of text and provides a summary. To use it, copy an excerpt from student writing and paste it into a new document. Then turn on the tool under the Tools menu. A menu offers four choices; we like the "highlighting the key points" option. After writing a rough draft, each student can try the auto-summarize tool to see if Word can find the same key points that the student planned.

A new software product, WriteOnline (www.cricksoft.com/uk/writeonline/), is an enhanced online word processor with built-in tools for writing support. Students can use its integrated speech, word prediction, word banks, and writing frames to help them write and save their documents online or to their computer.

Use vocabulary and word-study sites to strengthen vocabulary in a fun way. One of our favorites is the Text Twist Game at Yahoo! Games. Students are timed as they create words with a given set of letters. They cannot move to the next level unless they are able to create a 6-letter word. This game could be used with pairs of students, who track their progress on a tally sheet or spreadsheet. The word games Bookworm, Flip Words, and Word Mojo Gold are also fun and do not require downloads. BBC WordMaster contains games to improve vocabulary, grammar, and pronunciation skills.

Interactive Sites for Vocabulary and Word Study

BBC WordMaster Game:
www.bbc.co.uk/worldservice/learningenglish/flash/wordmaster

Bookworm on Yahoo!:
http://get.games.yahoo.com/proddesc?gamekey=bookworm

Flip Words on Yahoo!: http://get.games.yahoo.com/proddesc?gamekey=flipwords

Flip-A-Chip Word Study: www.readwritethink.org/materials/flip

Just Crosswords: http://justcrosswords.com/create_custom_crossword.html

Puzzle Maker: http://puzzlemaker.discoveryeducation.com

Text Twist Game on Yahoo!:
http://games.yahoo.com/console/tx;_ylt=AoiqKcFMB6Z6sfQfrAVbq4aO3X0u

Vocabulary Games: www.vocabulary.co.il

Word Central Dictionary: www.wordcentral.com

Word Mojo Gold on Yahoo!:
http://get.games.yahoo.com/proddesc?gamekey=wordmojo

WriteExpress Rhyming Dictionary: www.writeexpress.com/online2.html

Use WebQuest and ThinkQuest for research and literature exploration. Visit the WebQuest portal (http://webquest.org) and the ThinkQuest portal (www.thinkquest.org) for ideas.

ThinkQuest is an annual student competition that inspires students to think, create, and share their knowledge and skills. Students work in teams to construct inventive and educational websites to share. The ThinkQuest Library, including entries from previous competitions, is available to search and use. One of the past winners is WhosGotNews. com (http://library.thinkquest.org/C0126521/). You may also want to create your own WebQuest at http://questgarden.com or with web creation software or similar tools.

Include streaming media, podcasts, presentations, and games in your WebQuest. Language arts instruction may be enhanced and made more engaging by integrating short video clips, podcasts, presentations, and games that motivate students to learn.

For streaming media, your district may subscribe to a vendor that provides access to audio and visual resources. Discovery Education Streaming is a popular vendor, and there are others as well. We also like BrainPOP for interesting animated movies and quizzes that can be used prior to or after viewing each movie. BrainPOP's array of writing, reading, study skills, and grammar skills movies will certainly stimulate students' interests—and yours too.

Podcast (iPOD broadCAST) is an audio broadcast that has been converted to an MP3 file or other audio file format for playback on a computer or digital music player. Students will be able to practice listening skills when podcasts are used in the classroom. They can also make podcasts as a project.

Streaming Video and Podcasts

BrainPOP: www.brainpop.com

Discovery Education Streaming: http://streaming.discoveryeducation.com

Mabry Online Language Arts Podcasts:
http://mabryonline.org/podcasts/archives/teacher_podcasts/language_arts

Memorial Hall Library—Teens read their poetry: www.mhl.org/teens/audio

Moving Image Archive: www.archive.org/details/movies

Storynory (look at the Greek myths under the Educational section and the Classic Authors): http://storynory.com

The Common Crafts Show (explains technology in plain English):
www.commoncraft.com/show

The Education Podcast Network (check the Middle School and Subject Matter links): http://epnWeb.org

Presentations and Games

Students can learn from multimedia presentations and games created by others and by creating their own presentations and games. Research shows that students learned more "when they had access to laptop computers, were exposed to multimedia software, and created prjects with presentation software" (ERICDocs; Siegle & Foster, 2000). In addition to multimedia presentations, we have found that when students create board games using technology, their higher order thinking skills kick into high gear. Here are some sites that feature PowerPoint presentations and games that you may find useful for your classroom.

PowerPoint Presentations and Games Resources

Jeff Ertzberger PowerPoint Games:
http://people.uncw.edu/ertzbergerj/ppt_games.html

Jefferson County Schools—Language Arts Games and Presentations:
http://jc-schools.net/PPTs-la.html

Jefferson County Schools, Tennessee: http://jc-schools.net/ppt.html

Meade Schools, Kentucky:
www.meade.k12.ky.us/TRT/Teachers/PowerPoint_downloads.htm

Parade of Games in PowerPoint: http://facstaff.uww.edu/jonesd/games

PowerPoint in the Classroom: www.actden.com/pp

Webbes and Digital Stories

Along with biographies, five-paragraph essays, critiques, and all the other writing formats middle school students study and practice, there are two formats that really stand out in terms of piquing students' interest.

Webbes (Web Books for Everyone) began as 20-page books that used only three sheets of paper to produce. Invented by RealeBooks (www.realebooks.com), Webbes were initially produced by using a word-processing template. RealeBooks offers a free, downloadable version of the software or the Pro version, with expanded features, for a fee. Webbes have been used successfully in Grades 3 up to adult. Visit the Lopez Elementary School website (http://lopez.realelibrary.com) and the Adams 50 School District website (http://adams50.realelibrary.com) to see some Webbes created with the new software.

FIGURE **4.1** ■ Everything DI website   © 2007 www.everythingdi.net. Reprinted with permission.

At our website, Everything DI (www.everythingdi.net), we have downloads and directions for the modified Word template we used in making Webbes with students in Grades 5–8. Working with students to produce their Webbe books was a marvelous experience. It was exciting to see ideas being generated, the planning and searching for information and images stages, storyboarding, and finally completion of the product. Several classrooms held author parties at the end of the project, as well as round-robin reading sessions during which students read one another's books. Requests for extra copies for parents and grandparents were honored.

Digital stories are another adventure in ELA that must be embraced to the fullest. Similar to Webbes, which also tell a story, digital stories can be created using Photo Story 3, PowerPoint, iMovie, Movie Maker, and similar software.

The idea behind digital storytelling is to tell a tale with a personal touch, an ideal project for middle grade students. Photo Story 3, a free download for Windows users (www. microsoft.com/windowsxp/using/digitalphotography/photostory/default.mspx), is fun and easy to use. iMovie '09 is a similar downloadable product for Mac users (www.apple. com/ilife/imovie/).

To help students create their digital stories, provide guidelines, rubrics, storyboards, and training in the application you have available. Stories can center on a theme, such as a biography, a book report, an event, or a "how-to-do" something. The sky really is the limit. Student-created images, photos, and slides saved as digital images can all be imported into Photo Story 3 and then rearranged in the desired sequence. Along with text features, Photo Story 3 offers pan and zoom controls that produce motion or movie-like effects. JakesOnline has a great tutorial (www.jakesonline.org), and we have several resources for digital storytelling at our Everything DI website (www.everythingdi.net).

Chapter Resources

Here are some interactive sites, student materials, and related tech resources to enhance your language arts classes. We've discussed many, but not all in this chapter, so take a peek at the lists below. Note that many of the following links are from Read Write Think, an outstanding site with lessons and student materials and tools. We also like the specialized tools for producing comics and art/images.

Interactive Sites for Writing and Creating Products

Acrostic Poetry Maker: www.readwritethink.org/materials/acrostic

Book Cover Creator: www.readwritethink.org/materials/bookcover

CD/DVD Cover Creator: www.readwritethink.org/materials/cd-dvd

Comics: Comic Creator: www.readwritethink.org/materials/comic

Comics: MakeBeliefsComix: www.makebeliefscomix.com/comix.php

Comics: Strip Generator: http://stripgenerator.com/create

Compare and Contrast Map:
www.readwritethink.org/materials/compcontrast/map

Crossword Puzzle Creator: www.readwritethink.org/materials/crossword

Diamante Creator: www.readwritethink.org/materials/diamante

Doodle Splash: www.readwritethink.org/materials/doodle

Drama Map: www.readwritethink.org/materials/dramamap

Essay Map: www.readwritethink.org/materials/essaymap

Fractured Fairy Tales: www.readwritethink.org/materials/fairytales

Graphic Map: www.readwritethink.org/materials/graphicmap

Literary Elements Map: www.readwritethink.org/materials/lit-elements

Multigenre Map: www.readwritethink.org/materials/multigenre-mapper

Mystery Cube: http://readwritethink.org/materials/mystery_cube

Myths and Legends Story Creator: http://myths.e2bn.org/story_creator

Notetaker: http://interactives.mped.org/notetaker722.aspx

Persuasion Map: www.readwritethink.org/materials/persuasion_map

Plot Diagram: www.readwritethink.org/materials/plot-diagram

Postcard Creator: www.readwritethink.org/materials/postcard

Printing Press: http://interactives.mped.org/view_interactive.aspx?id=110&title=

Profile Publisher: www.readwritethink.org/materials/profile

Riddle Interactive: www.readwritethink.org/materials/riddle

Story Map: www.readwritethink.org/materials/storymap

Timeline: www.readwritethink.org/materials/timeline

Trading Cards: Flickr: http://bighugelabs.com/flickr/deck.php

Trading Cards: Read Write Think:
http://readwritethink.org/materials/trading_cards

Venn Diagram: Three Circle: http://interactives.mped.org/venn28.aspx

Venn Diagram: Two Circle: www.readwritethink.org/materials/venn

Webbing Tool: http://interactives.mped.org/Webbing127.aspx

WriteIt!: http://teacher.scholastic.com/writeit

Interactive Sites for Grammar

BBC Skillswise: www.bbc.co.uk/skillswise

Grammar Games from the British Council:
www.britishcouncil.org/learnenglish-central-grammar-grammar-games-archive.htm

Maggie's Earth Adventure Grammar Games:
http://teacher.scholastic.com/activities/adventure

Interactive Sites for Reading

Global Tales: http://library.thinkquest.org/06aug/01340

Houghton Mifflin English: www.eduplace.com/kids/hme/6_8

Into the Book: http://reading.ecb.org/student

Teen Reads: www.teenreads.com

Content Connections

Bullfinch's Mythology: www.bulfinch.org

My Brother Sam Is Dead **Google Lit Trip:**
http://web.mac.com/jburg/GoogleLit/6-8/Entries/2007/4/14_My_Brother_Sam_Is_
Deadby_James_Lincoln_Collier_%26_Christopher_Collier.html

RAFT Reading/Writing Strategies:
www.greece.k12.ny.us/instruction/ELA/6-12/Reading/Reading Strategies/RAFT.htm

Shakespeare Online: www.shakespeare-online.com

Teen Reads: www.teenreads.com

Thinking Reader Software: www.tomsnyder.com

Productivity Tools

Citation Maker: http://myt4l.com/index.php?v=pl&page_ac=view&type=tools&tool=bibliographymaker

Cornell Notes: http://coe.jmu.edu/learningtoolbox/cornellnotes.html

Create a Brochure: http://epnWeb.org/index.php

iMovie '09: www.apple.com/ilife/imovie

Inspiration Software: www.inspiration.com

JakesOnline: www.jakesonline.org

Photo Story 3: www.microsoft.com/windowsxp/using/digitalphotography/photostory/default.mspx

RealeBooks: www.realebooks.com

Web 2.0 Tools

Blackboard: www.blackboard.com

Bubbl: www.bubbl.us

ePals: www.epals.com

Google Docs: http://docs.google.com

Graphic Organizer Maker:
http://myt4l.com/index.php?v=pl&page_ac=view&type=tools&tool=graphicorganizers

Notestar: http://notestar.4teachers.org

PBWiki: http://pbwiki.com

Rubistar: http://rubistar.4teachers.org

ThinkTank: http://thinktank.4teachers.org

Rubric Maker:
http://myt4l.com/index.php?v=pl&page_ac=view&type=tools&tool=rubricmaker

Wikis in Plain English: www.commoncraft.com/video-wikis-plain-english/

WikiMatrix: www.wikimatrix.org

WikiSpaces: www.wikispaces.com

WriteBoard: www.writeboard.com

Zoho: www.zoho.com

Summary

Differentiating English/Language Arts (ELA) is easier than it was before computer and web technologies were available in schools. Technologies open up new and exciting doors that appeal to diverse learners with a variety of learning styles, reading levels, interests, and abilities. The abundance of resources, the collaborative nature of Web 2.0 applications, and a wide range of products that students can craft kick up ELA learning a notch or two! Technology supports student engagement, connections to the real world, group participation, and project-based learning, all of which enhance learning in the ELA classroom.

CHAPTER 5

Using Technology to Differentiate Math

"Math education in the United States is a broken system.... 'We have kids sitting in rows in the classroom, and they're bored to tears. It's just not the way they live. Teachers and parents need to understand that this is the life of children today. They have to really understand that it's important for kids to be engaged, and it's important for us to change with the times.'" (Smith, 2008)

Technology use is limited in most math instruction. In many of the math classrooms we've visited, the presentation of content is still driven by the textbook. Although students use calculators regularly and sometimes complete self/practice tests on textbook-based websites, technology integration appears to be minimal or virtually nonexistent. From time to time, we've encountered electronic white boards or video presenters/cameras, but they mainly serve to magnify calculator screens and other images related to the lesson. On rare occasions, we've come across a classroom with clickers (student response systems). While hairstyles, clothing fads, and textbook covers have changed, modes of mathematical instruction have remained similar to those of past decades.

In the world of work, scientists, mathematicians, and others rely upon numerous technologies, very few of which we introduce to our students. However, we understand that many teachers feel trapped by their districts' limited financial resources and standards/curriculum. For example, one of our sons (who had a marvelous teacher) and his middle school classmates completed a huge algebra textbook (some 1,000 pages plus). In order to finish the book (or whatever the expectation may be), educators feel pressured to stick to the text and to keep outside activities to a minimum. What some teachers and administrators don't realize is that technology can lighten the workload while motivating students.

At times, we tend to shy away from pair or group work in more objective content areas, such as math. Socializing can distract students from the work at hand, so ground rules are essential. In addition, there is some concern that our students will not fulfill their roles. Struggling students may ask more proficient students to complete their portion of the task, and upper-level students might assume the bulk of the work to ensure a good grade. The social nature of our students, however, can actually work to our advantage. Listed in Table 5.1 are some of the ways in which teamwork, interactive tasks, and technology energize our classrooms and our students. They also assist us to customize learning.

TABLE **5.1** ■ Technology Opportunities in Math Instruction

Focus/Skill Area	DI Strategy with Technology
Teaching others/demonstrating mastery of content	PowerPoint presentation or Webbe
Problem solving within/outside classroom walls	Blogging
Competition (to promote mastery) within/outside classroom walls	FASTT Math software, online competitions, clickers (student response systems)
Construction/manipulation of mathematical tools	Websites with virtual manipulatives and GoSolve software
Learning via digital content	Jigsaw with Discovery Education Streaming or other content-based video sites

Yet another extremely compelling reason to promote personalized learning and collaboration with technology in the math classroom is the need to attend to all four learning styles of mathematical thinking. Educators who practice differentiated instruction, are aware that a learning profile is one of the four student traits that guides differentiation. When we talk about a learning profile, it's customary to consider brain-based predispositions, such as Gardner's multiple intelligences; cognitive styles, such as auditory, kinesthetic, visual, and tactile; and gender and culture-influenced preferences, such as learning personality traits, and group preferences. Math, however, is unique in that as a core subject, it has four specifically identified styles, which resemble those of the Myers-Briggs Type Indicator, that must be employed by all students to ensure mathematical success and understanding. Following is a description of the learning styles:

Mastery: learns concretely, repetitively, and sequentially. Calculation and computation are easier for this learner, while the student struggles with abstract concepts and nonstandard problem solving. This is the procedural dimension of learning.

Understanding: learns via explanations, ideas, concepts, and proofs. This student has difficulty with collaborative work and drill and practice. This is the conceptual dimension.

Self-expressive: learns best via strategies that permit exploration and visualization. Drill and practice and sequential learning strategies are problematic for this learner. This is the investigative dimension.

Interpersonal: learns best collaboratively (socially) and with application to math in the real world. Students do not work well with abstractions or on their own in their seat. This is the contextual dimension.

In the article "Creating a Differentiated Mathematics Classroom," Strong, Thomas, Perini, and Silver (2004) stress how imperative it is that we attend to and assist our students in the development of all four learning styles of mathematics: "…any sufficiently important mathematical topic requires students to learn that topic in four dimensions: procedurally, conceptually, contextually, and investigatively." As the article mentions, one of the greatest obstacles to broadening our students' repertoire is math curricula, for they usually require and focus on only one learning style. Let's see how technology, collaboration, and other tools and strategies help bridge that gap and kick things up a notch by reaching all learners!

Teaching Others/Demonstrating Mastery of Content via Presentations and Webbes

Although it has become extremely popular and sometimes overused, presentation software has many benefits. The majority of our students are familiar with it because it is used in other core classes. In addition, our students enjoy spicing up their work with graphics, sound, and the like. If they have not learned to use presentation software, such as PowerPoint, prior to entering your classroom, most students find it easy to manage in a fairly short period of time.

How can you use presentation software to engage students in your math classroom? Allow them to play the role of teacher for a brief portion of a class period. To help students become more familiar with content, ask them to create a slide show that explains a specific mathematical operation.

Table 5.2 lists some topics that might be explained well by using presentation software. The content areas and grade levels are based on the Michigan GLCEs (Grade Level Content Expectations), which, in turn, are founded upon the national standards set by the National Council of Teachers of Mathematics (NCTM). In Table 5.2, we have listed the national math standards that correspond with the topics we've suggested.

TABLE **5.2** ■ NCTM Standards and Suggested Topics

Sixth Grade	Seventh Grade	Eighth Grade
Multiply or divide fractions NM-NUM. 6-8.3: Compute fluently and make reasonable estimates	Slope/$y=mx+b$ NM-ALG. 6-8.1: Represent and analyze mathematical situations and structures using algebraic symbols	Calculate volume for generalized spheres, cylinders, pyramids, and/or cones NM-MEA. 6-8.2: Apply appropriate techniques, tools, and formulas to determine measurements
Add, subtract, multiply, or divide positive and negative numbers NM-NUM. 6-8.1: Understand numbers, ways of representing numbers, relationships among numbers, and number systems	Convert ratio quantities between different systems of units (such as feet per second to miles per hour) NM-MEA. 6-8.1: Understand measurable attributes of objects and the units, systems, and processes of measurement	Calculate the area and circumference of a circle NM-MEA. 6-8.2: Apply appropriate techniques, tools, and formulas to determine measurements

Your student "experts" can share presentations/slide shows with their class as part of a chapter or section review, or the day after you have presented new material, the experts could teach the class again, using slides they've made the night before. For example, if you recently presented content on calculating volume, have students create a presentation on this topic and open class with a slide show. The students can display the presentation and remind their peers in appealing digital format of what they covered during the last class period. Although the intent is not to compare or to encourage students to outdo one another, we've found that the competitive nature of our students works in a positive way. Students search for innovative ways to communicate the material, and if they feel comfortable in your classroom, they will relate something to an individual interest or experience. When our students have the freedom to make the link between their personal curiosities and classroom content, learning becomes energized and more meaningful.

Another variation on this activity would be to have students explain a math operation via the generation of a Webbe (discussed in Chapter 4 and the following chapters). In this case, math students become authors and their products can serve in a variety of ways:

Pairing/grouping students according to levels of readiness. Pair/group struggling students with those who have mastered the topic. The stronger student creates a Webbe about the math operation and shares it with the struggling student, or they may design one together.

Buddies or tutors for younger students. Your middle school students design Webbes, read the printed Webbes with their buddies, autograph them, and give them to the younger students to keep. This activity provides for a great review for the older students, fosters a sense of responsibility and community, and offers the younger ones the thrill of working side-by-side with cool older students.

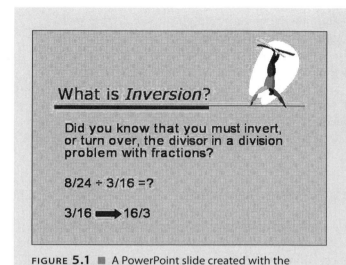

FIGURE 5.1 ■ A PowerPoint slide created with the included equation editor.

PowerPoint's Equation Editor

PowerPoint includes the Microsoft Equation Editor, which allows you to insert an equation into a presentation. To use the equation editor, click on Insert and then Object. Select Microsoft Equation 3.0 when it asks you to choose the Object type.

1. On the View menu, point to Toolbars, and then click Customize.
2. Click the Commands tab, and in the Categories list, click Insert.
3. In the Commands box, click Equation Editor, and then drag it from the Commands box to a gray area within any toolbar. Then click Close.
4. Click the new toolbar button to install and display the Equation Editor.
5. In the Equation Editor, use the buttons and menus to type your equation.
6. To return to Microsoft PowerPoint, on the File menu in Equation Editor, click Exit and Return to Presentation.

The equation appears on your slide.

Math Night. Parents, siblings, and friends can "meet the authors" of the Webbes as they share their artifacts and maybe even autograph copies and shake hands.

Review stations/Review resources. You and your class may use Webbes as a basis for review activities. You may create questionnaires, review sheets, and/or worksheets that refer to Webbes for additional help. Check out RealeBooks. com (www.realebooks.com), a fantastic online resource to produce a web-based version of a Webbe.

Problem Solving Within/Outside the Classroom via Blogging

As is the case with other Web 2.0 tools, educators and parents seem to be divided into opposite camps: those totally for or those completely against blogging. Those who are anti-blogging are most concerned about safety, which is a legitimate concern. Those who are pro-blogging claim that blogging helps students with writing and processing skills. Moreover, they contend that blogging is an everyday reality of our pre-teens' lives; so it is useless to ignore it or pretend it does not exist.

You might be asking yourself why and how blogging could play a role in your math classroom. Besides the fact that blogging may appear to be incompatible with mathematical computation, you, too, might find yourself worrying about monitoring and security issues. We hope that the pointers we offered on Internet safety in Chapter 3 were helpful to you. Our students spend ample time texting and conversing via cell phones, e-mail, and online chatting. Why not ask them to confer about math? Ideally, we want our students to think about and discuss math beyond the walls of our classrooms. Creating a unique opportunity to blog about their math work might intrigue students so much that even the reluctant learners get on board.

How Can You Use Blogging in Your Classroom?

As is the case with most technology tools, you don't have to be an expert to try out something new! Chances are that some of your students will be more experienced than you are, but you are the one who sets the pace. Following is a list of suggestions for different ways you might use blogging to invigorate your math classroom, and we move from simple to more complex tasks.

Entry Level. If you're a blogging novice, you can begin slowly by posting class announcements, reminders, and assignments.

Survey. Another easy option would be to post a survey-type question that requires input from each student. You could create an opportunity to learn more about your students' interests and learning styles, and they would appreciate the chance to talk about personal likes and dislikes. For example, you might ask them to comment on their most challenging or most enjoyable math content areas. You could ask them about their blogging background to determine how experienced they are: How much blogging have you done in the past? Where have you blogged, what was your motivation to do so, and what was the result? You can serve as a model by answering your own question(s) first. Although they might not openly admit to it, they are curious about their teachers' interests, and they are keenly observant.

If you've never tried an online survey poll, compose a questionnaire about blogging or math interests via SurveyMonkey, Zoomerang, Zoho Polls, FreeOnlineSurveys, or Poll Daddy. Allow your students to view the results and post some observational remarks about the patterns you notice.

Virtual Introductions. An activity that you could do with your students early in the school year is online introductions. Have them pair up in class to get to know one another, and then ask them to introduce each other to the entire class virtually. Of course, you'll want to give them some guidelines as to the information they can share.

Secretary. From here, you may step up your students' involvement by asking for volunteers to assume responsibility for posting class notes or summarizing what took place in class. Students can take turns, and if you're feeling comfortable, allow your posting volunteers to field questions from peers about the day's events. A good place to start with would be with your peer tutors or student experts if you have established such a program. If not, you know your students better than anyone. Look for volunteers who are proficient in math and able to express themselves clearly in writing. Another idea would be to request sample entries from all those who are interested, so that you can determine which students would best complete the task. If you would like your students to be involved in the selection process, have the potential volunteers all post a blog entry about the same class period. Ask the remaining students in your class to choose the blogger who did the best job of communicating what occurred in class. In order to protect feelings, you could generate an online survey for students that restricts access to the results so that only you may view them.

Guest Experts/Math in Everyday Life. To strengthen the connection between math and everyday life, consider inviting guest experts to talk about how they use math in the professional world. Provide your students with some background information about each guest, and then ask them to do a little investigative research so they can submit appropriate questions through the blog. A useful follow-up activity would be to require student entries on one or more of the following:

- Something new they learned from the guest blogger about math in everyday life

- Something new they learned from the guest expert about math as a profession

- A connection they made between current or past class content and something the guest mentioned

A fascinating website that you might take advantage of is The Futures Channel (www. thefutureschannel.com/hands-on_math/hands-on_math_movies.php). It has some movies about how various people use math in their professions and in the real world, such as a woman who designs Barbie dolls, finding space for furniture in an apartment, tracking bat populations with percent and ratio, and so on.

Annotated Website Reviews. Because our students are so tech-driven, let them find resources for one another. Collaboratively or individually, have them search for web resources related to something they are studying in class. When they suggest the links in their blog entries, require that they include three to four remarks explaining why they chose them and how the class will benefit. If students are working in teams to build resource lists on a particular theme, you could think about differentiating by interest in the following ways:

- Divide the students according to their favorite types of helpful academic sites, such as one group on gaming, a second on wikis, a third on other blogs, a fourth on movie tutorial sites, a fifth on test practice/ assessments, a sixth on online dictionaries or glossaries, another on manipulatives, and so on.

■ Group the students by contrasting interests, i.e., one student in the group is attracted to gaming, another student in the same group is fascinated by wikis, a third is captivated by blogs, and so on. If you wish to build teams according to levels of readiness, arrange them in groups of students who are of the same level, or deliberately place more capable students with struggling students.

■ Groups of students who are at the same level of mathematical ability can hunt for resources specific to their level that they share with peers and can use themselves, an effective motivator. You may also ask them to seek out links that they could use with a (future) project that involves pair or group work with a weaker student or younger buddy.

■ Heterogeneous groups that are based according to differing levels of readiness foster leadership skills in proficient students and afford a more personalized learning experience for less adept students who may benefit from working more intimately with stronger students.

By the way, social bookmarking tools like Daft Doggy make annotated website reviews a snap and have extra features that will enthrall your students. We mentioned a few options in Chapter 3, and here are several others that you can investigate. Daft Doggy (www.daft-doggy.com) allows users to build webpage tours online and to create voice recordings that enable comments, instructions, or descriptions. In addition, there is an automatic e-mail option to send the link to others for posting on a blog or webpage. Fleck (www.fleck.com) offers virtual post-it notes to stick on weblinks. Some other widely used bookmarking sites are Furl (www.furl.com), Simpy (www.simpy.com), Trailfire (www.trailfire.com), and Jump Knowledge (http://info.jkn.com). As students comb the web for this activity (or any other, for that matter), take the time to teach them about rating websites via selected criteria. The CyberSmart Curriculum provides a free lesson for middle school students called "Identifying High Quality Sites" (http://cybersmartcurriculum.org/researchinfo/lessons/6-8/identifying_high_quality_sites/). In addition, wikis are a wonderful resource for link collections, but we wanted to show you how blogs can serve as a platform for many learning tasks. Wikis are another Web 2.0 tool that we covered in Chapter 3 and will refer to in the following chapters.

Problem Solving. Finally! Did you think that we'd ever get to what should be the number-one reason for using blogs in the math classroom? Logically, math blogs function as a forum for problem solving in teams or as individual learners. Blogs give students chances to hash things out after we've left the school building, particularly when they are stumped and need assistance. Feeling alone or isolated when it comes to a challenging subject like math can be daunting. Blogs can foster a sense of community outside the physical walls of the classroom. Although cyberbullying and harassment are serious problems, we've also observed that the use of technology usually levels the playing field. Whether our students are athletes, artists, techies, or any combination thereof, all of them depend on and enjoy the same tech tools. When technology is used for collaborative purposes, all parties win, and social boundaries are broken down. Techies become stars because they know how to manipulate the tools and answer questions. Popular students realize that the techies can assist them. Levels of communication often increase with blogging, as students are less socially or emotionally intimidated when others are not physically present. Of course, a potential downside is students revealing more personal information than they should. Teachers can open discussions about the wisdom of keeping some information private.

The most common way to make use of blogs for problem solving is to ask students to post solutions to problems you've assigned. This provides an alternative venue for your students, and that in itself energizes them. However, if you're concerned that struggling students will copy others' solutions and fail to master the content, we have two additional tactics your students will welcome.

Tactic One: Permit your students to post questions individually or in teams to help review for upcoming assessments, or let them have some fun with math trivia or word problems by stumping others. You could make this a homework assignment that's worth few points or extra credit, if you allow it, and we're certain that your students will enjoy the chance to baffle their peers!

Tactic Two: One of Stephanie's favorite games from Spanish class can be transferred over to math. Math is a language of symbols and patterns. Use your class blog to solve math problems, step-by-step. Students can work in teams, which is how the exercise works in Spanish class. In Spanish, students would race to the board in relay teams to spell out, letter-by-letter, the correct verb conjugation of the infinitive, tense, and person specified. Here are the ground rules for our modification to the game that you may use in your blog: The first student begins by answering the first step or part of the problem. The next student may continue with the following step or correct an error in the previous step. He or she may not do both.

Again, you could easily differentiate by readiness by placing students in teams according to their ability levels. Give each team a problem appropriate to its skill level. For a variation, come up with an appropriate rotation or schedule that allows your students to assume responsibility for creating a problem of the day.

Review. If you're game for experimenting with embedding a visual or diagram into your blog, try out some of the document sharing links that we mentioned in Chapter 3, such as Google Docs, SlideShare, Zoho Show, and One True Media. You could upload your own and/or your students' presentations or create them online, and then embed them into the class blog for review purposes or for those who missed class. Another fantastic resource is Sketchcast (www.sketchcast.com). This application allows you to "draw" on a virtual whiteboard and even record an audio explanation to accompany your visual aid.

Construction/Manipulation of Mathematical Tools

A number of our elementary colleagues integrate concrete manipulatives into their math activities to enhance understanding. Although concrete manipulatives may be too unsophisticated for our middle school students, virtual manipulatives are not.

Virtual manipulatives are useful to teachers and students for several reasons:

- They enable concrete visualization of the abstract, more difficult to grasp math concepts.

- They are more game-like in nature.

- They accommodate diverse learning styles and readiness levels, including gifted students, challenged learners, and so on.

- They are not messy or difficult to store.

- With Internet access, you can use them quickly and frequently.

Are you aware that there are two different types of manipulatives? Static manipulatives are visual pictures that resemble concrete manipulatives and cannot be moved by users. They may change on the screen but not as a result of something that is controlled by the user. Dynamic manipulatives are virtual objects that users can move.

For example, imagine that your students are studying mean, median, and mode, measures of central tendency. In order for your students to understand the differences among them, as well as to experiment with how mean, median, and mode change when statistics are altered, allow them to test out these manipulatives with activities. In this activity, blocks are added to or removed from an axis within a set range using the PlopIt applet (Fig. 5.2).

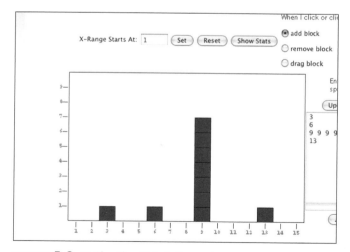

FIGURE **5.2** ■ The PlopIt! Activity applet

© 2009 Shodor's Interactivate (www.shodor.org/interactivate/)

Figure 5.3 shows an Illuminations applet (http://illuminations.nctm.org/ActivityDetail.aspx?ID=160) that allows students to investigate the mean, median, and box-and-whisker plot for a set of data that they create. The data set may contain up to 15 integers, ranging in value from 0–100.

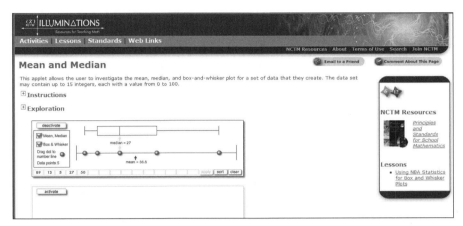

FIGURE 5.3 ■ The Illuminations applet

Reproduced with permission from the National Council of Teachers of Mathematics.

The following two Gizmos deal with box-and-whisper plots and line plots. Mean, median, and mode are calculated for a data set, and then the data values are changed. Students observe how the mean, median, and mode are affected.

ExploreLearning: Constructing Box-and-Whisker Plots:
www.explorelearning.com/index.cfm?method=cResource.dspDetail&ResourceID=259

ExploreLearning: Line Plots:
www.explorelearning.com/index.cfm?method=cResource.spDetail&ResourceID=225

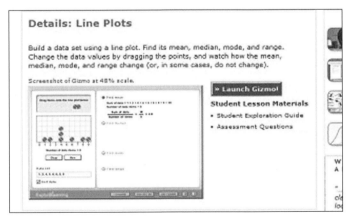

FIGURE 5.4 ■ ExploreLearning Gizmos

Reproduced with permission from ExploreLearning (www.explorelearning.com).

Whether you prefer static or dynamic manipulatives, or a combination of the two, virtual manipulatives are sure to add another dimension to your classroom. Take a look at some of these exciting sites and tools. Your students will beg for more, even if they say they don't care for math!

Virtual Manipulatives Resources

Algebasics: www.algebasics.com

Site includes Flash tutorials and step-by-step solutions.

Dimension M: Where There's Power in Numbers: www.dimensionm.com

Virtual games for algebra and pre-algebra with single or multiplayer capabilities, videos, interactives, and simulations. There is a cost involved.

ExploreLearning Math Gizmos: www.explorelearning.com/index. cfm?method=cResource.dspChildrenForCourse&CourseID=122

Very engaging site, but only a 30-day free trial is offered, and then the cost jumps significantly.

Illuminations—Activities: http://illuminations.nctm.org/Activities.aspx?grade=3

From NCTM with Java-based practiced that correlates with concepts from math strands.

Interactivate: www.shodor.org/interactivate

Interactive Mathematics Activities: www.cut-the-knot.org/Curriculum

Check out the mammoth listing of weblinks on this site, too!

Java Applets-Mathematics: http://edinfo.securesites.net/il/il_math.htm

Junior High Math:
www.learnalberta.ca/content/mejhm/index.html?launch=true

Site includes video and object interactives.

Math Manipulatives, Videos, and Games at Math Playground:
www.mathplayground.com

Maths.Net: www.mathsnet.net

MathTools: http://mathforum.org/mathtools/started.html

National Library of Virtual Manipulatives:
http://nlvm.usu.edu/en/nav/category_g_3_t_2.html

Manipulatives and online activities categorized by strand.

NEIRTEC Math Portal: www.neirtec.org/activities/math_portal.htm

Socha's Interactive Math Links:
www.fcps.edu/dis/OHSICS/math/socha

Villainy, Inc.: http://villainyinc.thinkport.org/default.asp

> An excellent, mission-based site to help middle school students with problem solving. It has animation, sound, and interactives.

Visual Fractions: www.visualfractions.com

Calculators and Other Helps

Awesome Talkster: www.awesomelibrary.org/Awesome_Talking_Library.html

> This site includes browser, search engine, and text-to-speech function that can read whole page or selected items in various languages.

CoolMath Online Graphing Calculator: www.coolmath.com/graphit

G-Calc: http://gcalc.net

Martindale's Calculators Online Center:
www.martindalecenter.com/Calculators.html

> This site has about 18,000 calculators to choose from!

ReadPlease: www.readplease.com

> This site will read the text on the computer screen out loud for you.

Talking Calculator: www.premierathome.com/products/TalkingCalculator.php

Solving Word Problems

What do students complain the most about in math? Word problems! No matter what the operation, word problems puzzle our students. Tom Snyder Productions has GO Solve Word Problems (http://tomsnyder.com/products/product.asp?SKU=GOSGOS), a handy piece of software to train your students to develop a systematic approach to solving word problems. GO Solve advocates the use of graphic organizers and provides adaptive leveling for differentiated instruction. Animated tutorials, text-to-speech features, graded and independent practice, hints, and options for personalization (add names of people, places, and things) combine to make a great product. Use this software to complement your math curriculum for sixth graders or for intervention with seventh and eighth graders.

Competition (to Promote Mastery) Within/Outside the Classroom Walls

As the saying goes, "A little competition is good for the soul." Have you attended one of your child's or students' sports events lately or perhaps, some type of competition involving the arts? While adults are busy teaching children important lessons about good sportsmanship and putting forth their best effort, children are keeping track of who's ahead. Of course, many adults are secretly or more overtly keeping track of it, too!

As humans, the quest to be the best may be instinctive or learned. The common perception is that with success comes power and recognition, albeit for a short time. In school culture today, we frequently downplay competition to avoid feelings of exclusion or alienation. While it is certainly essential to cultivate positive traits in our children, such as empathy, collaboration, and kindness, we believe that a healthy level of competition is vital to success in the marketplace of the future. As students vie for jobs with people of multiple nations and cultures, they must be ready to push their own limits. On top of all the statistical evidence, quick observation reinforces the fact that most students are inherently competitive, whether they vocalize it or not.

Just to make sure that we're on the same page, we are not advocating a learning environment that promotes cutthroat competition. The learning environment of the differentiated classroom is one of respect and teamwork. However, we've found that educators can effectively employ various forms of competition in math classes that boost students' levels of enthusiasm and active participation. As a general rule, don't you observe that the majority of your students perk up when you offer them the chance to play a game or take part in a contest? When they are outside the school environment, many of them are doing just that in their own homes or with friends via their Wiis, Playstations, X-Boxes, and online virtual games.

In our search for excellent resources, we came across several online contests that might intrigue you and your students. We've chosen just a handful; some are team-driven, and others are for individual participants.

Online Contests

ABACUS International Math Challenge (www.gcschool.org/pages/program/Abacus. html) came about as an outgrowth of a Hungarian printed journal about gifted students. Tivadar Divéki, a math and science teacher, posts eight problems a month for each of the three age groups. Solutions and mathematical explanations/reasoning are submitted via e-mail. Students have multiple opportunities to answer the question, if they respond incorrectly the first time. Teachers may provide tips to students to help them arrive at a successful answer. Students are encouraged to find all possible solutions to each problem and earn points based on the thoroughness of their responses. Standings are posted on the website, as well as an "International Hall of Fame." There is no charge to participate.

SIFMA Stock Market Game 2008-06-09 / 2009-06-13		Advisor: Team ID:SIA_72_A29		School: SIFMA Region: End of Day	
▸ MENU **Trading**		⑦ HELP		**Mutual Funds**	
Account Summary	Pending Transactions	Account Holdings	Transaction Notes	Gains and Losses	
Enter A Trade	America's Indices	Investor Research	Transaction History	News Update	
				Subtotal for 2008-11-01:	($17.32)
	INT	0.00	2008-10-25	$0.0000	($17.3000)
				Subtotal for 2008-10-25:	($17.30)
	INT	0.00	2008-10-18	$0.0000	($17.4800)
				Subtotal for 2008-10-18:	($17.48)
	INT	$10,000.00	2008-10-15	$0.0000	$264.5000
				Subtotal for 2008-10-15:	$264.50
	INT	0.00	2008-10-11	$0.0000	($17.6100)
				Subtotal for 2008-10-11:	($17.61)
	INT	0.00	2008-10-04	$0.0000	($17.6000)
				Subtotal for 2008-10-04:	($17.60)
	DIV	200.00	HPQ	2008-10-01	$0.0000	$16.0000

FIGURE 5.5 ▪ Sample screen from The Stock Market Game

Reproduced with permission from the SIFMA Foundation for Investor Education.

The Stock Market Game (www.stockmarketgame.org) is an innovative investment game. Students work in teams to build a portfolio that outperforms all others. They begin with a virtual cash account of $100,000, and they compete for the number-one spot via a live trading simulation. The website provides a free teacher login and teacher support center, as well as lessons and activities, standards information, assessments, and publications. Fees vary by state, but most seem to range between $15 and $25 per team.

Math Olympiads (www.moems.org/program.htm) are for individuals or teams. They suggest that students form math clubs that meet for one hour each week to practice for the five monthly contests or to discuss a specific strategy or topic. Each contest has five problems, and students may not use calculators to solve them. The contests are taken at the participating school, and results are either mailed in or submitted online. There is a charge for participation. Winners receive awards, such as trophies, patches, pins, certificates, and medallions. Division E is for Grades 4–6, and Division M is for Grades 6–8.

Middle School Madness (www.colstate.edu/mathcontest/problem.php?CategoryID=2& LinkID=Current) is sponsored by Columbus State University. A new problem is posted each Monday, and students have until Friday at midnight (EST) to submit an answer. If a student answers correctly, his or her name, school, city, state, and country will be displayed on the website. One t-shirt per week is given to a participant via a random drawing. Additional problems of the week are offered on the site, such as "Middle School Madness" and "Algebra in Action." This is a free service.

Online Math League (www.onlinemathleague.com/faq.asp#3) has three contests per year that may be taken online or on paper. Each test is 30 minutes long and has 15 multiple choice questions. Individual students and teams win physical awards, such as medals and plaques, but the site also supplies certificate templates for improvement and participation. All scores are displayed on the website. A student practice area is available. There is a charge for participation in this program.

In addition to the contests listed above, you could create your own problem of the day or have your students take turns preparing one. Taking time to solve the problem in class or generating a new problem of the day can serve as useful anchor activities.

FASTT Math

New software for academics is popping up more and more frequently, which means more alternatives for teachers and students. FASTT Math, created by Tom Snyder Productions (www.tomsnyder.com/fasttmath/), is a wonderful tool that delivers content based on three types of assessment. FASTT Math creates a personalized course of study for each student, based on results from the Placement Quiz. As students work to convert non-fluent facts to fluent, they complete frequent, automatic assessments that focus in on exactly where they need added practice.

In our experience, students are so enthralled by the software that there are few complaints about having to work on math facts! As students advance, they are allowed to play games that enable them to earn screen skins and to change the appearance of their screens. Although they do not compete against one another, they often make the rounds in the classroom or lab to see how many skins their classmates have, or what color their screens are as this will tell them who's at a higher or lower level in the program. During the pilot in Grace's district, the rising middle school students (fifth graders) cried when it was over!

Student Response Systems (Clickers)

Clickers are a more recent, kinesthetic tool that are a welcome addition to middle school math classrooms. They appeal to students for many reasons:

- They resemble and function like a TV remote or a cell phone. Some of them even allow for "text" type input, such as Promethean's Active Expression.

- Clickers increase frequency of response because students remain anonymous (and, therefore, do not feel embarrassed if they answer "incorrectly" in front of their peers).

- They encourage students' attentiveness because they have to be prepared for questions on the fly and when it is the correct time to respond. The visual images/graphics that often accompany automated response systems (such as those projected via electronic whiteboards or presentation software) catch their eyes.

- Clicker-based activities often feel more like games than hard-core classwork.

Now let's consider the teacher's point of view. There are many great reasons for you to choose to add clickers to your classroom repertoire:

- Automated response systems engage students and lengthen their attention spans.

FIGURE **5.6** ■ Examples of student response systems (clickers).
© Promethian 2009, © Quizdom 2009, © Turning Technologies, LLC, © Renaissance Learning. Used with permission.

- They provide for equity across the classroom. Even reluctant or struggling students are more willing to participate anonymously. Furthermore, many automated response systems supply an on-screen counter that displays the number of students that have responded and how they've responded. Teachers and students learn to wait a little longer for all responses before jumping ahead too quickly.

- Several clickers can accommodate questions on the fly—teachers can generate spontaneous questions to maintain student involvement and/ or check for understanding.

- Some automated response systems come with sufficient memory to plan and store questions/assessments in advance.

- Most automated response systems have a grade book that accompanies them and/or the ability to hook into other electronic grade books that your school might already have in place.

- If funds are a determining factor, some schools purchase only one or two sets that are shared by several classrooms.

At this point, you may remain unconvinced about the need for clickers. We realize that school budgets are not limitless, and one must be selective. However, let's take a moment to consider how you might incorporate clickers into your classroom tasks.

Clickers enhance Jeopardy-like review games created in a presentation program or other interface. All students can respond, or you can simulate the game itself by rotating three students at a time. Automated response systems can assist in all three types of assessment: pre-assessment, ongoing assessment, and post-assessment. For example, response cards are a common physical device to gauge comprehension. Teachers often use entrance cards prior to a lesson as a form of pre-assessment to determine students' prior knowledge about a particular topic. Exit cards, a form of post-assessment, allow teachers to verify mastery of comprehension of content at the end of a lesson, class period, or unit. Response cards that enable students to respond to teacher questions on cue as a group represent a form of ongoing assessment. Clickers offer an alternative to paper-created response cards. Further, some brands permit short/pop quizzes that are graded electronically, which mean less work for the teacher.

Learning via Digital Content: Streaming

We don't recall seeing a movie or filmstrip in any of our math classes, but teachers today can find a fair selection of math videos on Discovery Education Streaming or other web-based video sites. Wondering why you would ever want or need to show a video in math class? Simply put, a good number of our digital age students are visual learners due to the culture and their generation. Our students depend heavily on technology in their personal lives and are exposed to a barrage of visual images on a daily basis. In fact, they are so accustomed to it that many prefer the blitz of images, which mimics what they encounter in their video games. Even if they connect strongly with you in the classroom, they are eager to respond to tech-driven activities.

A differentiated activity interest that we enjoy using in math and other classrooms is video-based Jigsaw. For this activity, you will need to select a full-length video that is divided into manageable segments. You may also use a series of video clips that lend themselves to this activity and center on the chosen topic.

Jigsaw is a collaborative technique in which students are divided into home groups of students and expert groups of students. Each student is a member of one home group and one expert group, and no group has the same students in it.

For sake of example, we searched the Discovery Education Streaming site for a video on geometry. One of the available videos was Standard Deviants' "The Many-Sided World of Geometry, Program 4: Special Triangles." Here are the steps to follow to complete the video Jigsaw activity:

1. Divide the video into as many segments or subtopics as there are members in each home group and assign students to each home group. In the video that we chose as a sample, some of the possible segments or subtopics include:

   - Features of isosceles and right triangles and congruency

   - Names and definitions of polygons

   - Five categories of quadrilaterals and similarity

   - Review of triangles and triangle basics

2. In their home groups, students select the segment or subtopic they would like to investigate.

3. Separate the home groups of students into new temporary expert groups—the Jigsaw groups—in which they join other students assigned to the same segment or subtopic to research. In their expert groups, students view their video segment(s). If you choose, they may use additional resources (e.g., the Internet) to study further about their particular segment/subtopic. Members prepare a presentation to take back to their home groups.

4. Temporary expert group members return to their home groups and teach the home group members what they learned.

5. The home groups can then prepare a sequenced presentation that they deliver to the entire class.

Your middle school students will surely enjoy the combination of video, movement, and socializing with two different groups. The Internet offers an abundance of spectacular video-based math resources and tools.

Math-Based Resources

Brain Pop: Math: www.brainpop.com/math

Countdown Math: http://countdown.luc.edu

Free Math Videos Online: www.math-videos-online.com

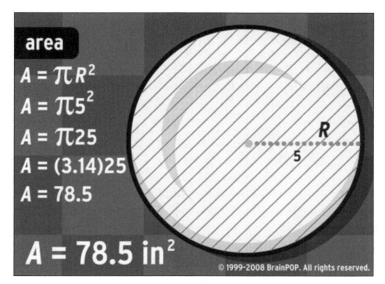

FIGURE **5.7**   ■   Calculating the circumference of a circle in BrainPOP
© 1999–2008 BrainPOP

Homework Video Tutors: www.phschool.com/webcodes10/index.
cfm?fuseaction=home.gotoWebCode&wcprefix=aee&wcsuffix=0775

Math TV: www.mathplayground.com/mathtv.html
This site has video word problems.

MathTrain.TV: www.mathtrain.tv
This site focuses on student-created screencasts or mathcasts.

Phenomenal Math Sites

At the Holt Rhinehart and Winston (HRW) Middle School Math Page (http://go.hrw.com/gopages/ma-msm.html) we explored resources for Holt Mathematics Course 2. HRW supplies a plethora of awesome resources, such as homework help with videos and practice sheets, a multilingual glossary, chapter projects in real-life math, lab resources, family involvement (letter to parents with overview activities, terminology, and formulas students will learn in class, game time at home), career resources, and web extra (an article and activity about the topic of study as it relates to a real-life example).

At the McDougal Littell ClassZone site (www.classzone.com/cz/) we selected our state and chose the pre-algebra text that our students use. McDougal Littell offers animated math, a homework tutor with problems, puzzles and games, math vocabulary, flip cards, critical thinking with real-world skills and extension, more examples with solutions, PowerPoint presentations, e-workbook, problem of the week, quick reference guides and tools, assessment, and parents as partners (lesson goals and exercises).

NutshellMath from Discovery Education (www.nutshellmath.com) has a very reasonably priced tool that could be of real benefit to your students as a home-based resource. The organization supplies explanations of math problems that appear in 60 textbooks with tutorial videos. All you have to do is choose the book and the page number on which the problem is located in the text. If your students struggle at home or can't remember what they learned in class, this could be very inexpensive help for them. The site also has a special section for parents.

Summary

As you can see, opportunities abound for differentiating math instruction with technology. Along with the benefits of differentiating to meet learners' needs, you will be combining math instruction with digital age skill sets and helping students prepare for the future. Choose a few of these strategies to move your classroom into the future.

CHAPTER **6**

Using Technology to Differentiate Science

In the course of writing this book, the number of resources that we reviewed was overwhelming. Thanks to the Internet, we have so many more materials at our fingertips! We can use them without leaving our own homes if we choose. We may search for and request books and CDs from libraries across the country and pick them up at our own local libraries when they arrive. As teachers, we have a vast array of pre-made activities that other teachers have made available for our use, reducing our preparation time. Organizations such as Discovery Education have developed amazing products that allow us to customize our students' learning experiences with a few mouse clicks. Publishers are creating online versions of textbooks that offer abundant interactive resources to our students. Struggling readers or auditory learners have the option of asking the computer to read web-based materials with text-to-speech capabilities.

Sounds fantastic, doesn't it? Unfortunately, in many of the classrooms we've visited, teachers are not taking advantage of these exciting resources. Students are still crafting projects on poster board and completing plenty of worksheets. The majority of the time, they're listening to their teachers drone on for a good portion of the class period, causing them to tune out. They literally have to decelerate or downshift ("power down") when they enter the school building because what they experience in school does not come close to the pace of their lives outside school—emotionally, academically, and physically.

It is absolutely critical that we fortify the connection between our learning activities in school and the outside world. If that link is weak or is never established, we lose our students academically and emotionally. Moreover, we fail in our charge to prepare them as future contributors to the global marketplace. If we do not make changes to educational systems by forging ahead and meeting the students where their technological skills and interests lie, students will continue to fall by the wayside in terms of academic and professional competitiveness. This is especially important in the core areas of science and math because they are the fields in which the number of jobs will multiply.

As we've visited different classrooms and conversed with teachers across the United States, we've found that the majority of teachers follow the steps listed below when teaching any science unit or lesson:

Pre-reading activities. Students predict what the topic is about, based on the chapter headings, subheadings, and graphics. The teacher introduces the unit or lesson in a way that makes students want to learn.

During-reading activities. The teacher uses during-reading activities to build understanding and provide food for discussion. Multimedia and website enhancements help to differentiate the text and appeal to a variety of learning styles. Students typically identify main ideas and details and sometimes make connections with math and/or other core subjects. Students research the topic at hand and use glossaries and dictionaries to understand new terms.

After-reading activities. Students demonstrate evidence of understanding via products and assessments.

To show how technology can absolutely empower science learning, we've created a sample differentiated unit on earthquakes. In many cases, students study earthquakes in sixth grade as part of a plate tectonics unit, and/or in eighth grade during a unit on severe weather or natural disasters/hazards. As students move ahead to the middle-school level, they have the ability to understand the phenomena of the geosphere (crust, mantle, and core), as well as the long-term processes involved in geological activity. Middle school is the time when students begin to develop investigative skills governed by ideas, knowledge, questions, and observations, the principles of scientific inquiry. However, they sometimes struggle with the use and effect of multiple variables in experiments, and they gravitate toward evidence that validates their current beliefs. As we constructed this unit, we tried to keep a clear focus on the abilities and tendencies of middle school science students.

We discuss each step and list resources you can use. Although we put this unit together in a specific order, you might opt to rearrange it or pick and choose from the steps detailed in the lesson.

Earthquakes Unit

Introduction/Pre-Reading Motivation

Show students pictures of damage caused by various earthquakes. Ask them to identify the type of natural disaster that caused the destruction. If possible, try to select locations that they might recognize, and ask them to identify where the earthquakes took place. Excellent pictures are available on these sites:

How Stuff Works Earthquake Gallery: http://science.howstuffworks.com/ enlarge-image.htm?terms=earthquake&gallery=1&page=1

BBC in Pictures: Peru Earthquake: http://news.bbc.co.uk/2/hi/in_pictures/6949478.stm

USGS Earthquake Photo Collections: http://earthquake.usgs.gov/learning/photos.php

San Francisco Public Library's 1906 Earthquake Photos: http://sfpl.org/news/earthquakephotos

Pre-Assess Readiness (Content Knowledge and Topical Vocabulary)

Choose from the following resources to pre-assess knowledge of content and key vocabulary associated with the topic. Print the completed activities.

Shorter list of vocabulary: www.quia.com/jg/1224204list.html

Longer list of vocabulary: www.quia.com/jg/115616list.html

Plate tectonics vocabulary: www.quia.com/jg/262313list.html
This site is useful to review past content, if needed.

LiveScience: The Big Quake Quiz: www.livescience.com/php/trivia/?quiz=quake

Quiz on Earthquakes: www.oswego.edu/geo_classes/geo100/q1eq.html

CBBC Newsround Quiz on Earthquakes: http://news.bbc.co.uk/cbbcnews/hi/newsid_4140000/newsid_4146100/4146125.stm

Earthquake Quiz: www.quizplz.com/science/earth/earthquake-quiz.htm

Pre-Assess Interest

In pairs, brainstorm a list of possible subtopics students might wish to study. Generate a web or map of ideas using one or more of the following online mapping applications: Glinkr, Gliffy, Thinkature, Bubbl, Mappio, Read Write Think Webbing Tool, or Mindomo. You might also choose to use Inspiration software. If needed, tailor your graphic organizers to simplify them for students, such as choosing a simplified Word document that allows students to type what they want to learn or a printable form that you can find below. Print the completed maps/webs.

Bubbl: www.bubbl.us

Eduplace Graphic Organizers: www.eduplace.com/graphicorganizer/
    These organizers are available in printable PDF format.

Gliffy: www.gliffy.com

Glinkr: www.glinkr.net

Mappio: www.mappio.com

Mindomo: www.mindomo.com

Read Write Think Webbing Tool:
http://interactives.mped.org/view_interactive.aspx?id=127&title=

TeAch-nology Graphic Organizer Makers:
http://teachers.teach-nology.com/web_tools/graphic_org
    This site generates organizers according to your specifications.

Thinkature: www.thinkature.com

Next, discuss maps and webs as a whole class, and determine the students' top five choices. Then ask them to confer with their partners and to pick their personal top three of the five. They must give compelling reasons why the class should study their selections; ask them to insert their rationales into their webs. You could also use a different organizer for this part of the task. Take a glance at these persuasive writing-based templates that you might modify:

My Opinion: www.worksheetplace.com/php_uploads/displaySheet.php?sheet=pw7

Persuasive Writing Opinion:
www.worksheetplace.com/php_uploads/displaySheet.php?sheet=pw5

Persuasive Writing Organizer:
www.worksheetplace.com/php_uploads/displaySheet.php?sheet=pw11

Print the completed organizers and be prepared to use the results from the Background Reading/Earthquake Basics and Terms/Anatomy section. If possible, make time for a fun game. Synthesize the results of the previous activity, and reveal the results via classroom, Family Feud style. Here are two sites with Family Feud templates:

Family Feud PowerPoint: www.ilovemath.org/index.php?option=com_docman&task=doc_details&gid=129&Itemid=31

PTT PowerPoint Game Samples: www.pttinc.com/ppgame.htm

Myths and Legends about Earthquakes

Students investigate myths and legends about earthquakes and then produce a comic strip to relate their own version of the myth or legend using an online comic creator.

The Chevron Cars Earthquake Myths and Legends: www.chevroncars.com/learn/wondrous-world/earthquake-legends

CERI Public Awareness, Earthquake Myths: www.ceri.memphis.edu/aware/myths.html

FEMA for Kids: Earthquake Legends: www.fema.gov/kids/eqlegnd.htm

Earthquake Legends and Science: www.msnucleus.org/membership/html/jh/earth/earthquakes/lesson2/earthquakes2a.html

Some of the following comic strip resources are very easy to use, offer a small number of pre-made templates, and are registration-free, but do not provide for embedding (into blogs and such). Others are sites that require registration but offer more creative options and embedding. Examine them for yourself to see what their policies are on appropriate content and to determine which ones you prefer. Print the completed strips, in color if possible, display, and/or have your students read creations aloud with a partner.

Make Beliefs Comix: www.makebeliefscomix.com

Bubblr: www.bubblr.com

Comic Creator: www.readwritethink.org/materials/comic

Myths and Legends 2: http://myths.e2bn.org
This site allows for Story Creator 2 and sound to be incorporated.

Toon Boom Animation has created some amazing animation software that is state-of-the-art, yet user-friendly. Toon Boom Studio is actually used by Hollywood giants in the animated movie industry. Flip Boom (kids' version), Toon Boom Studio Express 4 (a scaled-down version of Toon Boom), Comic Boom, and Animation-ish are incredible tools that your students will love, and they are reasonably priced.

ToonDoo: www.toondoo.com

Toonlet: www.toonlet.com

Comiqs: http://comiqs.com

Pixton: www.pixton.com

At this site, see the Pixton for Schools section.

Stripgenerator: www.stripgenerator.com

At the following sites, you can learn about the software, request trial downloads, see student showcases, and take product tours, among other choices.

Toon Boom Animation Software: www.toonboom.com/products

Toon Boom Animation Software for Kids: www.toonboom.com/products/kids.php

Background Reading/Earthquake Basics and Terms/Anatomy

Select from the following list of sites to allow your students to build fundamental content knowledge. Place your students in groups of three or four according to the interests they expressed in the interest assessment activities above. Each group is assigned a topic of interest, such as causes of earthquakes, fault types/motion, locations, hazards/side effects, types of earthquake waves, and earthquake preparation.

Using the Cornell Notes method, students should research basic facts about their category to share with the class. The intent is to provide an overview of main topics so that students can then move on to other steps, where they will study them in more detail. Preferably, have students use the Microsoft template to implement the Cornell Notes form into PowerPoint so that each group may project its information in front of the class for sharing purposes.

Cornell Notes Resources

Cornell Notes PowerPoint: www.geocities.com/kirkmsscience/Cornell_Notes.ppt#1

Cornell Note-Taking Method Custom PDF Generator:
http://eleven21.com/notetaker

Free Online Graphpaper: Cornell Note-Taking Lined:
http://incompetech.com/graphpaper/cornelllined

Cornell Notes Info (for students):
www.greece.k12.ny.us/instruction/ela/6-12/tools/cornellintro.pdf

Notalon: http://sourceforge.net/projects/notalon
>   Downloadable application for taking Cornell Notes, in an actual document.

Template to implement Cornell Notes form into PowerPoint 2007:
http://office.microsoft.com/en-us/templates/TC300006991033.aspx

Research Resources

Animations for Earthquake Terms and Concepts:
http://earthquake.usgs.gov/learning/animations

Earthquakes 101 Slide Show (Living with Earthquakes in Southern California):
http://earthquake.usgs.gov/learning/eq101/EQ101.htm

Earthquakes—Forces of Nature:
http://library.thinkquest.org/C003603/english/earthquakes/index.shtml
>   This site is an excellent, comprehensive resource.

Volcanoes, Earthquakes, Hurricanes, Tornadoes—Forces of Nature:
www.nationalgeographic.com/forcesofnature/interactive
>   This site offers some great resources, such as an earthquake simulation, case studies, animated fault motion, fly over the San Andreas Fault, and measure an earthquake.

Wikipedia: Earthquakes: http://en.wikipedia.org/wiki/Earthquake

BBC World Service: Science: Animated Guide: Earthquakes:
www.bbc.co.uk/worldservice/science/2009/09/090930_earthquakes_guide.shtml

BBC News: Science and Environment: How Earthquakes Happen:
http://news.bbc.co.uk/2/hi/science/nature/4126809.stm

Causes of Earthquakes/Fault Types/Animated Motion:
www.dsuper.net/~innotech/quake/causes.htm

Listen for Fun: http://earthquake.usgs.gov/learning/listen/allsounds.php

Earthquake Topics: Field Trips—Virtual, Real:
www.earthquake.usgs.gov/learning/topics/?topicID=62

McMillan/McGraw Hill's California Science Grade 6 text chapter 5 "Resources on Plate Tectonics and Earth's Structure" (http://activities.macmillanmh.com/science/ca/grade6/g6_ch5.html), provides several resources. Lesson 3 of chapter 5 focuses on earthquakes.

This is a spectacular online text with the following activities: an animated lesson on plate movement that includes a built-in "Whaddaya Know? Quiz Show," vocabulary game (crossword puzzle), an E-Journal on Earthquake Safety (with research, pre-writing activities, and writing online), an E-Review (Animated Summary and Quiz), and an E-Glossary with sound for each chapter. Translations of "concept summaries" are also available.

In addition, there is a Teacher/Parent View (http://activities.macmillanmh.com/science/ca/te/) that includes a sample lesson presentation in PowerPoint in the Classroom Presentation Toolkit, Sample E-Journal, and Online Teacher's Edition for those who adopt the text.

Another excellent feature is "Operation: Science Quest," an interactive CD that accompanies the text. Each grade level has a quest with a challenge that includes pre-assessment, mini-lessons, activities and interactives, post-assessment, and bonus interactive videos. Closed-captioning, a glossary, and notebook, are built-in. Check out the Internet resource page for Grade 6: Job for a Day: Earth's Moving Plates (http://activities.macmillanmh.com/science/ca/te/osq/G6_EarthMovingPlates_ALPHA/Build/G6/EarthsMovingPlace/PT_Master.html). In this challenge, a character (student) teams up with a seismologist to learn about plate tectonics. This is an interactive exercise with a glossary and notebook.

> **Exploring Earth: Chapter 10: Earthquakes (McDougal Littell's ClassZone):**
> www.classzone.com/books/earth_science/terc/navigation/chapter10.cfm
>> This is another excellent site with "Visualizations" (animations), "Investigations," "Careers" and "Data Centers."
>
> **Savage Earth Animation: Earthquake!:**
> www.pbs.org/wnet/savageearth/animations/earthquakes
>
> **Savage Earth: The Restless Planet: Earthquakes: All Stressed Out:**
> www.pbs.org/wnet/savageearth/earthquakes

Seismology

Group students in threes by readiness to research background information about seismology with some of the directed sites below. Choose the sites you would like them to visit, or give them an option of visiting particular sites. If desired, you may give each triad a different topic, which would require presentation and sharing at the end. Sample subtopics include seismic waves, how a seismograph works, reading a seismogram, finding the epicenter, and measuring an earthquake with the Richter and Mercalli scales.

Seismology Resources

> **Model of First Seismograph:** www.mssu.edu/seg-vm/pict0688.html
>
> **How a Seismograph Works:** www.wwnorton.com/college/geo/egeo/flash/8_3.swf

Aspire's Seismic Waves (with Mighty Wave Maker):
http://aspire.cosmic-ray.org/labs/seismic/index.htm#question6

> Be sure to click on the link "Discover More About the Earth's Interior."

What Is Seismology and What Are Seismic Waves?:
www.geo.mtu.edu/UPSeis/waves.html

How Do I Read a Seismogram?: www.geo.mtu.edu/UPSeis/reading.html

How Do I Locate That Earthquake's Epicenter?:
www.geo.mtu.edu/UPSeis/locating.html

Animations: Types of Seismic Waves:
http://nuWeb.neu.edu/bmaheswaran/phyu121/data/ch14/anim/anim1403.htm

UWM Virtual Seismograph Tour:
www.uwm.edu/Dept/Geosciences/recent_eq/station_info/virtual_tour.html

How Stuff Works: How Does a Seismograph Work? What is the Richter Scale?:
www.howstuffworks.com/question142.htm

IRIS Posters: www.iris.edu/hq/publications/posters

> At this site, you may request hard copies for your classroom.

Jet Propulsion Laboratory's Flash Movie:
www.jpl.nasa.gov/multimedia/earthquake1906

> This site provides an introduction to earthquake and tracking and data collection.

Rapid Earthquake Viewer: http://rev.seis.sc.edu
Instructions: www.iris.edu/edu/onepagers/REV_Insert.pdf

> This site allows you to view seismograms from every earthquake.

Exploratorium Faultline: Seismic Science at the Epicenter: Live Eye on the Earth:
www.exploratorium.edu/faultline/liveeye.html

> This site offers seismology tools and applications.

Ask students to take notes on paper or to use one of the following online note takers. Give them directives as to what you would like them to research. Students discuss findings with one another or with the class.

Online Note-Taking Resources

Penzu: www.penzu.com

Zoho Planner: www.zohoplanner.com/login

Google Docs and Google Notebook:
docs.google.com/, and notebook.google.com

NoteStar: http://notestar.4teachers.org

Read Write Think Notetaker:
http://interactives.mped.org/view_interactive.aspx?id=127&title=

Finally, students complete an activity in which they read and analyze eight seismograms.

Can You Read a Quake?:
http://cse.ssl.berkeley.edu/lessons/indiv/davis/inprogress/reading.html

Prediction/Prevention

As a means to investigate and solve problems about prediction and prevention of earthquakes, select one of the following websites with built-in resources. Several WebQuests with descriptions have been provided so that you may pick one or more, depending on whether you wish to differentiate by readiness, interest, process, product, and so on. In effect, we submit to you some "tiered" WebQuest options.

WebQuest: Exploring Earthquakes (http://express.howstuffworks.com/wq-earthquake. htm) resembles an Internet scavenger hunt. There are 12 questions, and students are directed to one or two specified websites for each question. Questions deal with probability, prediction, history, plate tectonics, and so forth.

In threes, students endeavor to prevent the next earthquake by journeying to its center with Journey to the Center of an Earthquake (www.oswego.edu/Acad_Dept/s_of_educ/ cigrad/WebQuest/earthquake_files/frame.htm). Students answer given questions and communicate their solutions via a collaborative PowerPoint presentation. This is described as a "short-term mission." There are only a handful of questions that students investigate.

With Rockin' Your World (http://zunal.com/webquest.php?user=3408), students work individually to conduct research and create a brochure that details the dangers and impact of a massive earthquake in our country. They need to describe what an earthquake is and why it occurs, investigate past and recent earthquakes in several states, explore how to prepare for an earthquake, and identify potential hazards following an earthquake.

What If New York Had an Earthquake? (www2.maxwell.syr.edu/plegal/tips/t2prod/ joneswq.html) prods students to imagine that seismic activity has been reported in New York, and they must conduct research to compile an informational brochure for citizens on preparedness. Students seek information and fulfill job roles in groups of four. This could be adapted for those outside of New York, but resources pertaining to New York would have to be changed.

In Earthquake Preparedness WebQuest (www.rockwood.k12.mo.us/selvidge/moser/EarthquakeWebquest/intro.html), students play roles in a three-person task force (Seismic Risk Specialist, Public Information Specialist, and Safety Preparedness Specialist) to address the lack of preparedness for earthquakes in the St. Louis area. Students create an earthquake risk report that includes a narrative, poster, and informational brochure.

With Earthquakes in Illinois (http://mtzion.il.schoolWebpages.com/education/components/links/links.php?sectiondetailid=86804&sc_id=1138635250), students work in pairs (each with a set role) to prepare informational articles about the threat of earthquakes in Illinois in order to increase public awareness and prevent future loss. They also determine the epicenter and the magnitude of an earthquake via Electronic Desktop—Virtual Earthquake (http://nemo.sciencecourseware.org/VirtualEarthquake/).

Using Shake, Rattle, and Earthquake Proof (http://questgarden.com/46/04/2/070129191949/), students collaborate in triads and perform specific roles to design buildings that can withstand earthquakes in Hawaii. Students create their own products according to their job descriptions, but all present the artifacts and results together as a group. This could easily be adapted for any geographic area and is designed to take (portions of) six class periods.

Earthquake (http://volWeb.utk.edu/Schools/bedford/harrisms/stuearth.htm) is a lengthier WebQuest that requires the generation of several products, including clay models to study folds and faults of rock layers. The main task is based on geographical standards (social studies). Students help a friend's father collect information on earthquake prediction for the president. This WebQuest lasts eight to ten days.

History/Famous Earthquakes

Students learn from an eyewitness's perspective by studying documents and sound recordings related to past quakes. In response, students create an illustration in Microsoft Paint of how they envision a portion of this person's earthquake experience or create a rap or poem about his experience. Print, record, or perform the finished product.

Exploratorium's podcasts, videos, and songs:
www.exploratorium.edu/faultline/activezone/media.html

This site contains information about older earthquakes.

Sound Records: http://Webshaker.ucsd.edu/soundRecords.html

Recordings of commentators and sounds from specific places as earthquakes struck are on this site.

Virtual Museum of the City of San Francisco: 1906 Great Earthquake and Fire:
www.sfmuseum.org/1906/06.html

This site features eyewitness accounts, police reports, photos, and timeline.

A Virtual Tour of the 1906 Earthquake in Google Earth:
http://earthquake.usgs.gov/regional/nca/virtualtour

Using Graph Master (www.tomsnyder.com/products/product.asp?SKU=GRAMAS/)
or Create a Graph (http://nces.ed.gov/nceskids/createagraph), students choose five to
seven countries or states and graph selected information about them, such as number of
volcanoes per state/country within a certain time period, or the top five to seven largest
volcanoes occurring within chosen locations in a certain time period, and so on. Print the
finished product. They may use the following directed sites for research:

USGS's Today in Earthquake History: http://earthquake.usgs.gov/learning/today

USGS's Earthquake Lists and Maps:
http://earthquake.usgs.gov/eqcenter/eqarchives

>   This site has lists on deadly earthquakes, largest earthquakes, significant
>   earthquakes, sorted by state, by country, and lots of statistics.

Latest Earthquakes in the World:
http://earthquake.usgs.gov/eqcenter/recenteqsww

If desired, extend this activity by comparing and contrasting results from different states
and countries, which would require that you limit the students' choices in advance. For
example, you would not want to allow 10 out of 25 students in your class to choose the
same states.

Whyville

Whyville is a social networking site for students ages 8–15, akin to Teen Second Life.
It was designed to increase interest in the sciences by offering engaging games and
hands-on learning activities. Students have the unique opportunity of learning via
conversing live with other students and working collaboratively by helping one another
complete activities in groups or by giving advice. In addition, they may post and read
messages and articles in *The Whyville Times.* All players are represented as animated
images. They attempt to acquire "clams" by earning a salary, playing educational games,
and starting a business.

In this unit, you could allow your students to participate in Whyville in various ways:
Write an article or message about a specific subtopic they've studied in this unit and post
to *The Whyville Times.*

Whyville Times' sample article on tsunamis:
http://h.whyville.net/smmk/whytimes/article?id=4848)

Investigate career possibilities in earth science and/or search for activities related to
subtopics you've studied. Ask for advice about facts to include in their culminating
project. Visit an area of the world that's been struck by an earthquake via the Warp

Wagon. See if any of the streamed events or virtual discussions that take place in the Greek Theater pertain to earthquakes and participate in one.

Whyville Times' sample posting about upcoming discussions:
http://h.whyville.net/smmk/whytimes/article?id=5087)

Culminating Project/Assessment

I-Search/Poster Format: Using the I-Search method, investigate a past earthquake for the International Earthquake Hall of Fame. Find out where, when, and how it happened. Give details about its size and duration. If possible, include authentic photos from the event and a map of where it took place. Describe the damage it caused and how it impacted the people near it. Use the Web Poster Wizard (http://poster.4teachers.org) to generate posters. Students may have to create two posters to accommodate necessary information.

R.A.F.T.T. Format: Various products accomodating assorted readiness levels and learning profiles appear in the chart below.

Role	Audience	Format	Topic	Technology
Governor of California	President	Letter	Earthquake aid for disaster area in state	Word processing or page layout (Word, Publisher, etc.)
Scientist/ Geologist	Other scientists and interested listeners	Radio interview/ podcast	Area most threatened by earthquakes in the 21st century	Audacity, GarageBand, or other podcasting software
Witness	Students and teachers	Monologue in costume	Narrate experience of living through earthquake	Presentation slide show in background with audio

Just for Fun/Possible Anchor Activities

If you wish to reward your students with some educational game time, here are a number of sites to check out. You could also use the following activities as anchors in your classroom.

Earthquake Terms Word Search Game:
www.abag.ca.gov/bayarea/eqmaps/doc/wordsearch/wordsearch.html

Rags to Riches (Millionaire) Game: Earthquakes: www.quia.com/rr/283672.html

Vocabulary Terms Games Earthquakes: www.quia.com/jg/460020.html

U.S. Top Ten States for Earthquakes: www.quia.com/rd/103394.html

U.S. Top Ten Earthquakes: www.quia.com/rd/8281.html

U.S. Top Ten (Largest) Earthquakes:
www.quia.com/pp/9404.html?AP_rand=47707210

Hidden Picture version: www.quia.com/pp/9404.html

Top Ten Earthquakes of the 20th Century:
www.quia.com/rd/20619.html?AP_rand=1078461854

Hidden Picture version: www.quia.com/pp/22007.html

Top Ten Deadliest (World) Earthquakes (sequential order):
www.quia.com/rd/20609.html

Hidden Picture version: www.quia.com/pp/21996.html

Outstanding Links and Resources to Use with Major Science Content Areas

As is the case with the other core content areas, state and national benchmarks require that we cover a vast amount of information in multiple strands in our science classrooms. A differentiated unit like the one on earthquakes could be done for any major topic area in any strand. You could use some of the suggestions we detailed, but you would have to modify your links and resources to accommodate the topic of choice. The Internet offers thousands of science resources for every strand, but listing even one hundred of them is beyond the scope of this book. To assist you in your effort to differentiate instruction with technology in other science strands (life science, physical science, the scientific method, Earth and space science, science in personal and social perspectives), we have included a list of online resources such as software, graphic images, video clips, interactive activities, and information. Using information garnered from these research topics as a basis, students can construct multiple products to share and demonstrate their learning. By "products" we mean posters, comparative timelines and charts, presentations, mini-booklets and Webbes, spreadsheets, wiki postings, and any other original works created by students.

In some cases, we've split out the major strands into their various subthemes, depending on the depth of the strand itself and the availability of resources on that strand. Sometimes we've combined the subthemes, when content overlaps. We believe that these tech-driven strategies will bring energy to you, your students, and your classroom.

Life Science

Heredity

The DNA Interactive site (www.dnai.org) offers a teacher's guide with 15 lessons and an extremely thorough series of modules that help students to "crack the DNA code," learn about DNA science, study the "book of life" (genome), discover the uses of DNA science, and consider past and future genetics research, theories, and shortcomings. Each module has several subsections, and within them students have opportunities to read articles, watch animations, and participate in simulations or games. Phenomenal!

At Kids Genetics @GlaxoSmithKline (www.genetics.gsk.com/kids/index_kids.htm), students may read narrative selections on DNA, genes, heredity, and disease and medicine response that are just right in length and style for middle school. Each selection is accompanied by an excellent interactive module with more information and a game.

Personalize your students' learning by asking them to create a digital story in Photo Story 3, iMovie '08, or PowerPoint that illustrates common traits in their families. To shorten or simplify the assignment for more challenged students, ask them to create one slide about this topic in PowerPoint. Another variation on this theme would be to ask each student to create one slide. Then compile them to produce a digital story or scrapbook about the interesting traits your students possess that they may pass on to their children.

Cells

CELLS *alive!* (www.cellsalive.com) presents amazing, interactive cell models and animations of processes cells undergo, such as mitosis, with text-based explanations and descriptions. There are other cool resources, such as image galleries, quizzes, bio cams, and helpful links. At The Virtual Cell webpage (www.ibiblio.org/virtualcell/), students may take a virtual cell tour with a pronunciation guide and tools to enlarge and rotate animations and also read a virtual text. The textbook's chapters are under construction, but the color and design of the animations is incredible.

Encourage your students to become experts in various types of cells via a flexible grouping task that relies on draw/paint software. Based on their interest, ask each group to create a series of labeled illustrations of a particular set of cells, such as muscle cells (striated, smooth, and cardiac) and then put them into book format to share.

Evolution, Adaptation, and Fossils

The University of California Museum of Paleontology K–12 Resources site (www.ucmp.berkeley.edu/education/) offers a wealth of resources to which we cannot devote enough time and space here! Something that we really appreciate about this site is that it usually provides teacher and student versions for online animations, guides, and so forth. "Getting into the Fossil Record," "Stories from the Fossil Record," "Understanding

Geologic Time," and "Life Has a History" are detailed modules that are must-sees. Other links that have loads of information are "Understanding Evolution" and "The Paleontology Portal." The Paleontology Portal provides details about the history of life through geologic time, and one of its neatest features is that it will present a list of virtual exhibits, research, and collections pertinent to the area of North America that you selected. The "Fossil Gallery" includes hundreds of images by time period or fossil type. The "Online Exhibits" link allows you to access other exhibits, one of which is a monthly "Mystery Fossil."

A Science Odyssey: You Try It: Human Evolution (www.pbs.org/wgbh/aso/tryit/evolution/) offers an activity that allows students to examine the relationships among human-like species and when they were discovered, along with other entries and articles related to human evolution.

Science Seekers (www.tomsnyder.com/products/product.asp?SKU=SSKHID) is a software series created by Tom Snyder Productions that includes three titles. The Changing Earth involves a quest for fossils, so students also learn about the Earth's structure and plate tectonics. Students work in teams to complete missions and analyze data. There is an on-screen video that students view together, along with a booklet for each student role.

Ask your students to create a newspaper about prehistoric times in your local, state, or regional area using these, and other, sites and publishing software, such as Microsoft Publisher Include some fun options for the newspaper, such as classified ads, obituaries, and the like, in addition to historical and scientific articles.

Populations and Ecosystems

Food Chains and Webs (www.vtaide.com/png/foodchains.htm) has information about the energy pyramid, roles animals and organisms play in the food chain, and the opportunity to create your own food web.

Blue Iceberg: Feature: Food Web 2.0 (www.blue-iceberg.com/featurefoodweb.html) is an interactive game about who's eating what in the ocean habitat.

Build-a-Prairie, presented by Bell Live! (www.bellmuseum.org/distancelearning/prairie/build/) asks students to construct a prairie from barren land by bringing in the correct mix of animals and growing the appropriate plants.

Science Seekers (www.tomsnyder.com/products/product.asp?SKU=SSKSSK) is a software series (described previously) created by Tom Snyder Productions that includes three titles. Ecosystems in Balance involves the study of the kelp forest ecosystem.

If you have access to the resources, try a clay animation project with your students to fortify their knowledge about food webs. In flexible groups, they could create a movie that depicts the workings of a food web of their choice. You could also divide the students into groups according to learning profile with tasks based on multiple intelligences. Bodily-kinesthetic students could craft the figures, musical students could produce a theme song or background music, verbal-linguistic students could take charge of the voiceovers/ narration, and so on. Here are some helpful links to get you started and some sample videos to view:

Ms. Daniels' Claymation with PowerPoint:
www-bioc.rice.edu/precollege/msdaniel/claymation.html

Clay Animation Made Easy:
http://education.wichita.edu/claymation/resources.html

Getting Started in Clay Animation: http://library.thinkquest.org/22316/start.html

Kim Flippin's Index of Clay Animation Files: www.earlyisd.net/~kflippin

If you do not have the resources to experiment with clay animation, your students could design a board game in a page layout or presentation program about the concepts they've learned. You could group them according to levels of readiness to fashion a product that would best reflect their abilities.

Either of the above activities would allow for wonderful connections with elementary students. Your students could have a movie viewing party in an elementary classroom or invite elementary students to their classroom. Your students could spend some time in an elementary classroom playing their board games with the elementary children, provided that they had designed them for younger children.

Physical Science

Matter

Interactive Practice on Chemical vs. Physical Properties (www.teacherbridge.org/public/ bhs/teachers/Dana/chemphys.html) offers a brief review of chemical and physical properties; it then presents different scenarios, and students have to choose whether a chemical or physical change has occurred.

Another short simulation on physical versus chemical changes can be found at the Class Zone (www.classzone.com/books/ml_sci_physical/page_build.cfm?id=resour_ ch2&u=1##).

Yet another interactive on Chemical and Physical Changes (http://virtual.yosemite.cc.ca. us/lmaki/Chem150-99/chapters/chapter1/lessons/phys_chem/phy_c_1.htm) is available with scenarios that students answer.

To ensure that your students have grasped the difference between chemical and physical properties and changes, how about asking them to create a flow chart that indicates the series of steps they would follow to identify a chemical vs. a physical change and property? They could use one of the tools below, Inspiration, or any of the mapping and webbing tools mentioned near the beginning of the differentiated unit in this chapter.

Read Write Think Webbing Tool:
http://interactives.mped.org/view_interactive.aspx?id=127&title=

Online Flowcharts at Vermilion Parrish:
www.vrml.k12.la.us/cc/gr_organ/flowchart/flowcharts.htm

Another possible means to reinforce comprehension of content would be to have students work in pairs to create a study guide in a word-processing document with hyperlinks. After students have completed the guides, collect and redistribute them so that each pair has another pair's guide to test out.

Energy, Motion, and Forces

The Physics Classroom Tutorial (www.glenbrook.k12.il.us/gbssci/phys/Class/newtlaws/u2l1a.html) has animation and four lessons.

GCSE Physics: Energy, Forces, and Motion: Forces (www.darvill.clara.net/enforcemot/forces.htm), along with the Energy Resources (www.darvill.clara.net/altenerg/), are animated sister sites created by Andy Darvill.

Forces Lesson: Physics Zone (www.sciencejoywagon.com/physicszone/02forces) provides several lessons with animation, movies, and interactive labs.

Take advantage of an excellent ThinkQuest called Fantastic Forces (http://library.think-quest.org/05aug/00769/index1.htm) with movie quizzes, a glossary, games, links, and teacher resources.

Take a look at PhET: Free online physics, chemistry, biology, earth science and math simulations from the University of Colorado at Boulder (http://phet.colorado.edu/index.php). You can run simulations online or download them, translate simulations, search for lesson plans by others that utilize simulations, and contribute ideas for use.

The Energy Kids' page (http://eia.doe.gov/kids/) includes a list of activities/experiments by grade, a timeline of energy history, biographies of famous scientists, and information on uses of energy, saving energy, science of energy, and sources of energy.

Get involved in a series of missions at Professor XYZ's lab at The Mission: A Great Scientific Adventure (www.onfjeunesse.ca/lamission/home_e.php). Some of the topics include waves, lightning, batteries, and simple machines; and there are games and quizzes, too.

Your student athletes will love this resource from San Francisco's Exploratorium called Sport Science (www.exploratorium.edu/sports/). Through video and audio clips, articles, and Q & A, students can investigate physics-based questions, such as "Why do curveballs curve?" and "What forces keep a bicycle from falling over?"

How about asking your students to design content for another link at the Sport Science site for a sport that is not covered? This presents a great opportunity to group students according to the sport that interests them.

To master some of the important terminology associated with energy, motion, and forces, students can create puzzles for each other using Discovery Education School's online puzzle generator (http://puzzlemaker.discoveryeducation.com).

Scientific Method

Click on the Scientific Method PowerPoint link at the bottom of this webpage for an overview of the process (www.chariho.k12.ri.us/faculty/kkvre/scimeth.htm).

Here's a teacher-created video on the scientific method (www.teachertube.com/view_video.php?viewkey=eac573fdaafa6dcedef6) as applied to a mud dauber problem in her home.

Check out the Scientific Method Lab interactive (http://sunshine.chpc.utah.edu/labs/scientific_method/sci_method_main.html).

We feel that it's important for our students to read different types of material about the content area they're currently studying, particularly because one of our goals is to help them become self-sufficient learners who are prepared for the future marketplace. They need to learn how to understand and evaluate all kinds of reading material. Why not have them read all or specific portions of "How the Scientific Method Works" (http://science. howstuffworks.com/scientific-method.htm) individually or in pairs? Perhaps you might select one or more of the sections titled "History of the Scientific Method," "Cell Theory," and "Pasteur's Experiment." Within those three sections, names of several scientists are mentioned with brief information about their scientific contributions. Ask students/pairs to scan the web to find three additional significant facts about their scientist of choice and to post that information to your class blog. Or have them use the information to prepare a brief entry for a biographical dictionary that the class compiles using word-processing or desktop publishing software.

Earth and Space Science

Structure of the Earth

Rader's Geography4Kids at www.geography4kids.com is very helpful, particularly when studying the four spheres, as well as other elements of the Earth's structure.

Take the time to use this resource with terrific imagery: JST Virtual Science Center Earth Guide (http://jvsc.jst.go.jp/earth/guide/english/). It addresses a variety of issues and basics about our planet using a question map as a guide. The "moving diagrams" are fantastic!

This site asks, "What is it like where you live?" Examine all sorts of biomes and animals who live there at MBGNet (www.mbgnet.net).

If your students need to examine properties of minerals, find images, and other resources, go to the World Minerals Exchange webpage (www.mineralszone.com).

Have a little fun with the Identify Rocks Game—Geology for Kids (www.kidsgeo.com/geology-games/rocks-game.php).

View and participate in this splendid animation: Interactives: The Rock Cycle (www.learner.org/interactives/rockcycle/about.html).

Science Seekers: The Changing Earth software mentioned previously would tie in well with a study of the Earth's structure.

How about a wiki to get students involved in tracking and describing rocks and minerals native to their own area or state? If rocks and minerals don't seem to appeal to them, they could do the same with animals. If you and your students are interested in a more global collaborative project, why not experiment with e-pals, Skype, or an online project that allows them to give and receive information about rocks or animals that are unique to each area?

Earth in the Solar System

Three spectacular tools for visualizing the heavens are the WorldWide Telescope (www.worldwidetelescope.org), Stellarium (www.stellarium.org), and Google Sky (www.google.com/sky/). With the WorldWide Telescope, your computer becomes a virtual telescope using a Web 2.0 visualization software environment. Stellarium is a free, open source planetarium for your computer that shows the sky realistically in 3-D. Stellarium also offers a user's wiki. Google Sky allows you to locate the position of the planets and constellations, as well as to view the universe at different wavelengths.

Rader's Cosmos for Kids (www.cosmos4kids.com) supplies slide shows, quizzes, and real world examples, just like the other 4kids.com science sites.

Try experimenting with one of the magnificent tools listed above, such as the WorldWide Telescope. The WorldWide Telescope has an unbelievable "tours" feature that allows you to take a guided tour (created by educators and astronomers) or to create one yourself. The tours are interactive so that you can pause along the way for exploration or information. They allow for background music, voice-overs, and the addition of text, objects, and pictures. Select one or two guided tours first so your students can get a feel for what it's like. Then give them the opportunity to create their own tour, work with a partner to create one together, or design a round-robin tour, as the WorldWide Telescope permits you to add to one another's tours.

Earth's History

Be sure to investigate the large collection of science videos from the Visual Learning Company (www.visuallearningco.com). One of their many DVD sets is called Geologic History. A license to stream, duplicate, or broadcast videos can be purchased, and the company also offers videos in high quality, digital H.264 format for use with iTunes and iPods. DVD features include indexes, labeled slides, glossary, animations, English subtitles, and an iMovie project. In addition, all videos come with a teacher guide with student activities and assessment tools, plus a video quiz. Also see the resources on fossils, evolution, geologic time noted in the Evolution, Adaptation, and Fossils section in this chapter.

FIGURE **6.1**   ■   Fossil image from Visual Learning Company video.   © Visual Learning Company. Used with permission.

Science in Personal and Social Perspectives

Personal Health

Depending on the grade level you teach and the maturity level of your students, see the TeensHealth homepage (http://kidshealth.org/teen/) or the KidsHealth homepage (http://kidshealth.org/kids/) on diseases, feelings, alcohol, drugs, and other topics.

If you are looking for some great health resources, examine the NIH Office of Science Education Educational Resources for middle school (http://science.education.nih.gov/home2.nsf/Educational+Resources/Grade+Levels/+Middle+School). You can download the plans or use a web version of them. Each set of plans includes super videos, flash simulations, and interactive, web-based activities.

Human Anatomy Online (www.innerbody.com) offers tutorials, text-based descriptions, and visual animations of the body.

The Franklin Institute is an exceptional site. If you're searching for resources on the heart, make sure to visit The Human Heart: An Online Exploration (www.fi.edu/learn/heart/) for some excellent activities, a glossary, and cool images.

Access Excellence at the National Health Museum (http://accessexcellence.org) has some engaging resources, such as mysteries to solve, collaborative spots for teachers for sharing ideas, a visual library, a just-for-students area, links to teacher websites, virtual labs, virtual dissections, simulations, and student links.

Rader's Chemistry for Kids (www.chem4kids.com) has a lot of useful chemistry resources, but explore the Biochemistry section in particular for bonus health information.

Your Gross and Cool Body (http://yucky.discovery.com/noflash/body/) screams middle school! At this site, students learn what causes dandruff, belches and gas, ear wax, and loads of other "gross" things that the body produces.

Enjoy these great sites and make them a part of some tech-driven tasks, such as a podcast or series of digital stories (interview-based) about students' feelings on, for example, bullying and/or peer pressure (and how to deal effectively with those issues). Students might appreciate the chance to come up with a new addition to the Your Gross and Cool Body site. Have students work individually or in pairs to determine what their addition would be to the site and create a descriptive poster or slide for display purposes. Decide on the most promising candidate via a class vote.

Natural Hazards and Populations, Risks and Environments

To assist you and your students in the area of "Science in Personal and Social Perspectives," we suggest a number of totally digital-age tools that will captivate your students. Experiment with these games, simulators, and virtual missions.

Smog City (www.smogcity.com) is an interactive air pollution simulator that shows how individual choices, environmental factors, and land use contribute to air pollution. Students' decisions increase or decrease ground-level ozone.

Windward (www.ciconline.org/windward/) is a game from Cable in the Classroom. The creators describe its mission as "outsmart the weather in a race around the world."

The River City Project (http://muve.gse.harvard.edu/rivercityproject/) is a team-based investigation in which students travel back in time to help the residents of River City understand why people are becoming ill. This excellent resource includes formative and summative assessments, videos, lab notebooks with scaffolding, and testing of hypotheses and collection of data online.

PowerUp the Game (www.powerupthegame.org) is a multiplayer game in 3-D. Students work collaboratively to save the planet, which is under destruction from a polluted atmosphere. The planet is also suffering from a loss of renewable energy. Students publish presentations at www.tryscience.com.

The JASON Project (www.jasonproject.org) is a "veteran" among the sites we've recommended, as it's been around for some time. As we pen this manuscript, two exciting missions are available to join: Operation: Resilient Planet "puts students on a mission to investigate the health of our environment and discover how to protect our planet's ecosystems," and Operation: Monster Storms "transports classrooms to the center of Earth's most extreme weather events. Fly into the eye of a hurricane or chase tornados through Tornado Alley."

Science Seekers (www.tomsnyder.com/products/product.asp?SKU=SSKSAF) is a software series (described previously) created by Tom Snyder Productions that includes three titles. Safe Groundwater requires that students pinpoint who is polluting the groundwater in the town of Fairview.

History of Science/Famous Scientists

To research or learn about famous scientists or the history of science, take advantage of these sites:

> **Famous Scientists:**
> www.clovisusd.k12.ca.us/learn/subjectlinks/science/famous.htm
>
> **Biographies:** www.sldirectory.com/studf/bio.html#science
>
> **The Case Files Online Exhibit:** www.fi.edu/learn/case-files

The Science Odyssey (www.pbs.org/wgbh/aso) is exceptional, with some of the following intriguing features: Then + Now (what we knew in 1900 vs. today); That's My Theory (game show about scientists who made history in the 20th century); On the Edge (comic book stories that describe scientists at the time of their discoveries); You Try It (interactives); and People and Discoveries (bank of biographies, events, and discoveries).

To continue to spark students' interest and deepen their knowledge in this area, try one of these exciting activities. Assign or permit groups of students to choose a handful of scientists about whom they generate trading cards. You might categorize scientists based on their nationalities, the time periods in which they lived and worked, the type of invention or theory they originated, and so forth. Students can access one of the useful sites below to generate the cards, print them, and discuss the scientists in small groups.

> **Character Trading Cards at Read Write Think:**
> http://readwritethink.org/materials/trading_cards
>
> **Trading Cards: Flickr:** http://bighugelabs.com/flickr/deck.php

If trading cards don't appeal to your students, survey them to find out which scientist they think is worthy of mention on a particular site or two above but does not currently appear. Initiate a campaign process for one or several scientists, depending on the procedure you decide to follow. Students could settle on one scientist, and you could assign each group a particular product-driven task associated with the campaign process: radio broadcast, newspaper ad, campaign speech, and so on. Another option would be to ask each group to prepare campaign materials for one of the scientists who was mentioned in the initial survey.

PBS Teachers: Science and Tech (www.pbs.org/teachers/sciencetech/) has oodles of resources just waiting for you that you can search for according to grade level.

The Franklin Institute (www.fi.edu/learn/sci-tech/) has a useful collection of artifacts at the History of Science and Technology (with blog discussion).

Superb Science Sites for Any and All Science Needs

Don't forget to pay a visit to one or more of the following sites to profit from outstanding lesson plans, applications, and resources, such as simulations, interactives, and general content information.

BrainPOP (www.brainpop.com/science/) is a remarkable site with animated movies that explain concepts in ways that are engaging and easy to understand. No matter what unit or subject you are teaching, check out BrainPOP.

Browse the collection of Gizmos at ExploreLearning (www.explorelearning.com/index. cfm?method=cResource.dspChildrenForCourse&CourseID=338&submit=Go) before you start a new topic or unit. Your students will thoroughly enjoy these virtual animations, simulations, and manipulatives.

BBC's KS3 Bitesize Science (www.bbc.co.uk/schools/teachers/keystage_3/topics/science. shtml) and Bitesize Teachers (www.bbc.co.uk/schools/teachers/) are phenomenal sites. Excellent resources include listening or downloading audio bites, e-mailable quizzes, a glossary of terms, animations for viewing, preparations of a "revision" (review) checklist, and hotlinks.

Discovery Education Science for Middle School (www.discoveryeducation.com/products/ science/middle.cfm) is a fantastic new suite of products including integrated science simulations, interactive video, virtual labs, and explorations. Make sure to investigate the K–12 sister site on Discovery Education Health (www.discoveryeducation.com/products/ health/).

TryScience (www.tryscience.org) provides field trips, live cams, adventures, Citizens for Planet Earth, experiments, and Find a Science Center.

How Stuff Works Express (http://express.howstuffworks.com) is the classic site for students that teaches them about careers, gives "autopsies" of how gadgets work, and features WebQuests, AskMarshallBrain, and puzzles.

The USGS and Science Education site (http://education.usgs.gov) is a treasure trove full of marvelous resources too numerous to mention. You'll find lesson plans, maps, images, data, and tons of other great tools for the study of natural resources, natural hazards, geospatial data, and issues that affect our quality of life.

NSDL Middle School Portal Science Pathway (http://msteacher.org/science.aspx) is a searchable site that will collect a wealth of resources for you.

Biozone (www.biozone.co.nz/links.html) is a thorough database of biology links. Choose a topic according to the image in the table, and the site will supply websites, newsfeeds, and search facilities on the subject of choice.

TeachersFirst's (www.teachersfirst.com) claim to fame is that it is created "for teachers, by teachers," and it provides super lesson plans, units, and web resources by the hundreds.

Take a glance at Extreme Science (www.extremescience.com) for heaps of information on earth and space science, animal kingdom, technology, and weather, along with a blog, science dictionary, science calculators, maps, news feeds, gallery of scientists, and on and on!

The purpose of The Whyfiles: Science Behind the News (http://whyfiles.org) is to explore connections in math, science, and technology in current news stories. This site has neat images, virtual animations, teacher activity pages, and a new story each week.

The Exploratorium: The Museum of Science, Art, and Human Perception (www.exploratorium.edu) has been in existence since 1993. It is an actual museum in San Francisco that offers online exhibits, podcasts, webcasts, hands-on activities, a digital library, a gateway to rich web resources, and many other tools worth exploring.

Drop by The Science Channel (http://science.discovery.com) for news, interactives, videos, games, puzzles, and access to companion networks, such as the Discovery Channel and Animal Planet.

VITAL, Virtual Immersive Technologies and Arts for Learning (http://vital.cs.ohiou.edu/secondlife.html), provides virtual science games using Second Life. See in particular "Nutrition Game," "Rafting Adventures," and "Interactive Science Lab."

SciberMonkey (www.scibermonkey.org/sitemap.htm) is a timesaver! It collects a handful of useful resources for each science topic and links you to them with one click, as opposed to a portal with lists and lists of resources. There are student pages and teacher versions of the same pages.

Summary

As you can see, science education is replete with software and web resources. There are many opportunities for students to craft artifacts using technology tools. Take advantage of the plethora of unique tools to engage developing young minds in your classroom! Technology adds the aspect of hands-on and exploratory learning that many young scientists crave. By bringing the science world into the classroom and making it exciting and alive, technology engages students' imaginations, and even those who thought they were not interested become fascinated by the structure and behavior of the world.

CHAPTER 7

Using Technology to Differentiate Social Studies

Today's social studies teachers and students are incredibly fortunate. More resources than ever are available through technology, making history and current events alive and interactive. Technologies help students conduct research, discuss issues, and create products as they discover how the past creates the present and learn about economics, geography, and civics.

We'd like to remind you that it's a good idea to begin the year by gauging your students' reading abilities. Reading is such an integral part of social studies that you will want to know right off which students struggle, which are at grade level, and which excel.

Many social studies textbooks are written at a fairly high reading level, so reading guides, pre-teaching of vocabulary, and other scaffolding strategies may be needed. Newer textbooks offer approaches for differentiating instruction for English-language learners and struggling learners. Graphic organizers, multimedia, glossaries, and technology tools can help students visualize and understand concepts and details.

This chapter is divided into three sections. The first section explores ideas for differentiating social studies, the second section provides an example lesson and resources for differentiating U.S. history, and the third section offers ideas for differentiating Western and Eastern Hemisphere studies.

Ideas for Differentiating Social Studies

For a differentiated social studies classroom to work well, it must be student-centered. The teacher manages time, space, resources, and activities and coaches learners in their tasks and projects. Students direct much of their own learning and are responsible for their own learning. This viewpoint is not always practiced in middle school classrooms, but in our own experience it works. In fact, research supports the use of student cooperative groups.

Cooperative efforts among students result in a higher degree of accomplishment by all participants. Cooperation, compared with competitive and individualistic efforts, typically results in (a) higher achievement and greater productivity; (b) more caring, supportive, and committed relationships; and (c) greater psychological health, social competence, and self-esteem. The positive effects that cooperation has on so many important outcomes make cooperative learning one of the most valuable tools educators have. (ERIC, 1985, summarizing findings from Slavin, 1983; Sharan, 1980; and Johnson, Mariyama, Johnson, Nelson & Skon, 1981)

The Big Picture

Along with student-centeredness in classrooms, we feel strongly about the method of teaching social studies. In our visits to middle school classrooms and in talking with middle school social studies teachers, we acknowledge that in many classrooms, the textbook and the teacher are the paramount sources for knowledge and not to be questioned. We don't subscribe to this practice. In fact, we believe that students benefit greatly from questioning sources as they move toward making sense of the past and how it connects with the present.

We prefer a holistic approach to teaching social studies: students wear many hats (some at the same time) as they learn to think like geographers, citizens, economists, historians, and cultural anthropologists. In a student-centered, holistic classroom, students learn to investigate and analyze primary and secondary sources, to look at cause and effect, to apply past to present, to query, and to debate. In short, these tasks engage students more effectively than memorizing facts that are disconnected and meaningless to them and give them lifelong skills.

When students repeatedly ask why they have to learn about Shays' Rebellion or John Brown's raid on Harpers Ferry or any of the myriad of topics taught in social studies classrooms, something is not working well in the classroom. We wonder how teachers respond to these questions.

We also know that students can get very excited about social studies. Take a look at what students have created using social studies topics as a basis for learning.

Civil War and Reconstruction Projects:
www.east-buc.k12.ia.us/00_01/CW/cw_intro.htm

Dragoenix: Imperial China ThinkQuest: http://library.thinkquest.org/C0122767

Global Tales ThinkQuest: http://library.thinkquest.org/06aug/01340/

Punjab Culture ThinkQuest: http://library.thinkquest.org/06aug/02374/

The Real Enslavement ThinkQuest: http://library.thinkquest.org/06aug/01071/

Time for Tolerance ThinkQuest:
http://library.thinkquest.org/07aug/00117/index1.html

Your authors are not alone in their thinking. Check out Bruce VanSledright's interesting article, "Can Ten-Year-Olds Learn to Investigate History as Historians Do?" (www.oah.org/pubs/nl/2000aug/vansledright.html) along with his list of resources. Mr. VanSledright's research "test" substantiates the belief that (his) upper elementary students are able to practice the craft of historical thinking effectively. How would your students do in such a test?

The book *Thinking Like A Historian: Rethinking History Instruction* by Bobbie Malone and Nikki Mandell is a terrific framework that will help you rethink teaching and learning. It's available from the Wisconsin Historical Society as a free download (www.wisconsin-history.org/ThinkingLikeaHistorian/), and you can also watch a 30-minute DVD online. The book's cover says it all (www.wisconsinhistory.org/ThinkingLikeaHistorian/images/cover-tlh.gif), as the authors have created a meaningful grid that will help you and your students understand historical thinking.

Arthur Costa and Bena Kallick's book *Activating & Engaging Habits of Mind* is another resource to consider. They write about using questions to challenge students' intellect and using thinking maps as visual tools to construct knowledge.

Two more worth-reading resources are *A Link to the Past: Engaging Students in the Study of History* by Michael M. Yell and Geoffrey Scheurman with Keith Reynolds and *21st Century Skills Maps* (www.21stcenturyskills.org/index.php?option=com_content&task=view&id=82&Itemid=185).

Key Strategies

In our teaching experiences, we have found that the following ten instructional strategies work very well with middle school social studies students. We talked about Robert Marzano's research in Chapter 1; correlations with his research are noted for each strategy. Please revisit Table 1.4 for applications and tech tools for consideration.

Collaborative/Flexible Groups. Structure activities and projects by student interest, learning style, or readiness. (Marzano #6: Cooperative/collaborative groups)

Compare/Contrast. Compare and contrast historical events with current events to bring relevancy to students. (Marzano #1: Recognizing similarities and differences)

Key Concepts/Main Ideas. Teach and summarize the main ideas of each topic or period and show students how to take notes. (Marzano #2: Summarizing information and taking notes)

Multimedia. Include as much multimedia (videos, software, images, cartoons, digital presentations, websites, and so on) as possible to engage learners and make social studies come alive. (Marzano #5: Nonlinguistic representations)

Praise and Recognition. Provide private and public praise of efforts and achievements. (Marzano #3: Reinforcing effort and providing recognition)

Product and Assessment Options. Give students choices via a tic-tac-toe board or menu. Use learning contracts and set ground rules and objectives. (Marzano #7: Setting objectives and providing feedback)

Provide Meaningful Assignments to Spark Thinking. Use content-related software, websites, and meaningful homework assignments. (Marzano #4: Homework and practice)

Sequence. Cover text sequentially to keep to the timeline of history and its events. (Marzano #9: Questions, cues, and advance organizers)

Think Like a Historian Investigations. Structure research as historical investigations of the past and how the past ties in with the present. (Marzano #8: Generating and testing hypotheses)

Timelines and Graphic Organizers. Have students use timelines and graphic organizers to help visualize and categorize information and understand cause and effect. (Marzano #5: Nonlinguistic representations)

Differentiating by Interest

Differentiating by interest means constructing activities that allow students to explore their own interests and develop new ones. When tasks promote curiosity, learning becomes more engaging to all students, even those who struggle most or are the most disinclined to learn. Giving students choices is at the heart of a differentiated classroom, so we describe seven tried-and-true instructional strategies to help you differentiate your social studies content by interest. Technology is used in all of the strategies.

I-Search. This strategy is student-driven, investigative research for a topic based on students' interest. Students individually or in groups use the web, electronic research tools, and other resources to investigate a topic of interest. Then they use technology as a tool to create a demonstration of their learning.

Jigsaw Group. Jigsaw is a collaborative technique where students are divided into home groups and expert groups. Each student is a member of one home group and one expert group, and no group has the same students in it. The teacher divides a topic into as many segments as there are members in each home group and assigns students to each home group. In their home groups, students select the topic they would like to investigate.

The teacher next separates the home groups of students into new temporary expert groups—the Jigsaw groups—in which they join other students assigned to the same segment to research. In their expert groups, students use resources and study about their particular segment. Members prepare a presentation to take back to their home groups. Temporary expert group members return to their home groups and teach the home group members what they learned. The home groups can then prepare a sequenced presentation that they deliver to the entire class.

R.A.F.T.T. R.A.F.T.T. stands for Role, Audience, Format, Topic, and Technology. The R.A.F.T. (without the technology component) coined by Nancy Vandervanter, a middle school English teacher who designed the strategy in the early 1980s (see pg. 129 here: www.eric.ed.gov/ERICDocs/data/ericdocs2sql/content_storage_01/0000019b/80/15/c6/bd.pdf) was originally designed to combine reading and writing in unconventional ways. Your authors coined the term R.A.F.T.T. in 2007.

Using the R.A.F.T.T. method, the teacher determines which content students are to learn and identifies the specifics of the five components. Students confer with the teacher about which role they are interested in assuming. Students individually or in pairs use library resources, web tools, and other resources to conduct research. Students individually or in pairs use technology to produce their final product (Smith & Throne, 2007).

WebQuests. WebQuests are team activities using the Internet to help students tackle multifaceted or open-ended questions. Tasks are research- or interest-based or both and require problem-solving skills, such as evaluation, analysis, and synthesis of resources. Working in a cooperative team, students use web tools to investigate a teacher-framed topic of interest. Then they use technology to create products that demonstrate their learning.

Digital Stories. Digital stories such as retold history, tales, diaries, fiction, and nonfiction can be formatted using technology. Tools include Webbes, Photo Story 3, iMovie, PowerPoint, and similar products. Games can be created by individuals or teams of students in the format of Jeopardy, board games, online tools, and interactive explorations using the action buttons in PowerPoint.

Choice Boards. Choice boards, tic-tac-toe boards, or menus are devices to give students assignment choices. These devices can be designed around students' interests, learning profiles, readiness, or a combination of elements.

Sequence of Teaching Steps

In teaching any history unit or lesson, social studies teachers by and large follow a sequence of steps.

Pre-Reading Activities. Students predict what the topic is about, based on the headings, subheadings, and graphics. The teacher introduces the unit or lesson in a way that makes students want to learn.

During-Reading Activities. The teacher uses during-reading activities to build understanding and provide food for discussion. Multimedia and website integration help to differentiate the text and appeal to a variety of learning styles. Students typically identify main ideas and details and make connections with geography, civics, economics, the arts, and literature. Students research the topic at hand and may compare it to the present. Students use glossaries and dictionaries to understand new terms.

After-Reading Activities. Students demonstrate evidence of understanding via products and assessments.

Essential Software: Timeliner Generators

Hands down, our favorite new software is Timeliner XE from Tom Snyder Productions. You may be already using Timeliner 5.0 or an earlier version, but this version is one of the best educational software products we have seen in many years. What makes it so terrific is that Timeliner XE is an all-in-one tool that helps students organize data into timelines or sequences, conduct online research, and create multimedia presentations all within Timeliner XE.

The program also contains ready-made projects, intuitive formatting tools, and a library of more than 1,000 media files and articles along with more than 300 customizable activities in language arts, math, science, and social studies.

"Students today are often overwhelmed with information and need tools to help them make sense of it all," said Rick Abrams, General Manager of Tom Snyder Productions. "Timeliner XE helps them to critically evaluate, synthesize and eventually communicate that information, and in the process transform it into knowledge."

Students can easily convert their sequences into multimedia slide show presentations without having to leave the program. Students can use included pre-made templates or create their own, as well as save their Timeliner XE projects in PDF format.

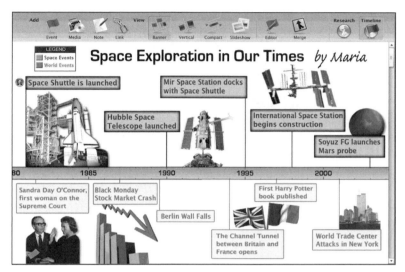

FIGURE **7.1** ■ A sample timeline created in Timeliner XE.
© Tom Snyder Productions, Inc. Reprinted with permission.

Because understanding timelines and creating timelines are key social studies skills, we think you will be impressed by Timeliner XE and want to use it with your students.

You can also use online time generators at:

Read Write Think: www.readwritethink.org/materials/timeline

Our Timelines: www.ourtimelines.com/create_tl_2c.html

Differentiating U.S. History

This topic is divided into two parts. In the first part, we provide an example of a differentiated lesson/unit for teaching about the Erie Canal, suggested technology resources, and a choice board. In the second part, we provide categorized starter links to use with some other units commonly taught in United States history.

Differentiating a Lesson or Unit on the Erie Canal

The Erie Canal was the first important national waterway built in the United States. It connected Lake Erie with Albany, New York, and the Atlantic Ocean via the Hudson River. Building the waterway improved political unity, created inexpensive transportation, and increased free trade between Midwest farm products and the East. Its route sparked immigration to the Midwest, helped to create numerous cities, and started a surge of canal building in the United States.

The building of the canal was promoted as early as 1809 by DeWitt Clinton, who served as canal commissioner during its early construction. A graduate of Columbia College, he served in the New York State Assembly and Senate, the United States Senate, as mayor of New York City, and as governor of New York.

The teaching of the Erie Canal usually falls within a unit on regional and national growth, covering the years 1800 to about 1840. The topic of the Erie Canal also aligns with the teaching of inventions, how technology changes society, and forms of transportation, such as roads, steamboats, and trains. You will want students to understand why the construction of the Erie Canal was a huge challenge, how the economy of New York and the midwestern and eastern regions were impacted, and how the canal fostered expansion to the Midwest and trade to the East.

Differentiated Lesson or Unit

To illustrate how we would differentiate a lesson or unit about the Erie Canal, we have created two graphic organizers. Figure 7.2 shows an overview of the time period from the proposal to the New York State Legislature in 1808 to the opening of the canal in 1825. Figure 7.2 was created using Timeliner XE.

In Table 7.1, we compare and contrast the typical, traditional instruction of teaching about the Erie Canal with technology-enhanced differentiated instruction of the lesson or unit.

To develop this table, we first looked at several social studies texts and online resources for teaching the topic. We compiled the typical steps teachers use for teaching the unit or lesson in column one. In column two, we added the tech-infused strategies that we would personally use in teaching the Erie Canal to our fictional class of eighth graders.

Please note that adding technology to differentiate instruction does not mean that you should use technology in every step of teaching a unit or lesson. There are many ways to differentiate instruction, and we provide enough choices to tech-enhance unit/lesson teaching so that you can pick and choose what works best for you. Start slowly and honor your comfort zone. Keep in mind that nearly any kind of technology will help to differentiate from straight text reading. On top of that, technology appeals to middle graders and may even motivate them to do more careful reading and thinking so that their technology piece is just right.

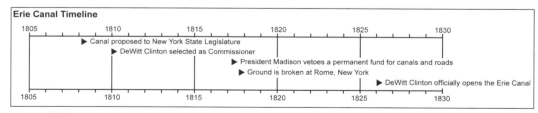

FIGURE **7.2** ■ Erie Canal timeline created in Timeliner XE.

TABLE 7.1 ■ Differentiating a Unit on the Erie Canal

Typical/Traditional Instruction	Tech-Enhanced/Differentiated Instruction
Pre-Reading Motivation	**Pre-Reading Motivation**
Have students look at the textbook illustrations and maps and ask why they think the building of a canal would be important. Lead a discussion in which ideas are captured on an overhead or chalkboard.	Show the movie *The Erie Canal: A Journey through History* from www.epodunk.com/routes/erie-canal/. Note that the movie includes clickable points along the route map. If you subscribe to Discovery Education Streaming, the Erie Canal is part of the film *New York Up Close: Immigration and the Industrial Revolution*. The first three segments are pertinent: Why Build the Erie Canal? (02:01) Construction of the Erie Canal (02:40) How the Erie Canal Influenced New York (02:46) Following the showing of some or all segments, lead a discussion about the building of the Erie Canal and why/how it was important. Ask students to pair/share and write out the key reasons. Share with the class. (Note: if you use a blog or wiki, students can post their notes to either application.) Another option is to project the image of the mural *The Pouring of the Waters* by Charles Y. Turner, painted in 1905. It isat www.nyscanals.gov/cculture/history/waters.html. Ask students to describe what is happening in the painting.
During-Reading Activities *Background Reading on the Erie Canal*	**During-Reading Activities** *Background Reading on the Erie Canal*
Map (text, encyclopedia, or paper handout) of the route Map of the region in 1817–25 Textbook	Pair students to investigate life while building the Erie Canal or life while traveling the Erie Canal. Students take notes and discuss with each other or in the whole group or post information to a blog or wiki. This research activity could follow the steps of the I-Search strategy where students investigate topics based on their research interest and then use the information they have found to create a product demonstrating their knowledge. **Suggested Links** Before and After Map: www.thirteen.org/edonline/ntti/resources/lessons/h_erie_canal/map.pdf Dewitt Clinton: www.eriecanal.org/UnionCollege/Clinton.html Diary excerpt: www.eduplace.com/ss/hmss/8/unit/act4.1.1.html Diary excerpts from Rachel Wilmer: www.archives.nysed.gov/projects/eriecanal/ec_questions1830_wilmer.shtml Diary of a young girl in 1822: Part 1: www.rochester.lib.ny.us/~rochhist/v62_2000/v62i3.pdf Diary of a young girl in 1822: Part 2: www.rochester.lib.ny.us/~rochhist/v62_2000/v62i4.pdf Diary of Marco Paul's travels on the Erie Canal: http://memory.loc.gov/learn/lessons/00/canal/teacher.html *(resources for the book and primary documents)* Erie Canal Time Machine: www.archives.nysed.gov/projects/eriecanal/ec_teachers.shtml Graphic organizer: www.history.org/history/teaching/enewsletter/volume6/images/jan/eriecanal_go.pdf

continued

TABLE **7.1** ■ **Differentiating a Unit on the Erie Canal**   *continued*

Typical/Traditional Instruction	Tech-Enhanced/Differentiated Instruction
	Suggested Links, continued History: http://pbskids.org/bigapplehistory/building/topic1.html (*includes video clip and slides*) History: www.eyewitnesstohistory.com/eriecanal.htm History: www.nyscanals.gov/cculture/history/erie-canal-history.pdf History: hwww.history.com/this-day-in-history.do?action=Article&id=7062 Images: http://memory.loc.gov/learn/lessons/00/canal/teacher.html and www.eriecanal.org/images.html Images, photos, and drawings: www2.libraryweb.org/index.asp?orgid=91&storyTypeID=&sid=& Locks: http://terrax.org/sailing/locks/lockflightjs.aspx (*interactive game on canal locks*) Locks: www.eriecanal.org/locks.html (*how a lock works*) Purchasing Power of Money from 1774–2007 Calculator: www.measuringworth.com/ppowerus/ Primary documents: www.mvcc.edu/academics/library/jackdaws.pdf Student resources at the Library of Congress: www.loc.gov/teachers/classroommaterials/presentationsandactivities/activities/ The Erie Canal: www.eriecanal.org (images and information) Timeline: http://mina.gc.cuny.edu/erie_canal/timeline.htm Tour the Old Erie Canal: www.eriecanal.org/tour.html
	Teacher Resources Erie Canal teacher's guide: www.laguardiawagnerarchive.lagcc.cuny.edu/eriecanal Word Wall: http://memory.loc.gov/learn/lessons/00/canal/wordwall.html Alphabet Book: http://memory.loc.gov/learn/lessons/00/canal/alphabet.html Related Illinois/Michigan Canal Lessons: www.canalcor.org/CCA2005/teachres.html#6-8
During-Reading Activities *Vocabulary Studies*	**During-Reading Activities** *Vocabulary Studies*
Glossary or word study using textbook	Students can use an online dictionary to create a glossary in a word-processing program, or if allowed, a wiki of Erie Canal terms. An online vocabulary quiz can be used as a checkpoint: http://xroads.virginia.edu/~ma02/volpe/canal/dictionary.html Visit the Erie Canal Time Machine, which offers vocabulary and document based questions: www.archives.nysed.gov/projects/eriecanal/ec_docindex.shtml

continued

TABLE **7.1** ■ **Differentiating a Unit on the Erie Canal** *continued*

Typical/Traditional Instruction	Tech-Enhanced/Differentiated Instruction
During-Reading Activities *Connections with economics, civics, geography, the arts, and literature*	**During-Reading Activities** *Connections with economics, civics, geography, the arts, and literature*
Textbook	Read about the canal in popular culture: http://mina.gc.cuny.edu/erie_canal/culture.htm View stock transfers and receipts: http://mina.gc.cuny.edu/erie_canal/construction.htm
After-Reading Activities *Culminating Project/Assessment*	**After-Reading Activities** *Culminating Project/Assessment*
Assessment/Test	Newsletter format: Create a 1–2-page newsletter with images and articles about the canal. Use publishing or word-processing software or try the printing press at Read Write Think: http://interactives.mped.org/view_interactive.aspx?id=110&title= Brochure: Using word-processing/desktop publishing software or free online software at www.mybrochuremaker.com, create a brochure to entice Europeans to travel to America to build the canal. Genealogical Interview/Tree: Students living in the Midwest and beyond may have ancestors who used the Erie Canal to migrate. They may be interested in interviewing their family genealogist and writing about the ancestor as well as creating a family tree. Digital Story: Ask a team of students to retell the story of building the canal, creating the story in Photo Story 3, PowerPoint, or similar software: Timeline (Our Timelines): Ask students to create a timeline of the world events prior to building the canal and after its completion, 1776 to 1840, at www.ourtimelines.com/create_tl_2c.html and another one of their own life. Ask them to analyze the timelines with respect to events in the United States and the world. Webbe: Ask students to create a Webbe about the Erie Canal.

Choice Board for Differentiating Student Products on the Erie Canal

We like to offer students choices based on their multiple intelligences and interests. As a result, we show a table of ideas for creating student products based on their research investigations about the Erie Canal. Consider the technology resources you have available in your building. Then look in Table 7.2 to see the sorts of tasks students may perform in a group project or individually to demonstrate learning. You can generate rubrics for these tasks at RubiStar (http://rubistar.4teachers.org).

TABLE 7.2 ■ **Erie Canal Choice Board**

1. Interpersonal	2. Intrapersonal	3. Math/Logic
Technology: Video camera and software, Internet research, and word-processing software. **Task:** Work with a partner to create a newscast about traveling on the Erie Canal in the 1840s. Broadcast the news to your class.	**Technology:** Word-processing or publishing software. **Task:** Write a series of diary pages about a student's journey on the Erie Canal in 1825. Share your product with the class.	**Technology:** Internet and word-processing or spreadsheet software. **Task:** Research and report on the cost of the Erie Canal. Calculate the cost in today's money along with the cost of common foods now and then using the calculator at www.measuringworth.com/ppowerus/.
4. Bodily-Kinesthetic	**5. Visual**	**6. Musical**
Technology: Internet research. **Task:** Create a costume in the style of persons traveling the Erie Canal in 1825. Use images, diaries, and primary documents for descriptions. Act out the role you chose to your class.	**Technology:** Draw/paint tools. **Task:** Create original images of life on the Erie Canal based on descriptions from diaries. Be able to project the images from the computer.	**Technology:** Music player installed on computer; Audacity, GarageBand, or similar free audio-editing programs. **Task:** Listen to "Fifteen Miles on the Erie Canal" at www.eriecanalvillage.net/pages/song.html and then rewrite the words into a rap. Record it and play it for the class.
7. Linguistic	**8. Existential**	**9. Naturalist**
Technology: Publishing software, online tools. **Task:** Design a newspaper advertisement that offers shipping services along the canal. Describe the benefits of using your shipping firm, the route and towns you serve, and why customers should choose your firm. Share with the class.	**Technology:** Word-processing or publishing software. **Task:** Design a plan for the canal and write a letter to the president to convince him or her to fund it. Share with the class.	**Technology:** Draw/paint and presentation software. **Task:** Find information about the plants and animals canal builders may have seen along the route. Project the images you have found or draw some of your own to share with the class.

Additional Resources for Helping to Differentiate United States History

We realize that there are thousands of social studies resources available on the web that you can use, but listing even one hundred of them is beyond the scope of this book. Instead, we point you to those we consider as excellent starting points for helping differentiate United States history.

All Units

America's Story: www.americaslibrary.gov/cgi-bin/page.cgi

Digital History: www.digitalhistory.uh.edu

Eyewitness to History: www.eyewitnesstohistory.com

Eyewitness: American Originals from the National Archives: www.archives.gov/exhibits/eyewitness

Growth of a Nation Animated Movie: www.animatedatlas.com/movie2.html

History Matters: http://historymatters.gmu.edu/browse/wwwhistory

HyperHistory Online: www.hyperhistory.com/online_n2/History_n2/a.html

NARA Online Exhibits: www.archives.gov/exhibits

Picturing America: http://picturingamerica.neh.gov

The Gilder Lehrman Institute of American History: www.gilderlehrman.org

The Library of Congress: www.loc.gov

The Presidential Timeline of the 20th Century: www.presidentialtimeline.org

Time Machine from the U.S. Mint: www.usmint.gov/kids/timemachine

Civil War and Reconstruction

A Day in the Life Simulation: http://pbskids.org/stantonanthony/day_in_life.html

Civil War at the Smithsonian: http://civilwar.si.edu/collections.html

Civil War Causes and Civil War, North and South: www.brainpop.com/socialstudies/ushistory

Civil War Photographs: http://memory.loc.gov/ammem/cwphtml/cwphome.html

Civil War Women:
http://library.duke.edu/specialcollections/collections/digitized/civil-war-women/

Gettysburg Camp Life: www.nps.gov/history/museum/exhibits/gettex/

Reconstruction: http://digitalhistory.uh.edu/reconstruction/index.html

The Valley of the Shadow: http://valley.vcdh.virginia.edu

Colonial

Archiving Early America: www.earlyamerica.com

Colonial Williamsburg: www.history.org/history

Do History: http://dohistory.org

English Settlement: www.learner.org/biographyofamerica/prog02/

Jamestown Rediscovery: www.apva.org/jr.html

Peter Zenger Trial: www.law.umkc.edu/faculty/projects/ftrials/zenger/zenger.html

Raid on Deerfield—1704: www.1704.deerfield.history.museum

Virtual Jamestown: www.virtualjamestown.org/interactive.html

Constitution

Ben's Guide to Government: http://bensguide.gpo.gov/6–8

Constitution, Branches of Government, Democracy:
www.brainpop.com/socialstudies/usgovernmentandlaw

Interactive Constitution: http://72.32.50.200/constitution

Gilded Age

The Great Chicago Fire and the Web of Memory: www.chicagohs.org/fire

Immigration

Immigration and Movement of People: www.brainpop.com/socialstudies/culture

Industrial Revolution

Industrial Revolution: www.brainpop.com/socialstudies/ushistory

Industrial Revolution Simulation (Britain):
www.schoolshistory.org.uk/Luddites/The Luddites.htm

Lowell Textile Mills WebQuest:
www.sun-associates.com/mercer/handouts/millgirls.html
www.sun-associates.com/mercer/handouts/millwebq.pdf

The Story of My Cotton Dress:
http://ehistory.osu.edu/osu/mmh/childlabor/cottondress.cfm

New Republic

At Home in the Heartland: www.museum.state.il.us/exhibits/athome

Gold Rush: www.brainpop.com/socialstudies/ushistory

Lewis and Clark: www.lewisandclarkexhibit.org/index_flash.html

Lewis and Clark Simulation: www.nationalgeographic.com/lewisandclark

War of 1812: www.galafilm.com/1812/e/index.html

Presidents

Abraham Lincoln Online: http://showcase.netins.net/web/creative/lincoln.html

Monticello Explorer: http://explorer.monticello.org

Presidential Timeline of the 20th Century: www.presidentialtimeline.org

Truman Library and Museum: www.trumanlibrary.org/kids

Virtual Tour of Mt. Vernon: www.mountvernon.org/virtual/index.cfm/ss/29

Slavery

The African American Odyssey:
http://memory.loc.gov/ammem/aaohtml/exhibit/aointro.html

Captive Passage: www.mariner.org/captivepassage

Expansion of Slavery 1790–1860:
http://wps.ablongman.com/long_divine_app_6/119/30484.cw/index.html#

Melrose Interactive Slavery Environment:
http://206.137.17.63/melrose/melrose.htm

Slavery in America: www.slaveryinamerica.org

The Underground Railroad: www.brainpop.com/socialstudies/ushistory

Underground Railroad: www.nationalgeographic.com/railroad

Transportation

America on the Move: http://americanhistory.si.edu/onthemove

Transportation in America before 1876:
http://americanhistory.si.edu/onthemove/exhibition/exhibition_1_1.html

Women's Rights

Women's Suffrage: www.brainpop.com/socialstudies/ushistory

Differentiating Western and Eastern Hemisphere Studies

In many classrooms across the United States, students study the Western Hemisphere in Grade 6 and the Eastern Hemisphere in Grade 7. Both curricula cover world cultures and geography as a way of understanding the Earth and its peoples.

In their lessons about the Western Hemisphere, teachers introduce geography and common geographical terms, the five themes of geography (location, place, region, movement, and human-environment interaction), the six essential elements (the world in spatial terms, places and regions, physical systems, human systems, environment and society, and the uses of geography), and present the essential question: In what ways does geography help people understand their world?

Because geography is the study of people, places, and environments, geographers try to answer such questions as, "Where are things located?" and "Why are they there?" To organize their data, geographers use the five themes and the six essential elements to detail their information. Once students understand the themes and elements, they will be able to think like geographers and apply their knowledge to understand. To help you out, there's an online teacher packet about maps from the U.S. Geological Survey (http://erg. usgs.gov/isb/pubs/teachers-packets/mapshow/) that you may wish to review.

Here are some ideas for differentiating instruction with technology when teaching Western and Eastern Hemisphere studies.

Geography

Mapping Themes and Elements

National Geographic's Xpedition Hall (www.nationalgeographic.com/xpeditions/hall/) features an interactive museum where students can learn about the world in spatial terms, the uses of geography, and more. Right off the bat, students can use technology to visualize the themes and elements. They could next use a graphic organizer to help them retell and classify the themes and elements. You, of course, could provide a graphic organizer; but why not have students use Inspiration or an online webbing tool like the one at Read Write Think (http://interactives.mped.org/view_interactive.aspx?id=127&title=) to classify their information?

Themes, Latitude and Longitude

BrainPOP has a terrific movie on "Geography Themes" and another on "Latitude and Longitude" to help students understand these essentials (subscription for a free trial, www.brainpop.com/socialstudies/geography). National Geographic outlines the five themes—location, place, region, movement, and human-environment interaction (www. nationalgeographic.com/resources/ngo/education/themes.html). Working in pairs or triads, students can explain the terms in two or three slides and present them to the class.

Geographers' Tools

Geographers also use a number of tools in their trade and many of them include technology, such as databases of information that can be sorted and stored (like Excel, Scholastic Keys, Access, and similar tools), photographs, globes, graphs, and maps.

Geographers use satellites to project views of the Earth in order to provide data for mapmaking and to obtain information about weather. The Satellite Site has clear explanations (www.thetech.org/exhibits/online/satellite). Remote sensing is also explained at

Earth from Space (www.earthfromspace.si.edu/online_exhibition_satellite_technology. asp).

Geographic information systems (GIS) and global positioning system (GPS) are terms you and your students will want to explore. You can learn how GPS receivers work (www. howstuffworks.com/gps.htm) and more about GIS (www.palmbeach.k12.fl.us/maps/gis/ giskids.htm).

This would be a good time for students to start a database or spreadsheet of the geographical terms they are learning or use a wiki to contribute their information. Or you might show them how to use a spreadsheet in Google Docs as a way to contribute information that all can access. Creating a common document that all can access empowers learners because everyone has a stake in the creation of an artifact.

Culture

Because geography also includes humans, consider connecting geography with culture at the Internet Public Library's Culture Quest World Tour (www.ipl.org/youth/cquest/), which describes cultural practices around the world. Or try the Big Wide World WebQuest (www.kn.pacbell.com/wired/bww/).

Following their exploration, students can think-pair-share and compare/contrast what they learned. You could provide students with a graphic organizer, but they can also use the online Venn diagram tool at Read Write Think (www.readwritethink.org/materials/venn/) or create a three-column table using a word processor.

During their culture and country studies, students will be using online resources to find facts about the countries they are studying. Here are several starter resources to use:

Atlapedia: www.atlapedia.com

Geographic.org: www.geographic.org

Geography Zone: www.geographyzone.com/new/index.php?t=2&b=0

Journey to Planet Earth: www.pbs.org/journeytoplanetearth/profiles

National Geographic: www.nationalgeographic.com

National Geographic's Map Machine: http://maps.nationalgeographic.com/map-machine/

The World FactBook: www.cia.gov/library/publications/the-world-factbook/

Plate Tectonics

Geography students also learn about the Earth's physical systems. One of the most interesting topics is the Earth's tectonic plates. Check out a movie about them at BrainPOP (subscription or free trial, www.brainpop.com/science/seeall) and look at the clearly explained information at Enchanted Learning (www.enchantedlearning.com/subjects/astronomy/planets/earth/Continents.shtml).

The 1906 San Francisco earthquake simulation (http://earthquake.usgs.gov/regional/nca/1906/simulations/) and a series of animations related to the 1906 quake (http://serc.carleton.edu/NAGTWorkshops/health/visualizations/SanFran1906.html) are excellent resources. The Virtual Museum of the City of San Francisco has photos of the damage that can be viewed (www.sfmuseum.org/1906/photos.html). BrainPOP also has fantastic movies on earthquakes, volcanoes, and tsunamis, and there's more information here at the Faultline Seismic Center (www.exploratorium.edu/faultline/). Students can practice "moving" plates in a simulation (www.pbs.org/wgbh/aso/tryit/tectonics/#).

In 1998, fifth grade students created the site Journey to the Center of the Earth (www.fi.edu/fellows/fellow4/nov98/). Your students could do an update by conducting online investigations and using digital tools, such as draw/paint software. They could start their research at Earthquakes for Kids (http://earthquake.usgs.gov/learning/kids/).

As a follow-up activity, students may wish to compare the San Francisco earthquake with another large-scale earthquake. The Epic Disasters site (www.epicdisasters.com) provides information about U.S. and world earthquakes as well as data about other disasters. The U.S. Geological Survey offers earthquake data, animations, and maps of recent earthquake activity (http://earthquake.usgs.gov/eqcenter/recenteqsanim). There's also a teacher lesson (http://earthquake.usgs.gov/learning/teachers/compare_intensity.php).

Plate tectonics is a perfect place for a R.A.F.T.T. in which students assume a role and write to a specified audience in a specified format and topic to create an informational piece.

Weathering and Erosion

Weathering and erosion are two concepts geography students study. Again, BrainPOP has terrific videos on these topics (www.brainpop.com/science/seeall/). National Geographic offers wonderful photos of these forces operating in the Grand Canyon (http://science.nationalgeographic.com/science/photos/weathering-erosion-gallery/arizona-rock.html), and there's a cool slide show to watch (www.teachersdomain.org/resource/ess05.sci.ess.earthsys.erosion/).

National Geographic provides an online article about weathering and erosion (http://magma.nationalgeographic.com/ngexplorer/0610/articles/mainarticle.html), and Geography4Kids explains erosion, deep erosion, and weathering (www.geography4kids.com/files/land_weathering.html). Erosion of a Sea Stack over 100 Years shows over time what erosion has done to sandstone (http://walrus.wr.usgs.gov/pubinfo/jump.html).

How to recap information learned? Students might produce a newsletter, webpage, or other product that shares their knowledge.

The Hydrological Cycle

Renewing the Earth's water is explained via a hydrological cycle. You can help students understand the cycle by using an interactive animation (www.nwlg.org/pages/resources/geog/hydro_cycle/hydro/cycle.htm or hwww.teachersdomain.org/resource/ess05.sci.ess.watcyc.hydrocycle/). How about asking students to use a word processing program to make a 3-column, 5-row chart that explains the four steps in the hydrologic cycle (evaporation, condensation, precipitation, and run-off), and the descriptions and areas of each step in the cycle? Another project that pairs could work on is using the tools in PowerPoint to make an animated hydrological cycle and explain it to the class.

Land Forms

Ask students to (1) use Inspiration or the Read Write Think Webbing tool (http://interactives.mped.org/view_interactive.aspx?id=127&title=/) to diagram water bodies and landforms, (2) create a presentation about landforms and water bodies, or (3) create an illustrated glossary about landforms and water bodies. There is an example of an illustrated glossary (www.enchantedlearning.com/geography/landforms/glossary.shtml) and another example with photos and related games (www.edu.pe.ca/southernkings/face.htm). Students could contribute data to a blog or wiki or shared spreadsheet if they choose option three.

Learning Games

Lighten up serious learning a bit and show students some educational geography games. Take a look at Quia games (www.quia.com/shared/geo) and the National Geography games (http://kids.nationalgeographic.com/Games/GeographyGames/).

There's also the GeoNet Game (www.eduplace.com/geonet/), and Sheppard Software offers online geography games for students (www.sheppardsoftware.com/Geography.htm).

Students can make their own board game or use a PowerPoint template to create a digital game. Directions for both are available at www.everythingdi.net.

Google Earth

If you and your students don't already use Google Earth in the classroom, you're missing out on a terrific free product (http://earth.google.com). Although downloading is required, as the Google folks say, "Google Earth lets you fly anywhere on Earth to view satellite imagery, maps, terrain, 3-D buildings, and even explore galaxies in the sky. You can explore rich geographical content, save your toured places and share with others."

The Google Earth User Guide (http://earth.google.com/userguide/v4/) provides a walk through and tips about using the product. There's a cool new feature—the Movie Maker—that you can use to record 3-D viewer imagery and save the recording as a movie file. After finishing your recording, you can place it on a website, blog, or wiki; use it in a presentation; or e-mail it. Talk about usefulness geared to social studies!

Once you teach students how to use Google Earth and its Movie Maker, they can make custom movies of a city, region, or country they are researching and share them with others. Google Earth Lessons at (www.gelessons.com/lessons) is another helpful site.

Civics/Government and Economics

Civics/Government

There are several decent sites to help with the teaching of civics or government. Ben's Guide to Good Government (http://bensguide.gpo.gov/6–8) offers information on how the government works as well as interactive games and links to U.S. government websites for students. Kids in the House (http://clerkkids.house.gov) and Congress for Kids (www.congressforkids.net) are also informative sites. Information about the United States House of Representatives (www.house.gov), the Senate (www.senate.gov), and the U.S. Supreme Court (www.supremecourtus.gov) are good resources.

Students can search the Biographical Dictionary of the United States Congress by name, state, or year (http://bioguide.congress.gov/biosearch/biosearch.asp). Centuries of Citizenship offers a great overview of our Constitutional timeline (www.constitutioncenter.org/timeline/).

The Charters of Freedom site (www.archives.gov/exhibits/charters/charters.html) is also valuable. The Democracy Project (http://pbskids.org/democracy/) and The White House Kids Home (www.whitehouse.gov/kids/) are worth visiting and using. We especially like the History section, America's Presidents, and the free download "My American Journal" pages. What can students do with this information? They could create timelines of key events; make a virtual museum in a wiki, blog, website, or PowerPoint; and make a podcast, game, or movie.

One of the ways students learn and understand a core democratic value is by retelling it themselves. Most middle schoolers seem to enjoy comics, so how about their using Make Beliefs Comix (www.makebeliefscomix.com) to retell or explain a concept they are learning? Read Write Think Comic Creator (www.readwritethink.org/materials/comic/) is a similar tool.

Economics

Economics is the study of the way money, goods, and services are made, sold, and used in a society, and how they are related to one another. BrainPOP has a series of economics movies available (subscription or free trial, www.brainpop.com/socialstudies/economics/). Topics include Comparing Prices, Stock Market, Money, Stocks and Shares, Supply and Demand, Taxes, and Interest. Also read "The Story of Money" article (www.frbatlanta.org/atlantafed/visitors_center/tour/story.cfm).

Young Investor (www.younginvestor.com), Peanuts & Crackerjacks (www.bos.frb.org/peanuts/indexnosound.htm), Smart Choices (www.moneysmartchoices.org), and Planet Orange (www.orangekids.com) are other places to visit.

The National Council on Economic Education (www.ncee.net) and EconEdLink (www.econedlink.org) and its online resource list (www.econedlink.org/weblinks) offer many fine resources for teachers.

So what can students do with economics using technology? You may want to look at the three links below for ideas. However, we think that taking a current topic, such as gasoline prices and supply/demand, would be a great issue for researching and clarifying the economic terms behind the problem. Students can conduct research, develop a timeline of prices, and explain the situation in economic terms. They can explain why the prices have fluctuated and make recommendations as to what should be done to raise or lower the prices. Using PowerPoint or a similar technology tool would be a great way to present the findings of their research.

> **Oil Market Basics WebQuest:** http://tonto.eia.doe.gov/kids/energy.cfm?page=6

> **The Story of Supply and Demand: Cabbage Patch Dolls, Beanie Babies, and White Power Rangers:** www.wvpt4learning.org/lessons/pdf02/storyof.pdf

> **Real Tree Farms:** www.realtrees4kids.org/ninetwelve/supply.htm

The Americas, Europe, Russia, and the Eastern Hemisphere

Students in Grades 6 and 7 study the Americas, Europe, Russia, and the Eastern Hemisphere. More recently, the study of ancient civilizations has been added back into social studies curricula, leaving some teachers scrambling for resources. For that reason, in this section we'll focus on a few of the early civilizations to represent content from these grades as we show examples of differentiating with technology.

In the series of ideas below, we present a combination of online resources, such as interactive activities, video clips, software, graphic images, and information. Using information gleaned from any of these research topics as a basis, students can produce any number of products to share and demonstrate their learning. By products we mean presentations, comparative timelines and charts, mini-booklets and Webbes, posters, spreadsheets, wiki postings, and so forth.

Maya, Aztecs, Incas

The Maya, Aztecs, and Incas lived in the Americas prior to the 1500s. They are known as pre-Columbian civilizations because they existed before Christopher Columbus arrived in the Americas. Information and timelines for these civilizations are available at History of Mesoamerica (www.elbalero.gob.mx/kids/history/html/conquista/). Below are two ideas for differentiating with technology.

Students can learn about archaeology and the pre-Columbian world of Maya, Aztecs, and Incas in a multimedia software package called Dig It! (www.mintmuseum.org/digit/learn.htm). Dig It! can be downloaded or played online with an Internet browser plug-in.

Students can also learn about the three cultures at a variety of sites including:

The MesoAmerican Ballgame: www.ballgame.org

Ancient Americas: www.carlos.emory.edu/ODYSSEY/AA/aafront.htm

Mystery of the Maya:
www.civilisations.ca/cmc/exhibitions/civil/maya/mmp01eng.shtml

Why Do Civilizations Fall?: www.learner.org/interactives/collapse

The Fall of the Mayan Civilization:
www.bbc.co.uk/history/ancient/cultures/maya_01.shtml

>   This site features the story of a fairly recent investigation about the collapse of the Maya.

Exploring the Early Americas:
www.loc.gov/exhibits/earlyamericas/online/interactives.html

>   On this site students can explore the Mayan Writing System.

Ice Treasures of the Incas: www.nationalgeographic.com/features/96/mummy

Cracking the Maya Code:
www.pbs.org/wgbh/nova/teachers/activities/3506_mayacode.html

>   At this NOVA site, students can watch the video "The Forgotten Maya Temples" and complete an activity sheet to decipher Maya code.

Following their investigations, triads of students may wish to construct a comparative timeline of the cultures. Timeliner XE would be a fantastic tool for constructing the timeline, but other tools, such as the word-processing and presentation software, could be used, too.

China, Egypt, Greece, Rome, India, Vikings, Anglo-Saxons and Celts, and Mesopotamia

The BBC Ancient History pages and the British Museum offer outstanding text and visuals and some learning games and tours about several ancient civilizations. Ancient Civilizations at the British Museum (www.ancientcivilizations.co.uk/home_set.html) opens with a movie about its collection of objects, some up to 6,000-years-old, related to buildings, cities, writing, trade, technology, and religion. BBC offers a number of interactive galleries, games, tours, timelines, simulations, and animations (www.bbc.co.uk/history/interactive/) .

HyperHistory Online at (www.hyperhistory.com/online_n2/History_n2/a.html) offers comparative timelines of several civilizations and cultures. By specifying events and time frames, students can view what is going on in the world in several places at the same time.

For example, when searching for events between 500 BC and 1 AD and scrolling the results of the search, students can see the comparative timelines of events in America, Europe, Rome, Greece, Middle East/Egypt, India, China, Japan, and Africa. Each culture or civilization is color-coded for easier viewing. Figure 7.3 shows part of the screen displayed after the search.

Because students often study cultures and civilizations in isolation, using the site with them to review what occurred in the world at a given point in time helps them to understand cause and effect, the rise and fall of civilizations, and to make a comparison of events across the world. They can also see the names of writers, musicians, politicians/leaders, and scientists who lived during the same period of time.

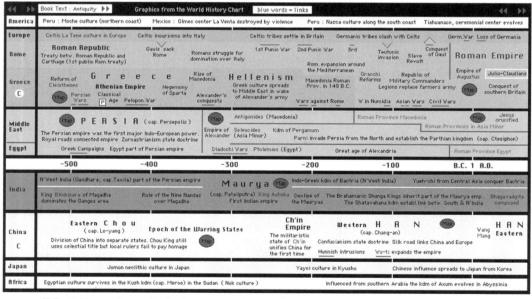

FIGURE 7.3 ■ HyperHistory Online's comparative timeline

Ancient China

The British Museum's websites on Ancient China (www.ancientchina.co.uk) and Early Imperial China (www.earlyimperialchina.co.uk/room.html) offer insights into the early history of China.

The "Great Wall of China" movie at BrainPOP (www.brainpop.com/socialstudies/worldhistory/) is also fascinating.

Ancient Egypt

At the NOVA site, The Mummy Who Would Be King (www.pbs.org/wgbh/nova/mummy/), students can see videos and read about undiscovered tombs, Rameses I, making mummies, and ancient Egyptian beliefs about the afterlife. There are Egyptian pharaohs and mummies movies at BrainPOP (www.brainpop.com/socialstudies/worldhistory/) to help with research.

Students can also visit a number of sites to research ancient Egypt:

The British Museum—Ancient Egypt: www.ancientegypt.co.uk

Egypt: Secrets of an Ancient World:
www.nationalgeographic.com/pyramids

Embalming (game):
www.bbc.co.uk/history/ancient/egyptians/launch_gms_mummy_maker.shtml

Pyramid Building Challenge (game):
www.bbc.co.uk/history/ancient/egyptians/launch_gms_pyramid_builder.shtml

The Egyptian Museum: www.egyptianmuseum.com

The Tomb of Perneb: www.metmuseum.org/explore/perneb_tomb/index.html

Royal Ontario Museum: www.rom.on.ca/schools/egypt/learn

Ancient Greece

The Golden Age of Greece, during which the Greeks flourished in art, philosophy, and government, began around 500 BC, but people lived in Greece as early as 1600 BC. At The Ancient Greeks site (www.bbc.co.uk/history/ancient/greeks), students can investigate the ancient Olympics, Athenian democracy, and other topics.

The British Museum (www.ancientgreece.co.uk) features information on the Acropolis, Athens, daily life, festivals and games, geography, gods and goddesses, knowledge and learning, Sparta, time, and war. Its school version offers similar topics (www.bbc.co.uk/schools/ancientgreece/).

Nova's Secrets of the Parthenon includes a webpage that details how the Parthenon is being restored (www.pbs.org/wgbh/nova/parthenon/restore.html).

Athens and Greek Gods movies are available at BrainPOP (www.brainpop.com/socialstudies/worldhistory/).

Ancient Rome

The Roman timeline extends from 753 BC, when the building of the city of Rome started, through 1453 AD, when the Roman Empire fell to the Turks. The following resources focus on many of the early events of Classic Rome.

The BBC site (www.bbc.co.uk/history/ancient/romans) speaks about Rome and its Empire, Roman Britain, Life in Ancient Rome, Gladiators, Pompeii, and other topics. Also offered is a school version (www.bbc.co.uk/schools/romans/).

Some interactive activities, such as building an aqueduct and touring a bath, are available from PBS (www.pbs.org/wgbh/nova/lostempires/roman/), along with The Emperor of Rome game (www.pbs.org/empires/romans/special/emperor_game.html).

Several videos, including the "Rise of the Roman Empire," "Roman Republic," "Pax Romana," and "Fall of the Roman Empire" can be viewed at BrainPOP (www.brainpop.com/socialstudies/worldhistory/).

Ancient India

Extensive urban civilization evolved in India around 2500 BC, and many groups and early societies have ruled India over time. These sites may help students to better visualize ancient India:

BBC's Ancient India: www.bbc.co.uk/history/ancient/india

The British Museum—Ancient India: www.ancientindia.co.uk

Vikings

Students generally regard the Vikings as people who sailed from Scandinavia to raid European rivers and coasts; however, not all Vikings were raiders. Some were farmers and traders who lived close to the sea in houses made of stone, wood, or sod. Eventually, land became crowded and more was needed; so the Vikings sailed in longboats that were constructed well enough to cross the ocean. As a result, the Vikings landed in England by 787 and in North America about the year 1000.

Explore a Viking Village: www.pbs.org/wgbh/nova/vikings/village.html

History of the Vikings (BBC Schools):
www.bbc.co.uk/history/ancient/vikings and www.bbc.co.uk/schools/vikings

Viking Quest (game):
www.bbc.co.uk/history/ancient/vikings/launch_gms_viking_quest.shtml

Vikings: The North Atlantic Saga and The Viking Voyage at the Smithsonian:
www.mnh.si.edu/vikings

Who Were the Vikings (NOVA): www.pbs.org/wgbh/nova/vikings

Anglo-Saxons and Celts

The Celts appeared in the British Isles about 450 BC and settled in Scotland, Ireland, and Wales. In the Middle Ages, tribes of Anglos and Saxons invaded and established small kingdoms in Britain until the Normans conquered England in 1066.

BBC's Anglo-Saxons: www.bbc.co.uk/history/ancient/anglo_saxons

BBC Schools' Anglo-Saxons: www.bbc.co.uk/schools/anglosaxons

Iron Age Celts: www.bbc.co.uk/wales/celts

Mesopotamia

The land between the Tigris and Euphrates rivers in the Fertile Crescent is referred to as Mesopotamia. People settled in Mesopotamia more than 12,000 years ago.

The British Museum: www.mesopotamia.co.uk

Mesopotamian Timeline: www.wsu.edu/~dee/meso/timeline.htm

Why Do Civilizations Fall?:
www.learner.org/interactives/collapse/mesopotamia.html

Summary

With an overload of web resources currently available, educators now have every reason to use them to bring in rich experiences for their diverse learners. Social studies teachers have an absolute treasure trove of resources from which to pick and choose, making social studies a fun and exciting place for learning. Students can listen to and create podcasts. They can investigate, interpret, and explain history. They can view videos of past historical events and create their own stories. Using Web 2.0 tools, students can become fully engaged in their learning, work with others around the world, and use real data.

CHAPTER **8**

Using Technology to Differentiate Encore Subjects
Art, Secondary Languages, Music, and Physical Education/Health

Money talks. Let's just get it out on the table.

As districts face repeated budget cuts, less and less funding from the state, higher utility and gas bills, and many other financial drains that affect our schools, educators recognize that none of our positions are guaranteed. Perhaps the encore teachers are the ones who best understand this reality, as elective classes are often perceived as "extra" or "nonessential." If courses and staff need to be cut, district administrators usually do not begin with those who teach core content, but rather, with the electives.

Enter Neil Diamond. Perhaps that might not sound too professional, but as we reminisce about the concerts we attended during his heyday, the countless reprisals of *Forever in Blue Jeans* come to mind. In the words of Neil Diamond, "Money talks, but it don't sing and dance, and it don't walk."

Our encore teachers are gifted, and we need them to bring a little song and dance to our middle school classrooms. In our opinion, middle school is the best time for these exploratory classes. Students need exposure to different fields, skills, and potential interests before they get to high school and college. Chapter 2 explains that the cerebral pathways our students fail to use in one area or another (music, art, athletics, drama, technology, and so on) wither away. If some of us had not had the opportunity to explore elective fields while in middle school, we may never have discovered a passion that we still enjoy. When students move on to the high-school level, many of them are consumed by "college prep" classes, leaving little room for electives within their schedules.

Furthermore, exploratory classes within the typical middle schooler's schedule provide some balance and relief from core classes that can be more stressful.

While innumerable encore teachers are fighting to convince their superiors of the value of and need for encore courses, others are enjoying a resurgence in popularity and demand. More recent research and "culturespeak" about the importance of the right brain and creativity are impacting our educational planning. We've discovered that math and music complement one another, and expertise in the fine arts is taking its rightful place alongside athletic ability. Those who are able to teach Spanish and other languages, such as Chinese and Arabic, find more employment opportunities are available to them. In addition, employers seem to be more attracted to job candidates who demonstrate well-roundedness.

A significant shift in the core content of encore classes has also occurred over the last few decades. This change isn't a surprising phenomenon, as curricular changes happen rather frequently in all grades and all subjects. However, a closer look is warranted.

In the past, the core content of most encore classes was skills-based. That is, teachers focused on instructing their students on *how* to develop a particular skill or talent, such as paint with watercolors, play the recorder, and so on. At present, they still train students to cultivate similar skills, but they also impart considerably more cultural, historical, health-related, and social knowledge about the artists and their works. By the term "artists" we mean those who create visual arts, music, drama, and literature, as well as the athletes who create physical art.

We can recall making the standard clay pot some 30 years ago without learning about María Montoya Martínez and Native American pottery. The same could be said for even more familiar artists, such as Henry Matisse, whom we never studied when we created collages. Without a doubt, encore teachers cross curricular areas in their classrooms, although we tend to label their courses as more specialized.

Many of the aforementioned factors make it seem like encore subjects aren't well suited for effective differentiated instruction. In our experience, however, we've discovered just the opposite. Differentiated instruction strategies can be incorporated successfully into encore classes and can bring about positive results.

Before adding our powerful ally, technology, to the mix, we begin with a brief overview of a variety of content and skills-based areas that could be differentiated in the encore classroom. In our earlier book, *Differentiating Instruction with Technology in K–5 Classrooms*, we listed starting points for differentiation in encore courses and believe that these suggestions are helpful to all educators, so we repeat them here. As we are addressing four subject areas in one chapter, fewer strategies and resources will be listed. There are countless websites, software programs, and webware applications available online. We've chosen the game-like strategy of Cubing and ThinkDots, as it's usable in all subject areas. We then provide tech-integrated sample activities that allow you and your students to break down all communication barriers via the World Wide Web: visually, audibly, and orally.

Beginning to Think about How to Differentiate in the Encore Classroom

As is the case with the majority of core subjects, there are many encore areas that could be differentiated to better serve our encore students. Today's encore teachers face a heavier load in terms of the amount of content-based knowledge and skills they must cover in the classroom. While many of you may already have experimented with one or more of the variations below, see if there are any suggestions you haven't tried.

The lists that follow are not comprehensive by any means; they are points of departure to get you started. They offer alternatives that you might draw on in your attempt to reach all students through differentiation. Think about additional options you might add to the lists and try in your classroom.

If you teach art, in addition to students' levels of readiness, consider the final products they could produce and how you might think about simplifying or making the creative process more complex/detailed. Our students' interests might factor into the equation, particularly in the choice of media used or genre. Here is a list of possible ways you might differentiate by product:

- Restrict creation to pure imitation of another's technique, or extend the liberty to create freely.

- Heighten or diminish the level of abstraction.

- Vary the type of media used.

- Expand or reduce the levels of dimension, such as three dimensional versus two dimensional.

- Minimize or maximize the complexity or intricacy of shape.

- Intensify or lessen the complexity or intricacy of pattern.

- Minimize or maximize the complexity or intricacy of shading.

- Reduce or expand the number of colors used.

- Add or eliminate the number or types of texture employed.

- Include options for different schools or genres of art.

If you teach a secondary language, you are probably familiar with the traditional four language skill areas: listening, reading, writing, and speaking. A more current trend in secondary language instruction is attention to the three "communicative modes"—interpersonal, interpretive, and presentational—that form the basis of the communication goal area included in the standards of the American Council on the Teaching of Foreign Languages (ACTFL). The standards center on five goal areas called the "5 Cs": communication, cultures, connections, comparisons, and communities.

The traditional four-skills approach treats writing, reading, listening, and speaking in the target language in a more isolated manner, whereas the communicative modes stress the purpose and the context of communication. The latter approach seems to strengthen and deepen the connection between real life and the activities inside the language classroom.

The incorporation of the remaining four "Cs" also encourages a well-rounded approach that enables us to prepare students for our global society. This approach embraces awareness and instruction on cultural topics, comparison and contrast of language patterns, multicultural and multilingual community experiences in the field, use of the Internet, and so forth. Glance at the ACTFL performance indicators for the communication standard (www.actfl. org/files/public/execsumm.pdf).

Standard 1.1: Interpersonal Communication

Students engage in conversations, provide and obtain information, express feelings and emotions, and exchange opinions.

Standard 1.2: Interpretive Communication

Students understand and interpret written and spoken language on a variety of topics.

Standard 1.3: Presentational Communication

Students present information, concepts, and ideas to an audience of listeners or readers on a variety of topics.

Although secondary language is sometimes taught as an exploratory subject at the middle school level (seventh grade in particular), its core content is similar to that of other primary subjects, such as ELA, in which teachers work on virtually identical skills in their native language. It would seem to be easy to accommodate differentiation within the secondary language classroom because it parallels academic instruction in the students' native language. However, due to the fact that secondary language instruction often occurs less frequently than that of core curricular subjects, teachers cannot always follow a comprehensive curriculum. Teachers of other encore subjects face similar time constraints that impact instruction, too. Many of the elective classes meet for just one quarter or semester, representing one-fourth or one-half of the time dedicated to core classes. In addition, in some middle schools, ELA and other core subjects have longer periods of instruction called double block or double period.

Secondary language teachers consider the readiness levels of their students, as well as the content to be communicated, in order to impart specific knowledge. Interests and learning profiles play a big part in terms of the students' receptivity and understanding of the material. Differentiation of process-based activities and diverse product formats are essential to accommodate all levels and types of learners. Teachers have multiple options in each of the traits and elements.

Here are a few basic ideas to consider for differentiation in a secondary language:

- Isolate or focus on a particular skill (such as writing), or require the use of two to four skills.

- Increase or decrease the number of tenses used.

- Intensify or lessen the level of vocabulary.

- Teach culture in students' native language or in the target language.

- Communicate facts only or incorporate feelings and emotions.

- Comprehend by listening only or comprehend by listening and then respond orally or in writing.

- Vary the length or complexity of an exercise, document, or text.

- Request structured responses or free responses.

- Incorporate simple or advanced realia and authentic documents.

- Invite recorded responses or spontaneous ones.

- Utilize group or individual presentations or assignments.

If you are a music teacher, ponder the readiness levels of your students and the final products they will generate. Your students' interests might play a role here, too, particularly in terms of the genres of music and the kinds of instruments they prefer. You might also challenge them in the process phase by asking them to play or sing at various tempos, using different dynamics, and so forth, which will affect their final products. Here are some suggestions:

- Lengthen or shorten the composition or piece.

- Vary the type of instruments used.

- Increase or decrease the number of instruments played.

- Play the treble clef or both the treble and bass clefs.

- Increase or decrease the range of the piece.

- Modify the rhythm.

- Speed up or slow down the tempo.

- Heighten or lessen the dynamics.

- Simplify or intensify the complexity or difficulty of the piece.

- Allow for various types of parts or harmony: solo, duet, trio, quartet, whole ensemble or choir, and so forth.

- Include pieces of various classifications of music.

If you are a physical education teacher, reflect on the readiness levels of your students and the skill levels you wish them to attain. Contemplate how you might alter the level of difficulty of each task as a part of the learning process. Some of the ways that you might challenge your students beyond their comfort zones are:

- Intensify or lessen the level of competition.

- Maximize or minimize the speed of the task.

- Increase or decrease the distance between performers.

- Reduce or expand the size of the playing area.

- Require the use of the weaker limb or permit the use of both limbs or the stronger limb.

- Change the levels of movement: stationary skills, tasks, or targets; moving skills, tasks, or targets; add or eliminate defenders.

- Place or remove restrictions upon game play or technique.

- Break skills development practice/tasks into parts or perform skills or tasks outright.

Take a second look at your subject area, and pinpoint one or two areas of differentiation you have not yet tried. Make a commitment to try out one in the next few weeks or months to see if it's effective for you and your students.

Differentiating Encore Subjects with Technology

Before we move on to our strategies of focus for this chapter, we'd like you to examine a table of resources. In Table 8.1, we have listed hardware, software/computer-assisted instruction resources, lesson plan resources, and virtual environments that you could use in *any* of the encore subject areas. The list is not comprehensive, but we wanted to get you thinking about technology right away. We're sure that most of you tech-savvy teachers are familiar with the majority of these resources, and we'll refer to some of them in our suggested activities. What resources could you add from your classroom experience?

Along with the technology resources that we can integrate into our plans for Cubing and other product generators, such as a PowerPoint e-book or digital story, each encore subject has a wealth of hardware, software, lesson plan resources, websites, and virtual environments specific to its particular curricular area. It is virtually impossible to provide an exhaustive listing of such resources in this chapter. While we recognize the wealth of some large-scale resources, such as labs, we have refrained from creating tasks dependent upon them, as some schools do not have a keyboarding lab for music or a language lab for secondary languages. Furthermore, the labs themselves vary greatly in terms of layout, size, availability, and software and hardware used, so it would be futile to make generalizations.

TABLE **8.1** ■ Technology Resources for Encore Subjects

Hardware	Software/ Computer-Assisted Instruction	Lesson Plan Resources	Virtual Environments
Digital cameras Interactive whiteboards Elmo projectors Tape recorders or DVD players Hand-held devices or PDAs Video cameras Laptops and desktop computers	Audio CDs or DVDs Online flashcards Clip art Online games and drills Drawing software (Paint) Online podcasts, videos, or clips E-mail Image-editing software (Photoshop) Graph Club or Graph Master Publishing software (Publisher) Presentation software (PowerPoint) Kidspiration or Inspiration Spreadsheet software (Excel) Online audio files TimeLiner Online dictionaries or glossaries Word-processing software	Graphic organizers, note-taking forms, or other templates Internet scavenger hunts Lesson plan links Surveys, questionnaires, or other pre-assessment tools ThinkQuests Video streaming WebQuests	Kids' chats and Keypals Virtual museums and other cultural institutions MUSHes, MOOs, CU-SeeMe Webcams Online collaborative projects Virtual field trips

Cubing and ThinkDots

Cubing and ThinkDots are related strategies that are extremely versatile, engaging, and adaptable enough to be used across curricular areas. They both involve the use of a "manipulative" to perform tasks that "work out" their assignment, so they're a strong way to differentiate by process. The ThinkDots strategy, developed by Kay Brimijoin, is a spin-off of Cubing. While both fulfill the same function and share the same benefits and components, their physical formats differ slightly. The term "Cubing" actually originates from a paper cube that students roll to work out their assignment. ThinkDots are six hole-punched cards that are joined together by a ring, yarn, string, or the like. Each card has a picture of one or more dots that correspond to the faces of a die. Instead of rolling a cube, students roll a die and complete the activity on the back of the card that matches the dot combination that appears on the face of the die.

Teachers often use a pre-made template for these strategies. We've provided ThinkDots and Cubing templates for you at the end of this chapter. Each face of the cube or back side of a ThinkDots card displays a different task, many of which involve a writing activity. These six key tasks encourage students to consider core concepts from six different perspectives. Task descriptions often contain a strong verb in the form of a command. We have compiled a list of possible suggestions that you might use to describe your tasks.

1. **Describe it.** Examine your topic closely and use descriptive words to tell about it. Name its shape, color, and size.

2. **Compare it.** Is your topic similar to another? Is it different from another? Explain by giving examples to show similarities and differences.

3. **Associate it.** Does your topic remind you of something? It could be a feeling, a person, a place, or a thing.

4. **Analyze it.** Identify the important parts of your topic.

5. **Apply it.** What is the purpose of your topic? How can you use it?

6. **Argue For/Against it.** Stand for or against your topic. Speak out in support of your topic, or protest against it.

Perhaps you might question the use of writing assignments in encore classes. We hope the following samples will show you some of the ways teachers can encourage students to utilize the historical and social knowledge they've learned as a part of the core content. The tasks we've listed suggest ways students may then apply that knowledge to an activity that mimics a possible "real-life" situation. As our world grows smaller and competition for jobs in the global marketplace increases, we believe that students who can demonstrate skills and knowledge in multiple areas (not solely in their areas of specialization) will be more employable. If we tie the content we're teaching to real-life tasks, students might be more receptive, particularly when technology is involved.

To prepare your students and your room for a ThinkDots or Cubing activity, organize the class into small groups at tables or desks with students who have cubes of the same color or identical card sets. You, the teacher, will first present a topic of focus. Students take turns rolling their cubes or dice, completing the tasks as they turn up. Tasks can be completed on a worksheet, on separate paper, or at a computer. If a roll turns up a task that they'd rather not do, you can give your students the option of "passing" on that task. As students work on their tasks, you may decide to allow them to ask for help from their classmates. When the activity is over, you might ask students to share their ideas with the other members of their groups. Yet another alternative would be to use Cubing or ThinkDots as a review tool, in which one cube or set of cards is shared by a group of students. Each student has a turn to roll the cube or die and must complete the task that appears.

At first, it might seem that Cubing and ThinkDots do not maximize technology integration, perhaps because students manipulate a physical cube or card that is template-generated. However, you can easily design tasks that require technology-driven responses or products. We've included examples typed into the Cubing template, but you could easily transfer them over to the ThinkDots template.

If you and your students would like to roll an animated die, instead of an actual, physical one, take a glance at these websites:

Animated Dice GIF Software Downloads:
www.download32.com/animated-dice-gif-software.html

Interactivate: Racing Game with One Die:
www.shodor.org/interactivate/activities/RacingGameWithOneDie/

> Although this site provides a game that involves a car race, it allows students to roll a virtual die with one click and actually see the die's face. It can be restarted over and over.

Sample Cubing and ThinkDots Tasks that Link Content and Technology

Following are three sample cubes in music, secondary language, and physical education that can also be converted to ThinkDots. Art teachers, don't feel left out. These examples are easy to follow and can be customized. Cubing and ThinkDots are kinesthetic activities that your middle schoolers will enjoy. They may seem elementary to you, but students find them appealing because they associate the rolling of the cube/die and the die-like image on the ThinkDots with games. Furthermore, the role of the cube or the die gives you a break, because chance, not the teacher, determines students' assignments!

FIGURE 8.1 ■
Music Cube

Compare and contrast blues and jazz using an online Venn diagram. How are they alike, and how are they different?

Create a bookmark of your favorite jazz musician. Use our bookmark template in Publisher (www.everythingdi.net/docs/explorerbmtemplate.pdf). You will have to modify, as the example is for Explorers. Draw his or her portrait in MS Paint, and insert it on the front side. On the back side, tell about his or her contribution to jazz and include biographical information.

What were three of the major cities where jazz took hold? Use Inspiration or another online Webbing application to map out details about each one.

Perform one of your favorite jazz or blues pieces or songs for the class. Dress in clothing appropriate for the time period. Record audio and/or video, if desired.

There are a number of different jazz styles, such as be-bop, Dixieland, swing, hardbop, big band, post-bop, and so on. Choose two or three and prepare a poster or brochure (with Web Poster Wizard, Letter Bop, or My Brochure Maker) to inform the class about the major characteristics of each one.

Does jazz exist today? Defend your answer in attractive letter format in MS Publisher with concrete examples.

FIGURE **8.2** ■
World Languages Cube

Create your family tree using Inspiration or another online mapping application. Identify your relationship with relatives in the target language.

Write a postcard to your favorite family member using My Postcard Maker. Tell him or her what you're learning in class about family.

Create an album or page for an album with My Album Maker about a favorite event that you shared with your family. Label your family members using terms in the target language, and include other sprinkles of the target language wherever possible.

Write a simple poem, such as a haiku, an acrostic (using person's name), or an adjective poem that describes your favorite family member. Type it into Publisher and spice it up with color and borders.

Craft a "WANTED" poster of one of your family members using Web Poster Wizard or Publisher. Include person's name, favorite color, age, hobby, location, when and where last seen, and so on.

Write a short dialogue and perform it with three other group members. Two of you are children, and the other two are parents. Introduce one another, making sure to include a greeting, a goodbye, some expression of pleasure about meeting one another, and an inquiry as to how they are. Record it if you wish.

FIGURE **8.3** ■
Physical Education Cube

Draw a diagram of a baseball diamond (in Paint or other drawing software) and label all positions.

Baseball has its own lingo. Identify some of the unusual terms learned in class and define them, such as tater, southpaw, grand slam, and so on. Accompany the words with clip art or a visual so a word and picture connection is made. Use PowerPoint or Publisher.

You are a pitcher who has to explain your pitching repertoire to your new catcher. Define the following pitches: curve, fastball, fork ball, knuckleball, slider, screwball, sinker, and change-up. Describe when you would use each one and how the ball moves. Use PowerPoint, Publisher, or begin your own wiki.

Watch Abbott and Costello's classic comedy routine, "Who's on First?" (available on YouTube). Perform it with a classmate and record it.

With a classmate, teach or perform two songs about baseball, or give a dramatic reading of "Casey at the Bat." Add some sound clips to accompany your reading.

Investigate the career of a baseball umpire. Research what it takes to achieve major-league status, how much umpires are paid, how many games they umpire, and how much travel is required. Prepare a brochure for "prospective umpires" using My Brochure Maker.

Get Gabby with the WWW

In addition to all the phenomenal visual resources available online, there are plenty of tools for speaking and listening. Not only is this useful for students who benefit from added features, such as text-to-speech and the like, but also for our music and secondary language students in particular. Gone are the days when we have to record something on cassette or videocassette and then physically carry it to someone or drop it off someplace. The Internet provides us with resources that enable us to make audio and video recordings in the comfort of our own homes and classrooms.

We mentioned back in Chapter 3 that podcasts can come in three forms: audio, visual, and video. Our students can profit from listening to and creating podcasts. Take a close look at and lend a good ear to these worthwhile encore projects.

Art

Digital Video. Students choose a work of art from the exhibition site, investigate the artist who crafted it, and then interview the artist on tape using prepared questions and answers (www.wyckoffschools.org/eisenhower/teachers/olejarz/digitalvideo/metmuseum.html).

Clay Animation. Students create a "story without words" in triads after watching a Wallace and Gromit video. They use a storyboard to develop a plot and then share design, video, and editing duties (http://rb043.k12.sd.us/art_tech_8th.htm).

Physical Education

Video Podcast. The PE Department begins to warm up for the creation of the movie for the annual Film Festival (www.cobbk12.org/~mabry/podcast_enclosures/UltimateMabry.m4v).

Music

Demarest Middle School. A video of the winner, James Chen, a fifth grader at the Demarest Middle School, performing his recital at the Young Pianist Competition of New Jersey (http://dmsmusic.podomatic.com).

Cranbrook Composers' Podcasts. This is a listing of podcasts created, produced, and cast by students in the Music Triarts Class at Cranbrook Kingswood Middle School in Michigan (http://cranbrookcomposers.blogspot.com).

Secondary Languages

Spanish Podcast Debut. Señora Rivera's eighth grade Spanish students' first podcast about the alphabet with great rhythm and music (http://mabryonline.org/podcast_enclosures/Spanish01.mp3.mp3).

Be sure to explore a simple, free resource to create, find, and view podcasts at podOmatic (www.podomatic.com).

If you haven't tried it yet, Gabcast is a user-friendly podcasting and audio blogging website that offers an incredibly easy way to create and distribute audio content. Students can use a telephone (cell or landline) to generate a recording. Check out www.gabcast.com. Yackpack (www.yackpack.com) is a free, web-based interface that enables communication between students and teachers via written notes and microphone recordings. Instructors must invite students to enter their "pack." This is such a versatile tool, as it can be used for feedback and grading, discussion, speaking in real time, global collaboration, reading, and a myriad of other possibilities. Yackpack could be useful in any subject area.

Yet another conversational tool that enables us to utilize the Internet as our delivery service is the audio dropbox. You may put a dropbox on a webpage, wiki, or blog. Since it's a virtual tool, you may access it anytime, anyplace, provided that you have access to the Internet. You could utilize this tool for speaking assignments for any subject area, but those who teach languages and the performing arts would find this tool particularly attractive. Students record themselves right from within the webpage, and then their audio files are deposited into your dropbox automatically. You don't have to do anything more. Take a look at Michigan State University's Rich Internet Applications for Language Learning (http://clear.msu.edu/teaching/online/ria/index.php). You'll find an application called Conversations that is excellent for role playing, virtual interviews, or simulations. There are too many others to mention, so plan to spend some time exploring.

A way we can converse with those who live around the world is by enlisting our students in a collaborative project with ePals Global Community (www.epals.com) or GSN's Internet Project Registry (www.globalschoolnet.org/gsh/pr/). While many of the collaborative projects of the past centered on communication via e-mail or traditional letters, more and more students are connecting through cool resources, such as Skype (www.skype.com), a communicative tool that you can download to call someone via computer. Classes are getting together with other classes around the nation and the world to share projects, debate issues, ask for advice—almost anything you can imagine—without being bound by time and space. These exciting projects are not limited to academic subjects, but can be done in athletics and the fine arts. Endless possibilities abound! Art students can take digital photos of their creations, insert them into PowerPoint or Adobe Photoshop, and then create an art exhibition in the form of a slide show. They can use the Record Narration function to describe their work. They can use PhotoStory 3, iMovie, or Movie Maker to put together a video-based version with sound of their exhibition. Similar projects can be done with concerts, solos, or any type of musical or dramatic performances, as well as athletic competitions or instructional pieces about how to perform particular sports techniques. Secondary language students can produce a video that demonstrates how to cook a simple dish or explains a particular cultural custom or celebration. To extend this type of collaborative exchange, classes that communicate with others around the globe can compile their shared knowledge and experiences in a wiki or blog, which could include intriguing content for the aforementioned suggestions, such as:

- recipes for the cooking videos

- historical/biographical information or a classification activity about the musicians, artists, and athletes

- comparisons that contrast and track changes that have occurred in the types of art, music, dance, drama, and sports over a certain time period

If you need some additional resources to encourage globalspeak and sharing of projects or ideas, see The Kidlink Project (www.kidlink.net/kidspace/). You can find resources in 30 languages, and it's totally free. There are numerous public and private virtual rooms where students and teachers may work in partnership and discuss how subject matter relates to life skills. According to the overview at Kidlink, its purpose is to help students "understand their possibilities, set goals for life, and develop life-skills," and the goal is to "motivate learning by helping teachers relate local curriculum guidelines to students' personal interests and goals." These are a great online resources to help you further differentiate instruction by interest and help build your students' character and self-worth.

If you're searching for a blogging resource, you might consider Global Voices Online (http://globalvoicesonline.org). We like the description of the site that we found at Wikipedia (http://en.wikipedia.org/wiki/Global_Voices_Online#Translations_of_Global_Voices_Into_Other_Languages): "…an international network of bloggers and citizen journalists that follow, report, and summarize what is going on in the blogosphere in every corner of the world.".

The Lingua project is the translation arm of Global Voices Online, and there are 15 available languages into which information can be translated. Seven additional languages are up and coming. While this site brings perspectives and information from around the globe right into your classroom, keep in mind that not everything may be appropriate for your middle school learners.

For additional resources to promote awareness of news, music, and culture in other countries, be sure to stop by All Newspapers.com (www.allnewspapers.com) and Radio Locator (www.radio-locator.com).

Virtual Trips

Speaking of visits, you and your students can tour the world in your encore classrooms! Even as recently as a few years ago, we were just beginning to talk about virtual field trips and museums. Now we have powerful tools, such as Google Earth and webcams, that can transport us to exact locations and make us feel as though we are really in the midst of it all. No matter what subject you teach, we're certain that you and your students can come up with significant places that you associate with your specialization. All encore students could visit a museum of sorts. Physical education students might wish to transport themselves to a stadium or golf course. Music students would appreciate attending a concert, and art students might wish to visit an outdoor art gallery in a city.

If time permits, each week we try to have a group of two to four of our encore students escort the remainder of the class on a trip they plan. We limit the time of the visit so that it does not consume the entire class period. The tour guides must prepare a travel itinerary ahead of time in the form of a brochure or one page sheet. They create a name for their tour company and create the document as if it were a publication from their organization. They must advise us of any potential travel hazards and be willing to answer questions from the tour group. At least one of the students must address some historical aspect of the tour. A great place to start is the Virtual Library Museums (http://icom.museum/vlmp/). Make sure to examine the following additional links:

Virtual Field Trips: www.Internet4classrooms.com/vft.htm

Walter McKenzie's Innovative Teaching—Virtual Field Trips: http://surfaquarium.com/IT/vft.htm

Utah Education Network: www.uen.org/utahlink/tours/fieldtrips2.cgi?core_area_id=0

FIGURE **8.4** ■ Discover Artists and Their Works virtual field trip website
© Utah Education Network (www.uen.org). Used with permission.

Online Flashcards

As we endeavor to prepare our students for life beyond the classroom and the world of work, we involve them in collaborative projects and interactive tasks. Although some of you might not agree, we believe that there is still some information that our students need to have at their fingertips without thinking twice. Examples are verb conjugations and essential vocabulary in a secondary language, anatomical and sports terms, music and art terminology, and so forth. However, we can't think of any reason that our 21st-century students should be required to create paper flashcards. Many of them are visual learners who are motivated by technology. Furthermore, online flashcard generators allow you to save your work and return to it, most of the time at no charge. Popular sites such as Quia offer flashcards; we'd like to share some sites that might be new to you and your students.

Quizlet: http://quizlet.com

StudyStack: www.studystack.com

Knowtes: https://www.knowtes.com

FlashcardExchange: www.flashcardexchange.com

The majority of online flashcard generators allow you to use existing stacks created by others for your own benefit. Some permit sharing, and some (such as StudyStack) also provide a hangman game, crossword puzzle, matching, word search, or word scramble options. You may also export your Study Stack flashcards to your cell phone, PDA, or iPod. With these great resources, paper flashcards should be passé.

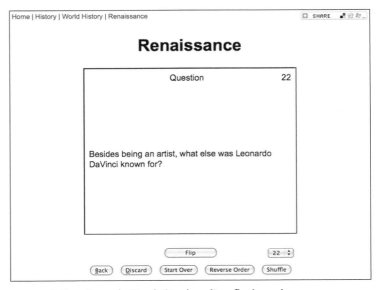

FIGURE 8.5 ■ Sample StudyStack online flashcard

© StudyStack (www.studystack.com). Used with permission.

Other Digital Tools and Interactive Sites that Jazz up Encore Classrooms

Physical Education/Health

In spite of the wealth of resources that we find at our fingertips at the beginning of the 21st century, some gaps still exist. We've encountered such a scarcity in the area of physical education, perhaps because the focus of most physical education classes is still traditional children's games and sports. With the current epidemic of childhood obesity and juvenile diabetes, we are certainly not trying to imply that physical education students should become more deskbound. More and more resources about nutrition, disease, and wellness are becoming available, as are traditional lesson plans for physical education. If you want to inspire students who are reluctant participants in the PE classroom, try some of these digital tools on nutrition, personal health, and wellness:

Calculate your BMI: www.nhlbisupport.com/bmi/

See the additional links at this site under "Aim for a Healthy Weight": "Assessing Your Risk," "Limitations of the BMI," "Controlling Your Weight," and "Recipes."

BrainPOP: Health: www.brainpop.com/health

This site has superb videos and animations.

Activity Calorie Counter:
www.primusWeb.com/fitnesspartner/jumpsite/calculat.htm

Of course, your middle school students would appreciate the opportunity to use practical tech gadgets, such as a heart monitor, GPS, pedometer, and the like. Allow your tech-inclined students to use these worthwhile devices to determine baseline levels of fitness and to measure improvements. There are free downloads for some of these tools, such as Stopwatch Plus 1.02 (http://handheld.softpedia.com/get/Business/Time-Tracker/Stopwatch-Plus-56906.shtml).

In our conversations with PE instructors across the country, many seem to be concerned that technology will take too much time away from physical activities. Although students could certainly take statistics home that they tabulated in class and conduct further research, we've found that it's rare for PE teachers to assign homework. We are not here to advocate piling on the homework! However, some of the basic Microsoft applications, such as Excel or PowerPoint, or online interactive sites, such as Create a Graph (http://nces.ed.gov/nceskids/createagraph), are definitely useful for PE. Even the tools that teachers perceive as more "complex,", such as those used to produce digital stories, wikis, and so on, would bring a renewed enthusiasm to your PE classroom.

Take a moment to peruse some of these valuable resources for PE:

Health for Grades 7–12 Interactives (Utah Education Network):
www.uen.org/7-12interactives/health.shtml

This site offers wonderful interactives on the body, nutrition, the media, and other socially and emotionally driven topics, such as mental health and respect.

Jefferson County Schools' PowerPoint Collection—Health:
http://jc-schools.net/ppt-health.html

This site provides fun games to review and master health-related content.

ThinkQuest Library: www.thinkquest.org/library/cat_show.html?cat_id=15&

This site offers a huge quantity of educational websites about sports and recreation.

Mary Pat Ferraro's PE website: www.visitation.net/ferraro_msphyed.aspx

A nice starting point if you need motivation to produce your own webpage.

Although Get Your Blog in Shape (http://jhh.blogs.com/getyourbloginshape/) is written by elementary PE teacher Stacy Roper, we like the fact that she encourages dialogue between students and faculty about health-related issues. Blogs kept up to date by middle school PE teachers are hard to come by. Marc Agnello has an interesting article about water versus Coke on his blog, written in 2007 (http://wellsville.ny.schoolWebpages.com/education/components/board/default.php?sectiondetailid=113026&threadid).

The Physical Education Resources at Grosse Pointe Public Schools (www.gpschools.org/ci/depts/pe/home.htm) may also be helpful.

World Languages

Unlike PE teachers, instructors of world languages have enjoyed an explosion of web-based materials and technology resources. The Internet supplies a wealth of information ranging from grammar instruction to periodicals, podcasts, satellite radio, software, cultural and geographical facts, tutoring, and on and on. While it's impossible for us to compile an exhaustive list of resources, we would like to help you get started.

BrainPOP, one of our all-time favorite video/animation sites is available en español at http://es.brainpop.com.

The following sites are useful for students telling digital stories in another language:

Tech Head Stories: http://tech-head.com/dstory.htm

Telling Stories: ESL Strategies Multimedia Page:
www.prel.org/eslstrategies/multimedia.html.

Teach with Music for Spanish: http://spanishplans.com

If you are in need of two super sites with virtually everything you can possibly dream of, check out Jim Becker's Super Language website (www.uni.edu/becker/) and Sue LeBeau's ESL and World Language Resources (www.suelebeau.com/languages.htm).

For your academically motivated students, as well as those who like to play with online tools, allow them to try a user-friendly language learning site like Mango Languages (www.mangolanguages.com).

Teaching and Learning Spanish (http://teachinglearningspanish.blogspot.com) is a very helpful blog for those who teach Spanish and want to polish their own language skills.

Learn English with Pictures and Audio (www.my-english-dictionary.com) is a photo dictionary with audio. On this site, you will also find links to Learn English with Audio and Transliterations, as well as Learn Spanish with Audio and Transliterations. The latter two sites offer videos and printable study sheets.

At the end of the chapter, you'll find a table of additional links for World Languages that you and your students might want to investigate.

Art and Music

Teachers of art and music also have some amazing resources available to them that are too numerous to count. First, don't forget some of the comic creation sites we mentioned earlier in the book, such as Stripgenerator, Toon Doo, Make Beliefs Comix, Comic Creator, and others. If you and your students are into creating your own music and art, these sites are must-sees.

With Art.com's artPAD (http://artpad.art.com/artpad/painter/) students can create their own masterpiece or watch the creation of someone else's picture, with the option of adding to it. The "replay painting" command is amazing! It replays each and every stroke and layer of the painting from beginning to end.

The National Gallery of Art NGAKids site (www.nga.gov/kids/kids.htm) has a treasure trove of resources for your students to experiment with interactive tools, such as BRUSHster, PHOTO OP (introduction to digital photography and image editing), Collage Machine, Still Life, Flow, and many others. In addition, there are gallery guides in five languages, and the NGAClassroom link offers videos, podcasts, online tours, and much more.

Art Education 2.0: Using New Technology in Art Classrooms (http://arted20.ning.com) is a social networking site created on Ning, an online platform. A forum and a chat are available, along with a number of specific groups you may join (one of which is "Middle School Art Educators"), a blog, and featured websites. Some of the neat tools we've mentioned earlier on in this book, such as VoiceThread, Flickr, Google Docs, and many others, appear on this site in relation to art. Make sure you visit the "Annex."

In the words of its creators, SmARThistory (http://smarthistory.org) is a "free multimedia web-book designed as a dynamic enhancement (or even substitute) for the traditional and static art history textbook." While many of the contributors are college-level teachers, this site has some attractive features. The podcasts and videos are intended to sound casual or entertaining. The speakers do not presume to sound authoritative, but simply converse about their thoughts and suggest possible theories, ideas about the artwork in question and the artist. This is a non-threatening site that most middle school art students would enjoy.

If you have never spent time at the Incredible Art Education Resources site via Princetononline (www.princetonol.com/groups/iad/lessons/middle/), you have missed a major treat. A former middle school art teacher developed this site, full of games, curriculum resources, lesson plans, Internet links, rubrics, art from different cultures, and countless other wonderful items.

Artsonia (www.artsonia.com/teachers) claims to be the largest online museum of artwork created by kids. Participation is free, and numerous lesson plans submitted by teachers are available. Here's a spot where your students can publish their artwork.

Olga's Gallery (www.abcgallery.com) boasts 10,000-plus works of art, classified by artist, movement, and country.

The Artist's Toolkit (www.artsconnected.org/toolkit/) offers students the opportunity to watch animated demonstrations, create their own works, check out an online encyclopedia of key terms, and find examples of the concepts they are learning in works of art.

Technology Integration Resources for Art (www.gpschools.org/ci/ce/elem/art/home.htm) and Technology Integration Resources for Music (www.gpschools.org/ci/ce/elem/music/music.htm) are K–5 sites, but many of the teacher tools, reference links, and museums are useful for the middle school level. Grace, coauthor of this book, played a large role in creating these sites.

Sound Junction (www.soundjunction.org/whatissoundjunctionandwhatcanido.aspa?nodeid=1) permits you to create music, take it apart, learn about instruments and styles of music, and listen to others perform it and find out how they make it. Teacher resources abound, as well as some excellent interactive tools for composing and remixing.

Virtual Keyboard—Piano (www.bgfl.org/bgfl/custom/resources_ftp/client_ftp/ks2/music/piano/) is a virtual keyboard with various drum beats and options to have the keyboard sound like another instrument. This site offers simple fun.

JamStudio (www.jamstudio.com/Studio/) states they offer "an online music factory" that people can use to compose their own music, but it also serves as an online band (drums and bass) to accompany those who need to practice guitar or another instrument.

Although Blast (www.bbc.co.uk/blast/music/tipsandtools) is for students aged 13–18 years, it has some useful tools and tips that are engaging for middle schoolers. Here you'll find an online music dictionary, information about music careers, genres, equipment, and various ways to craft different types of music.

Joseph Pisano, a professor at Grove City College, offers some practical links for music freeware and software on his MUSicTECHnology.net blog: http://mustech.net/freeware/, as well as at the Top 25 Music and Education-Related Web 2.0 Sites as Selected by My College Music Students: http://mustech.net/2008/03/15/the-top-25-music-and-education-related-Web-20-sites-as-selected-by-my-college-music-students.

The following links offer additional content-based interactives, games and role plays, and countless other features.

SAAM (Smithsonian American Art Museum) Interactives: http://americanart.si.edu/education/interactives/index.cfm

A Lifetime of Color: www.alifetimeofcolor.com

EduWeb: www.eduWeb.com/portfolio/visualarts.php

Learning at Whitney: http://whitney.org/learning/url=%2Flearning%2Fcollector%2Findex.php

ArtExplorer: www.artic.edu/artexplorer

Jefferson County Schools Art Presentations: http://jc-schools.net/PPTs-art.html

eMusicTheory.com Practice: www.emusictheory.com/practice.html

Interact: www.emusictheory.com/interact.html

Essentials of Music: www.emusictheory.com/interact.html

Enjoyment of Music: Online Tutor: www.wwnorton.com/college/music/enj9/shorter

Smithsonian Global Sound: www.smithsonianglobalsound.org/index.aspx

BrainPOP Arts and Music: www.brainpop.com/artsandmusic

Now let's turn to a more detailed strategy that is driven by student choice and accountability. Learning contracts offer a valuable means to differentiate instruction at all levels and in all subject areas.

Learning Contracts

The middle school years are a perfect time to use learning contracts. At this age level, students are beginning to transition emotionally from elementary dependence to teenage independence. They need to make the same kind of transition academically from dependent to self-sufficient learner. As a middle school teacher or administrator, you will not witness the completion of that conversion during the few years your students are in your building. However, perhaps our most important charge as teachers of future leaders is to guide them on the path to self-sufficiency. Learning contracts provide a comfortable means to steer students down that path, as directives are spelled out; additionally, options for interest-based learning are provided.

A learning contract is a signed agreement between you and an individual student. If you have not tried learning contracts with your students in the past, expect to encounter some resistance. Signing a document of any sort equals responsibility, and the same is true with the learning contract you present to your students. It might be overwhelming for students at first when they glance at the pages of outlined objectives, rubrics, timelines, and activities plus being held accountable for their own learning. These components clarify expectations and standards by which students will be assessed, thereby avoiding attempts to argue that deadlines have not been announced or that expectations were not clear. After students have the chance to become familiar with the learning contract, they will recognize that it offers some choices that will personalize their own learning experiences. Fortunately, learning contracts may be differentiated to accommodate diverse learning profiles, levels of readiness, and interests; teachers may do this without having to create 25 or 30 separate contracts.

The following steps will help you implement learning contracts:

1. As a general rule, develop three broad templates that relate to three typical levels of students:

   a. self-directed students who have a good command of core content,

   b. students who need to work through core materials from start to finish to comprehend them, and

   c. struggling students who don't understand core concepts.

2. Introduce anchoring at the beginning of the unit and help students elect their preferred anchor activities from a list of options.

3. Include tasks that involve choices from an assortment of interests or learning styles.

4. Build in assessment and progress checks throughout the contract.

   a. Pre-contract activity:

      ■ Use KWL charts to find out what your students know and what they'd like to investigate.

   b. In-progress activities:

      ■ Meet and consult with students as they work on individual assignments.

> ■ Record group participation and homework grades to make sure they're on target.
>
> ■ Fill out self-evaluations to help them improve time management and organizational skills (optional).
>
> **c.** Post-contract activities:
>
> ■ Assess student work.
>
> ■ Have students complete self-evaluations.

Once students get beyond the initial distress brought on by your "new teaching method," the majority will get on board and come to appreciate learning contracts. Learning contracts prevent boredom associated with re-learning material students have already mastered and eliminate busy work. In addition, students are usually excited about completing tasks that appeal to their passions, as well as the opportunity to work at their own pace. Learning contracts also go hand-in-hand with curriculum compacting, should you happen to use that differentiated strategy.

A Sample Differentiated Learning Contract Using Technology

It's possible you've never seen a learning contract before, so we're going to show you one designed for seventh or eighth graders. Often times, students are disengaged in the classroom because activities are very teacher-driven via whole class instruction. Many middle schoolers are still completing countless study guides with questions or textbook-based questions that they answer in writing. At the end of a unit, teachers assign a report and give a major test; and during the unit itself, students take quizzes and fill out worksheets.

In order to give encore teachers another example, we elected a topic that is studied in health class or science class: sun safety. It happens to be a part of the GLCEs for our state under the Personal Health and Wellness strand, and it matches up with several of the National Health Standards set forth by the American Cancer Society. We found it to be an intriguing topic for many middle grade students, as they are becoming more preoccupied with appearance and are influenced by what they see on TV, as well as by their peers' opinions. On top of that, most adolescents enjoy being in the sun, spending time on the beach, boating, and doing other outdoor activities.

We imagine that Mr. Sullivan, an eighth grade health teacher, has prepared the learning contract below for his students. Students are comfortable working individually or in flexible groups, and they are adept at using the software applications and web resources mentioned in the Learning Activities section of the contract. Mr. Sullivan has described how the learning contract works and what students will complete independently and in pairs.

On the following pages is a sample learning contract that Mr. Sullivan will present to the students in his class.

Sun Safety

Your Name: _____

Learning Contract

This learning contract covers your investigation of sun safety and products you will create. You will be able to do some of your work independently and some with a partner or group. Check off each box once you have completed an activity.

Warm-Up Activities

1. Find out what you already know about sun safety.

☐ Take the Sun Safety Quiz at www.chp.edu/CHP/Sun+Safety+Quiz.

☐ Print out the last page with your score and attach it to this contract.

2. Understand common facts and myths about sun exposure.

☐ In threes, play "Two Truths and a Lie" with the printed cards Mr. Sullivan gave to you. Each person has three cards containing common facts and myths about sun exposure. Two of your cards reflect factual information, and one is inaccurate. As you read your cards to your group members, they must decide which one is untrue.

☐ Report your results during sharing time with the whole class.

Required Activities

1. Familiarize yourself with the serious consequences of not practicing sun safety and how widespread the problem is in our country.

☐ Watch the "Harmful UV Radiation" video in groups of three or four at www.epa.gov/sunwise/media/forecastearth_4_300.wmv.

☐ Each member of the group should write down two facts that really shocked him or her. Share at the end of the video, and discuss why you were so surprised.

2. Begin to understand your genetic risks and predispositions.

☐ Print out, complete, and attach the Fitzpatrick Skin Type classification at www.skincancer. org/fitzpatrick-skin-quiz.html.

☐ Compare and contrast your results with a partner from the above exercise using this interactive graphic organizer: http://lexiconsys.com/graphic_organizers/candclndx.html. Enter the information; print and attach it to this contract.

☐ Survey your parents, grandparents (if possible), and siblings to find out the following: frequency of use of sunscreen (and use of other protective measures), most commonly used SPF, number of times they seriously burned (with blisters) before age 20, and names of relatives (and their relationship to you) who have suffered from skin cancer (and, if possible, what type).

continued

☐   Explore heredity and cancer at www.cancer.org/docroot/CRI/content/CRI_2_6x_ Heredity_and_Cancer.asp?/sitearea.+/.

☐   Take notes and prepare a table of the information in Word or Excel. Print and attach your table to the contract.

3. Investigate "The Skinny on Skin" at Discovery Education Science, an exploratory module and video to help you learn more about the skin and its layers and parts.

☐   After you complete the module, you and other members of a peer group will share the results of your surveys, the information you gleaned from them, and the Exploration module in Discovery Education Science.

☐   Complete a three-circle Venn diagram (http://interactives.mped.org/view_interactive. aspx?id=28&title=) that compares and contrasts the information each of you obtained about relatives' sun safety habits and sun-related conditions. Print the diagram and attach it to the contract.

4. With a partner, view information about teens and sunning behavior, and surf for any additional information related to that topic or other basic information.

☐   Share a computer to investigate either website number 1 or 2 from the table below, plus any three of the websites numbered 3–7. Take notes individually (on paper) to outline the major points of each resource, including the main idea and three or four important, supporting facts.

☐   Discuss the facts with your partner to make sure you understand them.

✓ when complete	Title and Webpage Address (URL)

	Sites that offer lots of information in many categories. Number one is written by teens, for teens:
	   1. It's Cool in the Shade!: http://coolshade.tamu.edu/index1.html
	   2. Sun Safe Colorado—Sun Safety at School: www.sunsafecolorado.org/mainSchool.shtml

	Sites that focus on problems associated with teen tanning, as well as the hazards of indoor tanners:
	   3. Teen Tanning video (excerpt from Today Show): www.youtube.com/watch?v=Vry088hiNz0
	   4. "Study Shows Tanning May Be Addictive": www.wpxi.com/health/14310710/detail.html
	   5. Young Tanners at Risk: www.skincancer.org/young-tanners-at-risk.html
	   6. The Case Against Indoor Tanning: www.skincancer.org/The-Case-Against-Indoor-Tanning.html
	   7. *Time* magazine article: "Why Teens Are Obsessed with Tanning": www.time.com/time/magazine/article/0,9171,1220506,00.html

continued

5. Opinion Paragraph

☐ Work independently and use your notes to write an opinion paragraph about your position on teen tanning and the possibility of addiction. Do you agree with what you read/viewed in the sources above? Why or why not? How risky would it be for you personally to tan frequently? Think about the results of your skin assessment and your family survey.

☐ Support your opinion with the facts you recorded from the websites. Facts can be checked for accuracy. An opinion is based on a personal belief or view.

☐ Attach your opinion paragraph after you type and print it.

Opinion Paragraph Rubric			
Categories	**Criteria**		**My Score**
	1 point	0 points	
Capitalization	I have zero to two errors in capitalization.	I have three or more errors in capitalization.	
Conclusion	My paragraph has a conclusion.	My paragraph does not have a conclusion.	
Descriptive Words	My writing has pizzazz. My word choices are descriptive. I may have used a thesaurus.	My writing isn't very colorful; it's somewhat dull.	
Format	My writing has a title, a body, and the author's name. It's neatly written.	My writing may be missing the title or author's name. It is not neatly written.	
Organization	My paragraph is well organized and in logical order.	My paragraph is poorly organized and hard to understand.	
Position Statement	My opinion position is clearly stated.	My opinion position is not clear.	
Punctuation	I have zero to two errors in punctuation.	I have three or more errors in punctuation.	
Sentence Structure	More than two-thirds of my sentences are mostly correct.	More than one-third of my sentences are incorrectly written.	
Source of Evidence	My sources for evidence are included.	My sources for evidence are not included.	
Supporting Evidence	My evidence supports my position.	My evidence is unrelated to or does not support my position.	
TOTAL POINTS			

continued

6. Choice of Learning Activities

Choose one option from each column and discuss with your teacher what you would like to do to learn more about sun safety. At the very end of the learning contract, you will find some useful "Starter Spots" on the Internet to help you with your research.

Scientist/Statistician	Dermatologist/ Public Health Expert	Writer	Artist
☐ Collect statistics from the last several years on the increase in skin cancer in various age groups. Graph your information and prepare a short paragraph that analyzes the results. (Use GraphMaster or InspireData.)	☐ Chart (or make a table) how the sun's rays can be beneficial and harmful to the human body. Include graphics. (Use MS Word or Inspiration.)	☐ Write a letter to the editor that highlights the dangers of teen tanning and what should be done about it. (Use MS Word.)	☐ Today's culture communicates to us through media that tan is better. Make a collage of media images of tanned TV, music, and/or movie celebrities. (Use MS PowerPoint or LetterPop.)
☐ Educate your peers about the ozone layer and the negative effects of its depletion via a brochure or newsletter. Include pictures and basic information about its location, how it protects us, and how we're destroying it. (Use MS Publisher, My Brochure Maker, or Letter Pop.)	☐ Design a poster that identifies effective forms of sun protection, not just sunscreen. (Use MS Publisher or Web Poster Wizard.)	☐ Research the best sunscreens on the market (popular and lesser known). Write a script for an infomercial about what you think offers the most protection and why. (Use MS Word.)	☐ Create a rap or other musical piece that emphasizes why it's important to practice sun safety and what happens if you don't. (Use music composing software or an online program, such as Band-in-a-Box, Music Ace, or Audacity.)
☐ Create a personalized weather report for the next several days that includes a UV outlook index and recommended SPF for your age group, based on your planned activities and skin type. (Use MS Publisher or PowerPoint.)	☐ Identify the types of skin cancer associated with poor sun safety. Include images of each type. (Design a Webbe in MS Word or with RealeWriter software.)	☐ Write several riddles about sun safety and/or limericks about people who practice smart and/ or unwise behavior in the sun. Include illustrations. (Use MS Paint.)	☐ You are a talk show host. Invite a panel to talk on the topic of sun safety. Form a group with your classmates. Roles are dermatologist, teen with melanoma, parent of the teen, and owner of a tanning salon. Record with a traditional video camera or a miniDV camera and Movie Maker software.

continued

Citizenship and Work Habits

I agree to the following learning conditions:

☐ I agree to follow our class ground rules.

☐ I agree to complete my work on time.

☐ I agree to do my personal best.

☐ I agree to give credit to sources that I use to complete my assignments.

Student's Signature: _____ Date: _____

Teacher's Signature: _____ Date: _____

Starter Spots for Choice Board Products

▷ **Cool Antarctica: Antarctic Ozone Hole:**
   www.coolantarctica.com/Antarctica fact 20file/science/ozone_hole.htm

▷ **National Weather Service Climate Prediction Center Stratosphere Home:**
   www.cpc.ncep.noaa.gov/products/stratosphere

▷ **Ozone Guarding Our Earth:** www.ec.gc.ca/ozone/DOCS/KIDZONE/EN/guardearth.cfm

▷ **Ozone Hole Tour:** www.atm.ch.cam.ac.uk/tour

▷ **Skin Cancer:** www.cdc.gov/cancer/skin/basic_info

▷ **Sun Safety:** www.nsc.org/ehc/sunsafe.html

▷ **Sun Safety:** www.emc.cmich.edu

▷ **Sun Safety Alliance:** www.sunsafetyalliance.org

▷ **Sunny Days, Healthy Ways Grades 6–8 Curriculum:**
   www.sdhw.info/curriculum/1_grades_6–8_written.asp

▷ **Sunsafe in the Middle School Years:** http://sunsafe.dartmouth.edu

▷ **Sunwise:** www.epa.gov/sunwise

▷ **The Ozone Layer: What's Going on Up There?:**
   www.ec.gc.ca/ozone/DOCS/KIDZONE/EN/ozoneupthere.cfm

▷ **The Science of Ozone Depletion:**
   http://dwb.unl.edu/Teacher/NSF/C09/C09Links
   www.epa.gov/ozone/science/science.html

▷ **Weather.com Rays Awareness Index:** www.weather.com/learn/raysawareness

An option that you might wish to include in the example learning contract, following the tic-tac-toe board (if time permits), would be an assignment for flexible groups based on readiness, learning profile, or interest. Students could devise a plan to make their school more sun safe. (The EPA has a program called "SunWise." Schools have to fulfill certain criteria to become qualified as "SunWise" schools. See www.epa.gov/sunwise/.) If you opted to differentiate by learning profile, you could ask each group to produce a product (one part of the project) that connected well with their learning style. Auditory learners could create a musical jingle or song; kinesthetic learners could perform a skit or create a physical/board game; visual learners could design posters, graphs, and so on. If you elected to differentiate based on interest, prepare a list of possible subtopics or products, and allow students to voice their preferences as to which group they'd favor based on their interest in the topic. If you decided to divide students by levels of readiness, you'd need to choose heterogeneous or homogeneous groups. At the end of the project, display the students' work, or better yet, ask your principal if you can present it in front of the school, parents, and/or other classrooms at grade level.

Learning contracts are extremely effective because they clearly outline the tasks that need to be completed and the requirements that students must fulfill. You might also want to supply additional supports, such as pacing guides and checklists to increase students' chances for success. Although you might be tempted to think that middle schoolers should be able to keep track of deadlines, remember that those overtaxed brains and bodies function more efficiently with lots of reminders about expectations, organization, and target dates. Self-evaluation and peer-evaluation, a collaboration rubric, and display and sharing of final products are other important activities. The learning contract we developed above is simply a model to give you an idea as to what one might look like and how you can use it with your students. You may embellish your contracts with color or clip art, or you can make yours even more detailed. There are no absolutes in terms of length, so do not feel pressured to include numerous tasks within the contract. In fact, it would be wise to start off with a short contract and then move to more elaborate contracts. Our intent here is to provide a "middle of the road" idea. Regardless of the contract's physical design, we think you'll encounter positive results in your classroom when you offer your students more learning choices. You'll also be pleased to discover that learning contracts modify your teaching responsibilities and engage you as you observe the development of their final products.

Summary

We hope that you and your students will be motivated to try out new formats that involve global communication and hands-on learning. As the world's population increases, the distance between people and cultures is shrinking, largely as a result of technology. Seize the unique instructional opportunities that you find before you! Make the world your classroom with some of these exciting digital tools and techniques as you bring new strategies and technology in to support encore learning.

Additional Resources
for Multiple World Languages

German Internet Project: www.uncg.edu/~lixlpurc/GIP

Japan @ UT-Martin's Globe-Gate: www.utm.edu/staff/globeg/japan.shtml

TeAch-nology: French Lesson Plans:
www.teach-nology.com/teachers/lesson_plans/languages/french

TeAch-nology: German Lesson Plans:
www.teach-nology.com/teachers/lesson_plans/languages/german

Tennessee Bob's Famous French Links:
www.utm.edu/departments/french/french.html

WebGerman: http://Webgerman.com

GlobeGate Spanish Language and Culture Pages: http://globegate.utm.edu/spanish

Foreign Language Teaching Forum WWW Resources for Language Teachers:
www.cortland.edu/flteach/flteach-res.html

iLoveLanguages: Your Guide to Foreign Language Resources on the Web:
www.ilovelanguages.com/index.php?category=Languages

Internet Activities for Foreign Language Classes: www.clta.net/lessons

Kathy Shrock's Guide for Educators: Regions of the World & World Languages:
http://school.discovery.com/schrockguide/world/worldrw.html

(Dr. Sass') Resources and Lesson Plans for World Languages:
www.cloudnet.com/~edrbsass/edwor.htm

(Dr. Sass') WebQuests Across the Curriculum:
www.cloudnet.com/~edrbsass/Webquest.html

Omniglot: www.omniglot.com

Spanish NewsBites: www.spanishnewsbites.com

Spanish Flashcards: www.online-spanish-course.com

Spanishpod, Chinesepod, Frenchpod, Englishpod, Italianpod:
http://spanishpod.com/about

"Mi vida loca": www.bbc.co.uk/languages/spanish/mividaloca
This site is a Spanish interactive video mystery/online application for beginners.

BBC Languages: www.bbc.co.uk/languages

Babbel: www.babbel.com

SpanishLingq: www.spanishlingq.com
This site also has links to other language Lingqs.

FIGURE **8.6** ■
Front side of
ThinkDots
cards

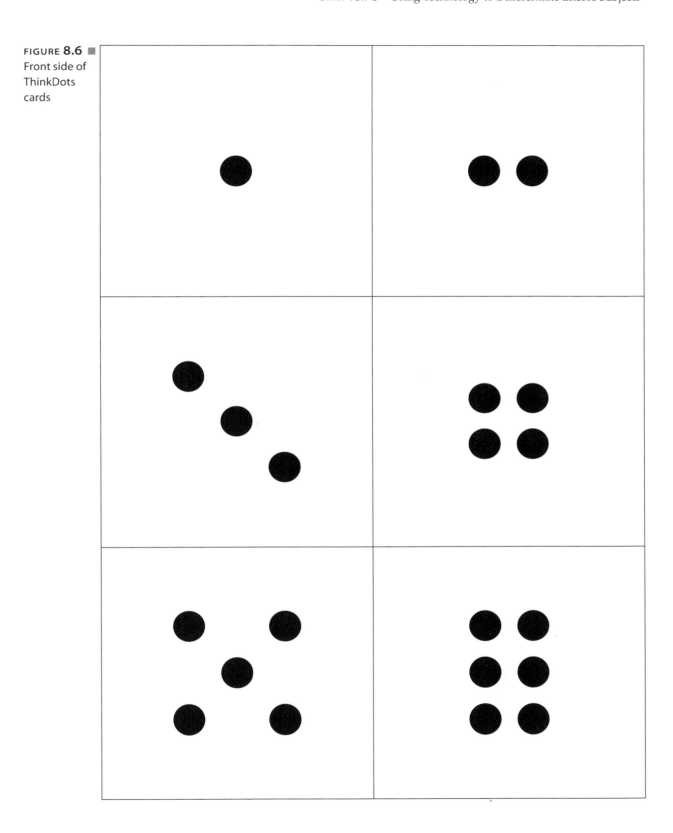

FIGURE **8.7** ■
Blank Cubing Template

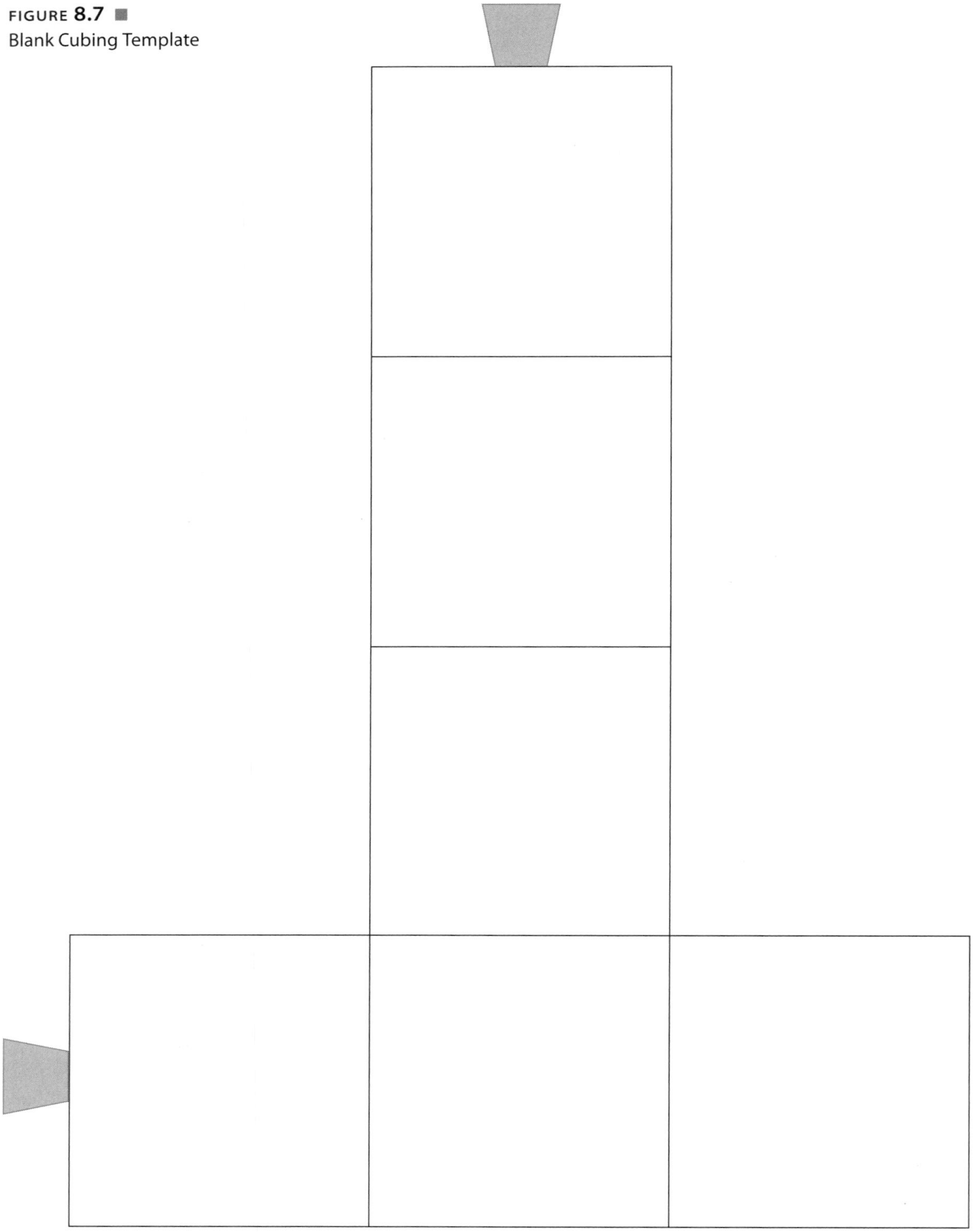

CHAPTER 9

Using Technology to Assess Learning

When educators and parents think of the term assessment, paper and pencil usually come to mind, probably because for many years teachers have traditionally used these tools to test learning. In today's classrooms though, many types of assessment strategies can be used to measure learning and discover information needed for differentiating instruction. Newer strategies include technology.

Educators are not always clear about the terms "assessment" and "evaluation;" however, in general, they believe that:

1. Assessment means the collecting of data to understand students' current knowledge, understandings, and skills more completely. Assessments can be large-scale; that is, the sort of assessment that is used in most districts and states to rank schools and students for accountability purposes. Or they can be the classroom assessments that teachers create. These teacher assessments are the tests, written assignments, quizzes, and homework papers that teachers assign to chart progress.

2. Evaluation refers to the summative or cumulative analysis of learners' skills, abilities, and performances at a given point in time in order to make judgments and compute letter grades. Evaluations are usually made at the end of a term, semester, or school year.

In this chapter, we discuss the three categories of assessment that teachers use and provide some strategies and resources for adding technology. We also want to show where assessment fits into the curriculum cycle, for assessment is not an isolated event outside of curriculum and instruction. Assessment is an integral part of the curriculum cycle, so let's start with the interconnectedness among curriculum, instruction, and assessment.

Curriculum, Instruction, Assessment, plus Technology

The three components of any course are (1) its curriculum or content, (2) the instructional strategies teachers use to deliver that content, and (3) assessment, which measures how well students have accomplished content learning goals. Assessment plays an important role because it measures student learning, provides feedback on instruction, and provides data and direction for modifying and differentiating curriculum.

We very much like the rotating diagram portrayed on the USD 204 Bonner Springs/ Edwardsville, Kansas website (www.usd204.k12.ks.us/cia) and the model at the Field-Tested Learning Assessment Guide (FLAG) site (www.flaguide.org/start/assess_in_ context.php). Both illustrations show the traditional interrelationship among curriculum, instruction, and assessment with the three parts making the whole.

However, we propose an updated model that includes the technologies that both students and educators use in instruction, curriculum, and assessment. Instructional technologies have such a powerful impact on teaching, learning, and assessment, as well as 21st century skills, that the technology component can stand on its own and, therefore, be included in the curriculum cycle as an equal part. That said, our model consists of the four components fitting tightly together as pieces of the learning and teaching puzzle.

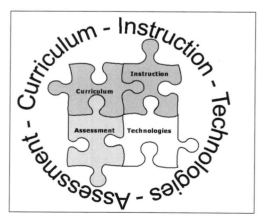

FIGURE 9.1 ■ Model depicting the interrelationships among curriculum, instruction, assessment and technologies.
© 2007 Everythingdi.net

You've probably noticed that technology is changing and continues to change the ways curriculum is provided, delivered, and assessed. Most of the newer software products, for example, have built-in assessment tools so assessments can be made and feedback can be provided to students and teachers. Here are some examples of technology-driven products on the market right now.

FASTT Math, a Codie Award Winner (2006), is a terrific example of newer software for Grades 2–8 that delivers content based on three types of assessment. The "Placement Quiz" pre-assesses students' fluent and non-fluent facts. Based on this assessment, the program creates a customized course of study for individual students. During instruction, the program generates frequent, automatic assessments to ensure that students are receiving the correct amount of practice exactly where they need it. Finally, the "Fact Fluency Foundations" guide provides assessments for teachers to determine where students need additional help. More information is available at www.tomsnyder.com.

In the examples below, student Kayla Holland's screen shows the results of her placement assessment in FASTT Math. Color shading indicates the facts in which Kayla is already fluent, which facts that she will currently focus on, and the facts to be learned.

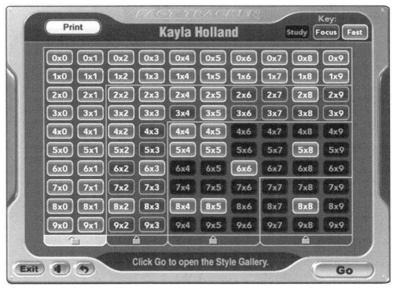

FIGURE **9.2** ■ FASTT Math's placement assessment
© Tom Snyder Productions, Inc. Reprinted with permission.

The "Study Facts" screen illustrates customized instruction to help Kayla visualize and learn her facts. In FASTT Math software, the computer assesses students' progress and specifies individual instruction based on students' responses.

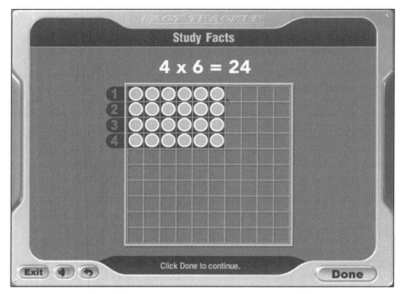

FIGURE **9.3** ■ FASTT Math features adaptive instruction, customizing instruction to target fluency gaps. © Tom Snyder Productions, Inc. Reprinted with permission.

Cognitive Tutor Algebra I by Carnegie (http://carnegielearning.com) is another content-delivered program with built-in assessments and tracking. This product is a 2007 Codie Award winner.

Another type of software is the Measures of Academic Progress (MAP) and other products from the Northwest Evaluation Association (NWEA) that assess learning in several subjects. NWEA (www.nwea.org) offers state-aligned computer adaptive tests to measure student achievement and growth, and resources for teachers to apply test results to instructional grouping and differentiated instruction.

Pre-Assessment, Formative Assessment, and Summative Assessment

First we will describe three types of assessment. We'll then compare and contrast their attributes in a table to illustrate how they are alike and how they differ.

Pre-assessment refers to the types of assessment that occur prior to an instructional segment, including the assessments that identify learners' traits, preferences, and skills. Pre-assessments are sometimes called diagnostic because they help teachers diagnose learners' similarities and differences in skills and content knowledge so that teachers can make instructional decisions tailored to students' needs.

The purpose of pre-assessment is to gather information and to diagnose learners' entry levels. Pre-assessments determine students' current levels of readiness, interests, or learning profiles and allow teachers to meet students at their various levels. In other words, the intention of any pre-assessment is to know as much about learners as possible.

Formative assessment refers to the ongoing and frequent assessment that takes place simultaneously with instruction and learning to modify instruction and provide feedback to students. Just as pre-assessment is an important strategy, so is ongoing assessment.

The purpose of ongoing assessment is to take a "temperature check" of the classroom climate and provide specific feedback to teachers for the purpose of guiding teaching to improve learning. Teachers will also want to offer corrective feedback in a timely manner so that students have opportunities to improve. Simultaneously, teachers document students' performances to guide instructional decisions.

In *Classroom Instruction that Works* (2001), Robert Marzano et al. quote researcher John Hattie (1992) who says, "the most powerful single modification that enhances achievement is feedback. The simplest prescription for improving education must be 'dollops' of feedback."

Marzano discusses four generalizations about the use of feedback that are helpful to teachers:

1. Feedback should be corrective in nature.

2. Feedback should be timely.

3. Feedback should be specific to a criterion.

4. Students can effectively provide some of their own feedback.

Summative assessment refers to the assessment that follows instruction and is used for evaluation purposes. These assessments usually require demonstration or mastery of essential understandings. Summative assessments are usually reported as a score or grade. Typical evaluative assessments include final exams and culminating projects with a grade recorded on a transcript or report card.

Comparing Pre-Assessment, Formative Assessment, and Summative Assessment

In Table 9.1 we list the characteristics of each form of assessment, when it is used, why it is used, and how it is used to give you a better idea of similarities and differences.

Now that you have some descriptions, a comparison-contrast chart, and hopefully a better understanding of the three types of assessment, we want to show you how you can modernize your assessment practices by bringing in technology tools.

TABLE 9.1 ■ Comparing pre-assessment, formative assessment, and summative assessment

Element	Pre-Assessment	Formative	Summative
What	Diagnostic	Assessment *for* Learning	Assessment *of* Learning
When	Before content is taught	During teaching of content	After content is taught
Why	Identifies learners' individual needs to design instruction. Measures students' pre-knowledge and skills. Determines what students already know and understand about a unit of content. Clarifies which areas of content will require review, reteaching or enhancement. Expands knowledge of students' interests, readiness, and learning profiles to help determine flexible groups.	Used to adjust instruction. Provides feedback to students in the form of praise, constructive criticism, or guidance. Provides students with information about what they currently understand. Provides students with information for improvement. Provides correct instruction. Identifies gaps in learning and/or where students exceed expectations.	Assesses students' success in attaining knowledge, concepts, and skills that were the goals of instruction. Evaluates the effectiveness of an instructional program. Represents a culmination of learning experiences.
Who	Classroom teacher	Classroom teacher	Classroom teacher
How (Traditional)	Paper and pencil	Observation Practice activities, such as ungraded quizzes Homework, worksheets, checklists Student self-checking lists, rubrics, journals, logs	End of chapter/unit/year tests Standardized tests Statewide or district accountability tests
How (Using Technology)	Online survey	Clickers Blogs or discussion boards Handhelds Online surveys E-portfolios Software	Online or computerized
Where	Classroom	Classroom	Classroom
Grading	None	No Final Grade	Graded or Scored

In the next sections we cover both pre-assessment and formative assessment strategies, kicking them up a notch via technologies. Bear in mind that the same instrument could be used for both a pre-assessment and a formative assessment. How? Teachers could use the end of a unit test as a pre-test to measure what students already know. Or, last year's released items could be used as a pre-assessment for teaching a unit. That's why assessment types are a little confusing—because you can use them in more than one way. We've found that the easiest way to understand and classify an assessment is by its use. No matter what the instrument, tool, or practice is, how you use it is what counts!

To prevent muddying the waters, we have placed some information in tables. For the most part, Table 9.2 addresses pre-assessments and Table 9.3 addresses formative assessments. We do not cover evaluative or summative assessments, for many of the ideas in Table 9.3 can be expanded for summative assessments. Remember that you can use computer software, hardware, and web resources to generate pre-tests, make response cards, create surveys, and much more. The emerging technologies of Web 2.0 greatly help with assessment, and you will have fun learning them. In the following pages are some ideas to get you started.

TABLE **9.2** ■ Pre-Assessment Ideas

Example/Description	Traditional Pre-Assessments	Using Technology
1. **Checklists:** Checklists can be set up in different formats, ranging from very simple yes/no questions to more complex surveys that rate skills on a scale. For example, you might create a writing assessment checklist in which students check off whether they know writing mechanics and story elements and can identify or define them. Or you might create an assessment checklist for evaluating technology skills.	Paper/pencil	A checklist can be created using word processing in table format with the assessment items in the first column, space for checkmarks in the second column, and space for comments in the third column. Checklists can be easily set up in Word or Excel by creating a table with several columns and rows. You can also customize a checklist by using the online PBL Checklist Generator at http://pblchecklist.4teachers.org. Electronic documents can be e-mailed or posted for students to complete. You can also create a survey in Zoomerang and collect the results. A tech assessment would start off like the example below. _See nested table below._
2. **Entrance Cards:** Before a lesson, students respond in writing to a question or set of questions posed by the teacher or physically move to a part of the classroom that defines their knowledge about a certain topic.	Paper/pencil	Create questions in Word or Publisher and print them. Technology can help you make classroom signs. You can create your signs in word processing or publishing software or use the online tool Web Poster Wizard at http://poster.4teachers.org. Make four signs, such as "Hardly Ever," "Sometimes," "Often," and "All the Time," or words of your choice. Print the signs and post them in four corners of your room. Ask students to respond to your prompt by moving to the corner of the room sign that most closely matches their learner knowledge of the topic. Use clickers or similar technology such as student response systems.
3. **Games:** These are a fun way to pre-assess what students already know so you don't spend time reteaching content.	Paper/pencil	PowerPoint games are very popular and many of them are on the web for you to use. You can also design your own games/quizzes at Quia. See the chapter resources section at the end of this chapter for online locations of these tools.

Nested table within Checklists "Using Technology" cell:

Technology Skill: Multimedia Students will plan, design, and communicate a simple multimedia project for an audience.	Level: N = Novice D = Developing H = High			Comments
	N	D	H	
1. I can choose an appropriate design layout.				
2. I can choose an appropriate background.				
3. I can present the multimedia project in digital/ printed formats.				

continued

TABLE **9.2** ■ Pre-Assessment Ideas   *continued*

Example/Description	Traditional Pre-Assessments	Using Technology
4. **Interest Inventories:** Use an interest survey or inventory to get to know your students better.	Paper/pencil	You can create your own online student interest survey free at Zoomerang or Survey Monkey and then share the results with students. Check out the chapter resources to explore these tools. Students can use mapping software like Inspiration to create an interest map or the free webbing tool at Read Write Think (http://interactives.mped.org/view_interactive.aspx?id=127&title=).
5. **KWL Charts:** These are used to assess what students already know (K), what students want to know (W) and what students have already learned (L). KWL charts are an effective pre-assessment tool as well as a tool for evaluating students' level of understanding.	Paper/pencil	A KWL chart can be created in Word by inserting a table with three columns. You can also use one of the KWL charts found in the resources at the end of the chapter or Inspiration software.
6. **Multiple Intelligences Surveys:** These are used to identify students' preferred/customary learning styles. We have found it useful to assess students in their multiple intelligences and then hold a discussion about their results with the class.	Paper/pencil	One of our favorite online surveys is Pick an Alien (www.ncwiseowl.org/kscope/techknowpark/LoopCoaster/eSmartz2.html). We also like Caves of the Code Breakers (www.ncwiseowl.org/kscope/techknowpark/Secret/Welcome.html).
7. **Observations:** Students complete a task or activity as the teacher observes, takes notes, and/or records progress using a checklist or form. Observation is a fine assessment tool that can be used at any time.	Paper/pencil	You can create your own custom form in word processing software and print several copies to use on a clipboard in the classroom. If you have a handheld computer, you could create a form for that device and use it to record your observational notes. Later you would connect your handheld to your laptop or desktop computer to upload the data. More information about handheld assessment and two forms from Saskatchewan Learning are listed in the chapter resources.

continued

TABLE **9.2** ■ Pre-Assessment Ideas   *continued*

Example/Description	Traditional Pre-Assessments	Using Technology
8. **Pre-tests:** Designed to point out where students are in particular content areas and skills and can be used for guiding differentiated instruction. Pre-tests are often used in conjunction with curriculum compacting.	Paper/pencil	Teachers can use technology for pre-testing and scoring. Many teachers use post-tests or a derivation of them as pre-tests. Newer software also empowers you to create your own. The Electronic Assessment Tools section of the chapter resources provides several sites for you to explore. You may also want to look at some of the Microsoft tutorials for creating your own assessments. Quia (www.quia.com) is an online tool that features some shared tests created by teachers. You can also search for shared tests based on publishers' texts. Take a look at this geography quiz created by Mrs. D. Johnson as an example: www.quia.com/quiz/1202605.html?AP_rand=1450312346.
9. **Response Cards:** Students use paper cards to respond to questions posed by the teacher. The students hold up their answers for the teacher to check responses. Example: Yes/No Cards are cards students make with Yes on one side and No on the opposite side. Teachers ask a question (review or introductory). Students who know the answer hold up the Yes card; students who do not know the answer hold up the No card. This tool is especially useful when introducing new vocabulary words that students need for a new unit of study.	Paper/pencil	Response cards can be made with word processing software and laminated for long-term use. Better yet, have your students design the cards using similar software. New handheld response devices made by EInstruction, Turning Point, and other companies make responses really exciting. These tools are about the size of a TV remote control device. Students press buttons on the tools to respond to questions and other content posed by the teacher. Each response is recorded, and the sum of responses can be shown statistically. The teacher can also see who has/has not answered questions because each remote device has its own tracking number.
10. **Surveys/Inventories:** Surveys, questionnaires, and inventories are forms that contain a set of questions for gathering information.	Paper/pencil	Surveys and inventories can be designed using word processing. You can create a form and protect it so that it cannot be altered. You can also create a form for posting on the web. However, exciting new web-based software does a lot of the work for you in terms of design. Both Zoomerang and Survey Monkey offer free (limited) teacher accounts.

TABLE **9.3** ■ Formative Assessment Ideas

Example/Description	Traditional Formative Assessments	Using Technology
1. **Anecdotal Records:** These are short accounts or descriptive notes that describe students' behavior.	Paper/pencil	Since anecdotal records are really teachers' notes, teachers can use technology to set up forms for recording, or they can use handheld devices to record information as they walk around the classroom. The chapter resources section of the chapter offers sample forms and information about using handhelds for assessment.
2. **Checklists:** With these formatted lists of behaviors, teachers check off specific actions carried out or skills that have been mastered. Checklists should be specific, with easily observable behaviors that are age appropriate. Checklists can be set up in various formats ranging from simple, such as checking yes or no, to more complex, such as rating skills on a scale.	Paper/pencil	A checklist can be created using word processing in table format with the assessment items in the first column, space for checkmarks in the second column, and space for comments in the third column. Checklists can be easily set up in Word or Excel by creating a table with several columns and row. You can also customize a checklist by using the online PBL Checklist Generator at http://pblchecklist.4teachers.org. Electronic documents can be e-mailed or posted for students to complete. You can also create a survey in Zoomerang and collect the results.
3. **Discussion Questions:** These open-ended questions help teachers gather information on students' readiness.	Discussion	The contemporary format of classroom discussion questions is the blog or electronic discussion group. As long as a blog can be contained on a secure server (non-public), it can be safe for students to use. Commercial products, such as Gaggle (www.gaggle.net) and Class Blogmeister (http://classblogmeister.com) offer safe and secure settings; however, any blog must be monitored. Blogs can be used for almost any topic, including novel discussion, sharing ideas, and ongoing assessment.

continued

TABLE **9.3** ■ **Formative Assessment Ideas**   *continued*

Example/Description	Traditional Formative Assessments	Using Technology
4. **Games:** Games for middle school include simulations often used in social studies and science, vocabulary and related topics in ELA, and math/computational games. Games can be used to assess learning during teaching content. For example, what percent of the students in your class grasp the content you are teaching?	Paper/pencil or verbal	An engaging way to assess a group of students is through an electronic game format, such as Jeopardy or Millionaire. There are free PowerPoint game templates available on the web. We especially like the commercial products from FTC Publishing. Links and sample games are available in the chapter resources section at the end of this chapter. The sample screen shots in Figures 9.4 and 9.5 illustrate two Jeopardy-like games that can be purchased from FTC Publishing. We also like the concept of students' creation of board games using MS Publisher, PowerPoint, or Word to design the game boards and question cards. Designing a game requires critical thinking, and students can work in small teams to design their games based on a novel, topic, or current events.
5. **Learning Logs:** These are short, ungraded, and unedited writing that reflects on learning activities. The writings serve as a sort of journal for students to promote thinking in their writing.	Paper/pencil	Learning logs can be created in Word and used electronically or in print format. The chapter resources section offers an example of a learning log form. If your school allows it, try using Google Docs. See Chapter 3 of this book on Web 2.0 tools.
6. **Observations:** This is a method for circulating among flexible groups to learn how students are processing ideas and understanding concepts.	Paper/pencil	You can create your own custom form in word processing software and print several copies to use on a clipboard in the classroom. If you have a handheld computer, you could create a form for that device and use it to record your observational notes. Later you would connect your handheld to your laptop or desktop computer to upload the data. More information about handheld assessment and two forms from Saskatchewan Learning are listed in the chapter resources. Use the anecdotal forms described above, or create a checklist using technology, or consider Student Response Systems.
7. **Peer Review:** This process allows learners to give written or verbal feedback to other learners. Peers can use checklists, rubrics, or give a written or verbal response to peers' work.	Paper/pencil	Peer review documents can be created in Word and used electronically or in print. The chapter resources section offers several examples of peer review forms. If your school allows it, try using Google Docs. If not, try a shared folder on your server. See chapter 3 on Web 2.0 tools.

continued

TABLE **9.3** ■ **Formative Assessment Ideas** *continued*

Example/Description	Traditional Formative Assessments	Using Technology
8. **Portfolios of Work Samples:** These contain artifacts of students' work. Traditional portfolios are paper/pencil while electronic portfolios may be entirely digital. That is, students' 100% digital portfolios contain products made only with technology tools.	Paper/pencil	Electronic portfolios can be created with PowerPoint, word processing programs, blogging or similar software, or with commercial portfolio software. These digital portfolios contain artifacts created with technology software or some scanned materials. Students can create a portfolio in PowerPoint, for example, and hyperlink to digital art and artifacts created in MS Paint, MS Office and other software. An example of a student-led conference/portfolio template is available as a download at www.rst2.edu/ctee/files/elecPort.ppt. Helen C. Barrett's page (http://electronicportfolios.com) offers guides to creating portfolios in several software applications. Check our website at www.everythingdi.net/ for directions for making a portfolio in PowerPoint.
9. **Product Assessment Tools:** These assess student products constructed according to guidelines and rubrics presented prior to product development. Students can use project scoring guides to self-grade their products as well as self-assessment exercises.	Paper/pencil	Product assessments can be created in Word or Publisher in the form of rubric tables or Likert scales for self-grading of products. Open-ended student-reflective exercises can also be created to assess self and team.
10. **Reflective Journals:** This process can be used for students to reflect on their own learning. They can be open-ended, or the teacher can provide guiding, reflective questions for the students to respond to. Journals provide insight on how the students are synthesizing their learning, but they also help the students make connections and better understand how they learn.	Paper/pencil	Journal page samples are provided in the chapter resources section; however, it's easy for you to make your own template in Word or Publisher or a similar program.
11. **Response Cards:** This strategy is used with the whole class for responding on cue to teacher questions at the same time. Response cards are similar to exit cards except they are used during instruction and before the end of a unit.	Paper/pencil	Previously described in the pre-assessment section of this chapter, response cards are also useful for ongoing assessment.

continued

TABLE **9.3** ■ Formative Assessment Ideas *continued*

Example/Description	Traditional Formative Assessments	Using Technology
12. **Rubrics:** These scoring tools list the criteria for a product or performance. Rubrics show gradations of quality for each criterion in a range from poor to excellent.	Paper/pencil	Construct your own rubrics by looking at those created by other teachers. Examples abound at RubiStar and Kathy Schrock's Guide. One caution about rubrics. Many rubrics are not high quality. Rubrics should be both qualitative and quantitative. Use specific language to help students understand goals.
13. **Running Records:** This tool is used to record the errors/miscues students make while reading. Running records help to determine the difficulty level of texts so that teachers select appropriately leveled books and materials.	Paper/pencil	Forms for running records used in reading assessment can be created in Word. Samples and printable forms are listed in the chapter resources.
14. **Self-assessments:** These are assessments in which learners reflect on their own learning and evaluate specific criteria in order to assess their learning. Teachers may use checklists, rubrics, or open-ended questions to prompt students in their self-assessments.	Paper/pencil	Teachers can use Word to set up checklists or surveys or use self-assessment examples from the chapter resources section.
15. **Teacher-made Tests:** Assessments constructed by teachers to determine what students have learned after teaching a skill or unit of instruction. Teacher-made tests may include open-ended and essay questions, multiple choice and true/false questions, fill in the blank and matching questions, and blank-page assessments in which students write what they know about the topic.	Paper/pencil	Tests can be easily crafted in Word or any word processor. However, newer online test creation software (see the Electronic Assessment Creation Tools section of the chapter resources) is fun to use as well as productive. If you use Discovery Education Streaming, the Quiz Center is a unique way to combine assessment with video streaming content.

Along with the formative assessment examples shown in Table 9.3, we like the idea of using digital games with students.

The communication game in Figure 9.4 features a Jeopardy-like board in a colorful format. Using this template, we created a Women's History Month game for students. As in the real Jeopardy game, three individual players or three student teams select a category and answer in the amount of $100–$500. The answer is revealed, and the correct question must be asked to gain credit. Scores can be added as the game continues. A final challenge and wager complete the game.

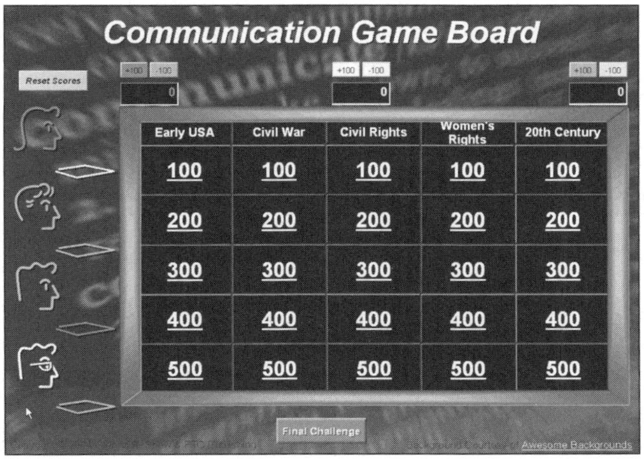

FIGURE **9.4** ■ Communication game
© FTC Publishing. Reprinted with permission.

Chalkboard Challenge, another Jeopardy-like game, offers a more traditional look for two classroom teams or group assessment. Using this game template, we created a Revolutionary War game with five categories for eighth graders (Figure 9.5). It is played in the same way as the Communication game.

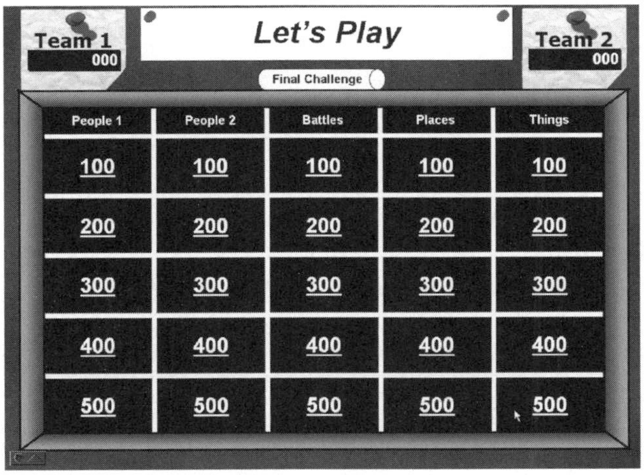

FIGURE **9.5** ■ Chalkboard Challenge Game
© FTC Publishing. Reprinted with permission.

Summary

We expect that you can see numerous new ways to use technology to assess the various stages of student learning. Please take time to visit our suggested resources to investigate strategies to use in your classroom, as well as our website (www.everythingdi.net), for additional help. Pre-assessment, formative assessment, and summative assessment all have an important role in the learning cycle. Although it is chiefly the teacher's job to assess, students can also take on some assessment functions as part of their responsibilities.

Chapter Resources

Assessment and Rubric Links

A Checklist for Effective Questioning: www.pgcps.org/~elc/isquestion7.html

Assessments: http://school.discovery.com/schrockguide/assess.html

Authentic Assessment Toolbox: http://jonathan.mueller.faculty.noctrl.edu/toolbox

Blogs

Class Blogmeister: http://classblogmeister.com

Education World: www.education-world.com/a_tech/tech/tech217.shtml

Gaggle Blogs:
http://gaggle.net/gen?_template=/templates/gaggle/html/blog/index.jsp

Checklists

Computer Skills:
www.kgcs.k12.va.us/tech/ss/elementary_middle_school_curriculum.htm

Make a Checklist in Word:
http://office.microsoft.com/en-us/assistance/HA011624511033.aspx

PBL Checklist Generator: http://pblchecklist.4teachers.org

Reading Skills:
www.pvsd.k12.pa.us/salisbury/Reading%20Skills%20Lists/ReadingSkills.htm

Curriculum, Assessment, and Instruction Models

Field-tested Learning Assessment Guide (FLAG):
www.flaguide.org/start/assess_in_context.php

USD 204 Bonner Springs/Edwardsville, KS: www.usd204.k12.ks.us/cia

Electronic Assessment

Online Assessment Resources for K-12 Teachers:
www.uwstout.edu/soe/profdev/assess.shtml

Using Electronic Assessment to Measure Student Performance:
www.nga.org/Files/pdf/electronicassessment.pdf

Electronic Assessment Hardware

Einstruction:
www.einstruction.com/index.cfm?fuseaction=K12.Display&Header=K12

Handheld Assessment:
http://thejournal.com/the/learningcenters/center/?msid=14
www.tribeam.com/educator.html

Turning Technologies: www.turningtechnologies.com

Examples and Forms

Create Class Surveys with Excel:
www.educationworld.com/a_tech/techtorial/techtorial082.shtml

Design a Survey Using Microsoft Word, Then Evaluate the Data Using Microsoft Access: www.microsoft.com/education/designsurvey.mspx

Journal Pages: www.abcteach.com/MonthtoMonth/June/journal1.htm

Journal Forms: www.sdcoe.k12.ca.us/score/actbank/sjournal.htm

Journal Writing Everyday (article):
www.education-world.com/a_curr/curr144.shtml

KWL Chart:
www.eduplace.com/graphicorganizer/pdf/kwl.pdf
www.nwrel.org/learns/resources/organizers/kwl.pdf

KWL Form: http://teacher.scholastic.com/lessonplans/graphicorg/kwl.htm

PowerPoint Flash Cards:
www.thinkbright.org/teachers/viewResource.asp?contentid=4401

Self-Assessment Rubric:
www.readwritethink.org/lesson_images/lesson277/rubric.pdf

Student Interest Survey:
www.union.k12.sc.us/ems/Teachers-Forms--Student Interest Survey.htm

Student Grid Assessment:
www.readwritethink.org/lesson_images/lesson851/grid.pdf

Technology Self-Assessment:
www.bham.wednet.edu/technology/documents/StaffRevisedMnkto2004.pdf

Electronic Assessment Creation Tools

A+ FlashCard Creator: www.aplusmath.com/Flashcards/Flashcard_Creator.html

Creating Tests with Microsoft Word:
www.educationworld.com/a_tech/techtorial/techtorial020.shtml

Discovery School Quiz Center:
http://school.discovery.com/quizcenter/quizcenter.html

Easy Test Maker: www.easytestmaker.com

E.L. Easton: http://eleaston.com/quizzes.html

Game-O-Matic: http://clear.msu.edu/dennie/matic

Hot Potatoes: http://hotpot.uvic.ca

Personal Educational Press: www.educationalpress.org

Quia: www.quia.com

Quiz Star: http://quizstar.4teachers.org

Survey Monkey: www.surveymonkey.com

RubiStar: http://rubistar.4teachers.org

Kathy Schrock's Guide: http://school.discovery.com/schrockguide/assess.html

SurveyMonkey: www.surveymonkey.com

Test Pilot: www.clearlearning.com

Zoomerang: http://zoomerang.com/online-surveys

Exit Cards

Exit slips: www.saskschools.ca/curr_content/bestpractice/exit/index.html

Sample card:
www.animalrangeextension.montana.edu/amazgraze/images/exitcard3-large.gif

Portfolios

Create Student Portfolios with Hyperlinks:
www.educationworld.com/a_tech/techtorial/techtorial044.shtml

Electronic Portfolios in the K–12 Classroom:
www.educationworld.com/a_tech/tech/tech111.shtml

Electronic Portfolios: Students, Teachers, and Lifelong Learners:
http://eduscapes.com/tap/topic82.htm

E-portfolio Fever: www.educationworld.com/a_tech/techtorial/techtorial038.shtml

PowerPoint Games

FTC Publishing: http://ftcpublishing.com

Jefferson County Schools: http://jc-schools.net/ppt.html

Parade of Games in PowerPoint: http://facstaff.uww.edu/jonesd/games

PowerPoint Games:
http://jc-schools.net/tutorials/PPT-games
http://jc-schools.net/write/games

Pre-Assessments

Counter Squares:
www.amblesideprimary.com/ambleweb/mentalmaths/countersquare.html

Dolch Site Words: www.mrsperkins.com/dolch.htm

Multiplication Table: http://office.microsoft.com/en-us/
templates/TC060900071033.aspx?CategoryID=CT063739921033

PowerPoint Collection: http://jc-schools.net/ppt.html

Scribble Square:
www.amblesideprimary.com/ambleweb/mentalmaths/scribblesquare.html

Multiple Intelligences Online Test:
www.bgfl.org/bgfl/custom/resources_ftp/client_ftp/ks3/ict/multiple_int

Running Records

Forms: www.readinga-z.com/guided/runrecord.html

Forms, tips, and codes:
www.hubbardscupboard.org/guided_reading.html#RunningRecords

Software

Fastt Math: www.tomsnyder.com/Products/product.asp?SKU=FASFAS

FTC Publishing: http://ftcpublishing.com

FINAL SUMMARY

We hope that reaching the end of this book opens, rather than closes, a new and exciting door in your mission as an educator. Combining technology and differentiated instruction can be challenging. However, the rewards far outweigh the work and the risks. If you already are a technology advocate and enjoy its benefits in your classroom (media center, school, and so on), we trust that you will try out some of the new ideas and strategies that we shared throughout the book to help you better differentiate instruction for your diverse learners. If you are not a technology enthusiast, perhaps we've been able to inspire you to begin experimenting with it so that you can prepare the students in your classroom even more effectively.

Perhaps the most important message that we've tried to communicate throughout this book is that technology should no longer be considered an "optional" tool, "afterthought," or "addition" to lesson plans and classroom content. We've emphasized how powerful technology can be as a differentiator because it engages students' imaginations and needs for visual, aural, and kinesthetic stimulation. Technology strengthens our teaching effectiveness because it enables us to customize the learning experience for all of our unique students. Connections between the real world and the classroom are enhanced and reinforced through a variety of technological tools and resources. If we persist with conventional instructional strategies, not only will we lose our students intellectually, physically, and emotionally in our classrooms, we will fail in our calling to prepare them for what they encounter beyond school walls today and in the future. We must question the relevance not only of the content that we are communicating to our students, but also the relevance of our techniques. The gap between what and how students are taught in school versus how the real world operates with technology to plan, educate, communicate, evaluate, and create is widening to become a chasm. What are educators going to do about using technology in meaningful ways? What should our 21st-century role include? Where do we go from here? Research over the last 30 years has indicated that we teachers are the most important factor in student learning. Let us celebrate and embrace the imprint we are still able to make on our students, though we may come from different technology backgrounds, generations, and experience. If we are willing to take a step in their direction to bridge the digital gap, most students will meet us and even help to carry us across as we, too, further our learning journeys.

Glossary of Strategies

Centers or Stations: To engage students in active learning tasks (adjusted by readiness, learning profile, or interest) at various stations to apply and extend specific skills, content-based knowledge, exploration, and/or enrichment.

Cubing: The term actually originates from a paper cube that students roll to work out their assignment. The series of tasks printed on the sides of the cube empower students to consider a concept from several different viewpoints.

Curriculum Compacting: A strategy for streamlining curriculum to allow more able students to work at a faster pace in order to pursue an alternate topic or investigate an area of study in greater depth rather than holding them to basal or grade-level curricular objectives, which they may have already mastered.

Flexible Grouping: A more recent term for arranging students into teams according to their interests, readiness levels, and learning profiles, as well as by random selection or student choice. Flexible grouping challenges learners to take on new roles in work teams and better prepares our students for relationships and cooperative projects in the real world.

I-Search: Student-driven investigative research paper or other product based on a "genuine itch" (interest or passion), as defined by creator Ken Macrorie.

Jigsaw: A peer teaching strategy in which students focus on a specific interest or topic with the assistance of a Jigsaw group. In the Jigsaw (or expert) group, students discuss definitive aspects of their shared interest or topic and brainstorm how they'll present key information to their home groups.

Learning Contract: An agreement between the student and teacher that provides for a mix of both required and self-selected tasks. Students usually design a new product that demonstrates their conceptual understanding of teacher-identified skills and ideas.

R.A.F.T.T.: R.A.F.T. traditionally stands for Role, Audience, Format, and Topic, and was created originally to combine reading and writing in unconventional ways. In our article entitled "Tech-Enhanced Strategies That Capture Student Interest," (Smith & Throne, 2008) we renamed it "R.A.F.T.T.," adding on the last "T" for technology. Today, teachers of all subjects rely upon R.A.F.T.s to strengthen conceptual understanding using deep thinking and allow for multiple product formats.

Scaffolding: The teacher breaks a complex task down into smaller tasks, models the desired learning or task, and provides support as the students work on each task. Scaffolding provides the necessary support to students as they progress to higher levels of skill or knowledge.

ThinkDots: Six hole-punched cards that are joined together by a ring, yarn, string, or the like. Each card has a picture of one or more dots that correspond to the faces of a die. Instead of rolling a cube, students roll a die and complete the activity on the back of the card that matches the dot combination that appears on the face of the die. Similar to Cubing, the series of tasks printed on the cards empower students to consider a concept from several different viewpoints.

Tic-Tac-Toe or Choice Board: Students select multiple tasks, in the form of a horizontal, diagonal or vertical line, from a choice board that enable them to practice skills they've learned, exhibit mastery of content, and/or extend learning. The choice board offers a range of options that are differentiated by learning profile, interest, and/or readiness.

Tiering or Tiered Assignments: Building on students' prior knowledge, teachers vary the depth of a lesson that centers on specific concepts, big ideas, and skills in order to meet students' diverse interests, learning profiles, and levels of readiness.

WebQuest: Team or individualized activities using the Internet to help students grapple with complex, open-ended questions. Tasks are research- and/or interest-based, and require problem-solving skills, such as evaluation, analysis, and synthesis of resources.

Bibliography

Adelman, H. S. & Taylor, L. (2005). *Classroom Climate.* In S. W. Lee (Ed.), *Encyclopedia of School Psychology.* Thousand Oaks, CA: Sage. A prepublication version of the chapter is available at http://smhp.psych. ucla.edu/publications/46 classroom climate.pdf

Armstrong, T. (2000). *Multiple intelligences in the classroom* (2nd ed.). Alexandria, VA: Association for Supervision and Curriculum Development.

Beck, J., & Wade, M. (2004). *Got game: How the gamer generation is reshaping business forever.* Boston: Harvard Business School Press. Cited in Simpson & Clem (2008).

Bloom, B. (1956). *Taxonomy of educational objectives, Handbook I: The cognitive domain.* New York: David McKay Co., Inc.

Boster, F. J., Meyer, G. S., Roberto, A. J., & Inge, C. C. (2002). *A report on the effect of unitedstreaming application on educational performance.* Cometrika, Inc., Baseline Research, LLC., & Longwood University. Available at www.iste.org/AM/Template.cfm?Section=Home&CONTENTID= 3069&TEMPLATE=/CM/ContentDisplay.cfm

Bransford, J. D., Brown, A. L., & Cocking, R. R. (Eds.) (1999). *How people learn: Brain, mind, experience, and school.* Washington, DC: The National Academies Press. Available at www.nap.edu/openbook. php?record_id=6160

Bushweller, K. (2006). Tune in, turn off. *Teacher Magazine, 17*(5), 49. Available at www.edweek.org/tm/ articles/2006/03/01/05classtech.h17.html/. Cited in Simpson & Clem (2008).

Campbell, L., & Campbell, B. (1999). *Multiple intelligences and student achievement.* Alexandria, VA: Association for Supervision and Curriculum Development.

Chapman, C., & King, R. (2005). *Differentiated assessment strategies: One tool doesn't fit all.* Thousand Oaks, CA: Corwin Press.

Davidson, R. (2007). Presentation recorded on Dec. 10, 2007, in New York City, at the CASEL forum to raise awareness about social and emotional learning (SEL). Available at www.edutopia.org/richard-davidson-sel-brain-video

Deubel, P. (2006). Game on! *T.H.E. Journal* (Jan 1.). Available at www.thejournal.com/articles/17788/. Cited in Simpson & Clem (2008).

Duncan, D., & Lockhart, L. (2000). *I-search, you search, we all learn to research.* New York: Neal-Schuman.

Edutopia. (2001a). *Emotional intelligence: The missing piece: Social and emotional learning can help students successfully resolve conflict, communicate clearly, solve problems, and much more.* Retrieved July 31, 2008, from www.edutopia.org/emotional-intelligence-missing-piece

Edutopia. (2001b). *Emotional-intelligence research: Indicators point to the importance of SEL.* Available at www.edutopia.org/emotional-intelligence-research

ERIC Clearinghouse for Social Studies/Social Science Education. (1985). *Cooperative learning in social studies education: What does the research say? ERIC Digest No. 20.* Retrieved July 16, 2009, from www.ericdigests.org/pre-923/cooperative.htm (ERIC Document Reproduction Service No. ED264162).

Gagné, R. (1985). *The conditions of learning* (4th ed.). New York: Holt, Rinehart & Winston.

Gardner, H. (1993). *Multiple intelligences: The theory in practice.* New York: Basic Books.

Glasser, W. (1998). *Choice theory in the classroom.* NY: HarperCollins. Cited in Simpson & Clem (2008).

Goleman, D. (1995). *Emotional intelligence: Why it can matter more than IQ.* NY: Bantam Books.

Jacobs, H. H. (1997). *Mapping the big picture: Integrating curriculum and assessment K–12.* Alexandria, VA: Association for Supervision and Curriculum Development.

Kelly, M. G., & Haber, J. (2006). *Resources for student assessment.* Eugene, OR: International Society for Technology in Education.

Kirk, K. (2007). *What is the affective domain anyway?* Workshop summary. Student motivations and attitudes: The role of the affective domain in geoscience learning. Carlton College, Northfield, MN, Feb. 11–13, 2007. Retrieved July 31, 2008, from http://serc.carleton.edu/NAGTWorkshops/affective/intro.html

Kruse, K. (n.d.). *Gagné's nine events of instruction: An introduction.* Available at www.e-learningguru.com/articles/art3_3.htm

Lemke, C., Coughlin, E., Thadani, V., & Martin, C. (2003). *enGauge 21st century skills: Literacy in the digital age.* Los Angeles, CA: Metiri Group; and Naperville, IL: NCREL. Available at www.metiri.com/features.html

Lepper, M. R., & Malone, T. W. (1987). Intrinsic motivation and instructional effectiveness in computer-based education. In R. E. Snow & M. J. Farr (Eds.), *Aptitude, learning and instruction. Vol. 3: Cognitive and affective process analysis.* Hillsdale, NJ: Erlbaum.

Lorain, P. (n.d. a). *Squirming comes naturally to middle school students: Physical changes trigger behavioral changes.* National Education Association. Retrieved April 21, 2009, from www.nea.org/tools/16616.htm

Lorain, P. (n.d. b). *Can't stop talking: Social needs of students in the middle.* National Education Association. Retrieved April 21, 2009, from www.nea.org/tools/16641.htm

Macrorie, K. (1988). *The I-search paper: Revised edition of searching writing.* Portsmouth, NH: Boynton/Cook.

Maday, T. (2008). Stuck in the middle: Strategies to engage middle-level learners. *The Center for Comprehensive School Reform and Improvement Newsletter.* Retrieved July 31, 2008, from www.centerforcsri.org/index.php?option=com_content&task=view&id=551&Itemid=5

Marzano, R. J., Pickering, D. J., & Pollock, J. E. (2001). *Classroom instruction that works: Research-based strategies for increasing student achievement.* Alexandria, VA: Association for Supervision and Curriculum Development.

Mayer, R. E., & Moreno, R. (2003). Nine ways to reduce cognitive load in multimedia learning. In R. Bruning, C. A. Horn, & L. M. PytlikZillig (Eds.). *Web-based learning: What do we know? Where do we go?* pp. 23–44. Greenwich, CT: Information Age Publishing. Cited in Metiri Group/Cisco Systems. (2008).

McKenzie, W. (2002). *Multiple intelligences and instructional technology.* Eugene, OR: International Society for Technology in Education.

Metiri Group/Cisco Systems. (2008). *Multimodal learning through media: What the research says.* Available at www.cisco.com/web/strategy/docs/education/Multimodal-Learning-Through-Media.pdf

National Education Association. (2008). *Access, adequacy and equity in education technology: Results of a survey of America's teachers and support professionals on technology in public schools and classrooms.* Available at www.digitaldivide.net/comm/docs/view.php?DocID=451

North Central Regional Educational Laboratory (NCREL) & Metiri Group. (2003). *enGauge 21st century skills: Literacy in the digital age.* Available from www.grrec.ky.gov/SLC_grant/Engauge21st_Century_Skills.pdf

O'Reilly, T. (2005). *What is web 2.0: Design patterns and business models for the next generation of software.* Retrieved July 16, 2009, from www.oreillynet.com/pub/a/oreilly/tim/news/2005/09/30/what-is-Web-20.html

Partnership for 21st Century Skills. (2002). *Learning for the 21st century: A report and mile guide for 21st century skills.* Partnership for 21st Century Skills Report. Retrieved July 14, 2008, from www.21stcenturyskills.org/downloads/P21_Report.pdf

Pitler, H., Hubbell, E. R., Kuhn, M., & Malenoski, K. (2007). *Using technology with classroom instruction that works.* Alexandria, VA: Association for Supervision and Curriculum Development.

Prensky, M. (2001). *Digital game-based learning.* NY: McGraw-Hill. Cited in Simpson & Clem (2008).

Public Broadcasting Service (PBS). (2002a). *Inside the Teenage Brain: Adolescent Brains are Works in Progress: Here's Why.* S. Spinks, producer. Jan. 31, 2002, program # 2011. Retrieved July 31, 2008, from www.pbs.org/wgbh/pages/frontline/shows/teenbrain/work/adolescent.html.

Public Broadcasting Service. (PBS) (2002b). *Inside the Teenage Brain: Adolescent brains are works in progress: Here's Why.* Interview Jay Giedd. Retrieved July 31, 2008, from www.pbs.org/wgbh/pages/frontline/shows/teenbrain/interviews/giedd.html

Public Broadcasting Service (PBS). (2002c). *Inside the Teenage Brain: One reason teens respond differently to the world: Immature brain circuitry.* Interview Deborah Yurgelun-Todd. Retrieved July 31, 2008, from www.pbs.org/wgbh/pages/frontline/shows/teenbrain/interviews/todd.html

Reis, S. M., Burns, D. E., & Renzulli, J. S. (1992). *Curriculum compacting: The complete guide to modifying the regular curriculum for high ability students.* Mansfield Center, CT: Creative Learning Press.

Richardson, T. L. (2002). Research on middle school renewal. *Middle School Journal, 33*(3), 55–58. Retrieved July 31, 2008, from, www.nmsa.org/Publications/MiddleSchoolJournal/Articles/January2002/Article10/tabid/411/Default.aspx.

Siegle, D., & Foster, T. (2000). *Effects of laptop computers with multimedia and presentation software on student achievement.* A paper presented at the annual meeting of the American Education Research Association. April 24–28, 2000. New Orleans, LA. Abstract available at http://www.eric.ed.gov/ERICDocs/data/ericdocs2sql/content_storage_01/0000019b/80/16/44/d7.pdf

Simpson, E. & Clem, F. A. (2008). Video games in the middle school classroom. *Middle School Journal, 39*(4), 4–11. Available at www.nmsa.org/Publications/MiddleSchoolJournal/Articles/March2008/Article1/tabid/1627/Default.aspx

Smith, G. E., & Throne, S. (2007). *Differentiating instruction with technology in K–5 classrooms.* Eugene, OR: International Society for Technology in Education.

Smith, G. E. & Throne, S. (2008, January). Tech-enhanced instructional strategies that capture student interest. *Instructional Leader, 21*(2), 1–5.

Smith, L. (2008). *Winning equation: How technology can help save math education.* Available at www.edutopia.org/technology-math-education

Speak up 2008 for students, teachers, parents, and administrators. (2009). Project Tomorrow, a national education nonprofit group based in Irvine, CA, is the sponsoring body for Speak Up reports. Available at www.tomorrow.org/speakup/pdfs/SU08_findings_final_mar24.pdf

Spires, H. A., Lee, J. K., & Lester, J. (2008). The twenty-first century learner and game-based learning. *Meridian: A Middle School Computer Technologies Journal 11* (1: Winter). Available at www.ncsu.edu/meridian/win2008/21st/index.htm

Sternberg, R. (1999). *Thinking styles.* New York: Cambridge University Press.

Strong, R., Thomas, E., Perini, M. & Silver, H. (2004). Creating a differentiated mathematics classroom. *Educational Leadership, 61*(5) 73–78. Retrieved July 16, 2009, from http://pdonline.ascd.org/pd_online/assessment/el200402_strong.html

Technology Counts (2007). *Technology counts 2007: A digital decade.* Education Week and Editorial Projects in Education (EPE) Research Center. Individual state reports are available at www.edweek.org/ew/toc/2007/03/29

Technology Counts (2008). *Technology counts 2008: The push to improve STEM education.* Education Week and Editorial Projects in Education (EPE) Research Center. Individual state reports are available at www.edweek.org

Technology Counts (2009). *Technology counts 2009: Breaking away from tradition.* Education Week and Editorial Projects in Education (EPE) Research Center. Individual state reports are available at www.edweek.org

Tomlinson, C. A. (2001). *How to differentiate instruction in mixed-ability classrooms* (2nd ed.). Alexandria, VA: Association for Supervision and Curriculum Development.

Tomlinson, C. A. (2003). *Fulfilling the promise of the differentiated classroom: Strategies and tools for responsive teaching.* Alexandria, VA: Association for Supervision and Curriculum Development.

Varlas, L. (2002). Getting acquainted with the essential nine. *ASCD Curriculum Update* (Winter). Available at www.middleweb.com/MWLresources/marzchat1.html

Wormeli, R. (2006). *Fair isn't always equal.* Portland, ME: Stenhouse Publishers.

Zins, J. E., & Elias, M. J. (2006) Social and emotional learning. In G. G. Bear, & K. M. Minke. (Eds.) *Children's needs III: Development, prevention, and intervention.* pp. 1–13. Bethesda, MD: National Association of School Psychologists. Available at http://www.nasponline.org/publications/booksproducts/cn3.aspx/. Chapter PDF available at www.nasponline.org/educators/elias_zins.pdf

National Educational Technology Standards for Students (NETS•S)

All K–12 students should be prepared to meet the following standards and performance indicators.

1. Creativity and Innovation

Students demonstrate creative thinking, construct knowledge, and develop innovative products and processes using technology. Students:

    a. apply existing knowledge to generate new ideas, products, or processes

    b. create original works as a means of personal or group expression

    c. use models and simulations to explore complex systems and issues

    d. identify trends and forecast possibilities

2. Communication and Collaboration

Students use digital media and environments to communicate and work collaboratively, including at a distance, to support individual learning and contribute to the learning of others. Students:

    a. interact, collaborate, and publish with peers, experts, or others employing a variety of digital environments and media

    b. communicate information and ideas effectively to multiple audiences using a variety of media and formats

    c. develop cultural understanding and global awareness by engaging with learners of other cultures

    d. contribute to project teams to produce original works or solve problems

3. Research and Information Fluency

Students apply digital tools to gather, evaluate, and use information. Students:

    a. plan strategies to guide inquiry

    b. locate, organize, analyze, evaluate, synthesize, and ethically use information from a variety of sources and media

    c.   evaluate and select information sources and digital tools based on the appropriateness to specific tasks

    d.   process data and report results

4. Critical Thinking, Problem Solving, and Decision Making

Students use critical thinking skills to plan and conduct research, manage projects, solve problems, and make informed decisions using appropriate digital tools and resources. Students:

    a.   identify and define authentic problems and significant questions for investigation

    b.   plan and manage activities to develop a solution or complete a project

    c.   collect and analyze data to identify solutions and make informed decisions

    d.   use multiple processes and diverse perspectives to explore alternative solutions

5. Digital Citizenship

Students understand human, cultural, and societal issues related to technology and practice legal and ethical behavior. Students:

    a.   advocate and practice the safe, legal, and responsible use of information and technology

    b.   exhibit a positive attitude toward using technology that supports collaboration, learning, and productivity

    c.   demonstrate personal responsibility for lifelong learning

    d.   exhibit leadership for digital citizenship

6. Technology Operations and Concepts

Students demonstrate a sound understanding of technology concepts, systems, and operations. Students:

    a.   understand and use technology systems

    b.   select and use applications effectively and productively

    c.   troubleshoot systems and applications

    d.   transfer current knowledge to the learning of new technologies

INDEX